Code Connected Volume 1

Pieter Hintjens

Code Connected Volume 1

Learning ZeroMQ

Professional Edition for C/C++

To my children Noémie, Freeman, and Gregor

Code Connected Volume 1

Copyright © 2010-2013 Pieter Hintjens

First Printing: January 6th, 2013

Licensed under CC-BY-SA-3.0

Published by iMatix Corporation

"Code Connected" is a trademark of Pieter Hintjens. "ØMQ", "ØMQ", "ZeroMQ", and the ØMQ logo are trademarks of iMatix Corporation.

Edited by Andy Oram at O'Reilly

This text originated as "ZeroMQ - The Guide" at http://zguide.zeromq.org, with examples from the ØMQ community in C, C++, C#, Clojure, Delphi, Erlang, Go, Haskell, Haxe, Java, Lisp, Lua, Node.js, Objective-C, Perl, PHP, Python, Ruby, Scala, Tcl, and other languages.

ISBN 978-1481262651

Contents

7		**Preface**
	7	ØMQ in a Hundred Words
	7	How It Began
	7	The Zen of Zero
	8	How This Book Came To Be
	9	Audience
	9	Code Connected
11		**Chapter 1. Basics**
	11	Fixing the World
	12	Starting Assumptions
	13	Getting the Examples
	13	Ask and Ye Shall Receive
	16	A Minor Note on Strings
	17	Version Reporting
	18	Getting the Message Out
	22	Divide and Conquer
	26	Programming with ØMQ
	28	Why We Needed ØMQ
	32	Socket Scalability
	32	Upgrading from ØMQ v2.2 to ØMQ v3.2
	34	Warning: Unstable Paradigms!
35		**Chapter 2. Sockets and Patterns**
	35	The Socket API
	40	Messaging Patterns
	56	Handling Errors and ETERM
	60	Handling Interrupt Signals
	62	Detecting Memory Leaks
	63	Multithreading with ØMQ
	67	Signaling Between Threads (PAIR Sockets)
	69	Node Coordination
	72	Zero-Copy
	73	Pub-Sub Message Envelopes
	75	High-Water Marks
	76	Missing Message Problem Solver

79   Chapter 3. Advanced Request-Reply Patterns

    79   The Request-Reply Mechanisms
    83   Request-Reply Combinations
    86   Exploring ROUTER Sockets
    88   The Load Balancing Pattern
    98   A High-Level API for ØMQ
    107   The Asynchronous Client/Server Pattern
    111   Worked Example: Inter-Broker Routing

135   Chapter 4. Reliable Request-Reply Patterns

    135   What is "Reliability"?
    136   Designing Reliability
    137   Client-Side Reliability (Lazy Pirate Pattern)
    141   Basic Reliable Queuing (Simple Pirate Pattern)
    144   Robust Reliable Queuing (Paranoid Pirate Pattern)
    152   Heartbeating
    155   Contracts and Protocols
    156   Service-Oriented Reliable Queuing (Majordomo Pattern)
    178   Asynchronous Majordomo Pattern
    184   Service Discovery
    185   Idempotent Services
    186   Disconnected Reliability (Titanic Pattern)
    198   High-Availability Pair (Binary Star Pattern)
    214   Brokerless Reliability (Freelance Pattern)
    234   Conclusion

235   Chapter 5. Advanced Pub-Sub Patterns

    235   Pros and Cons of Pub-Sub
    237   Pub-Sub Tracing (Espresso Pattern)
    239   Last Value Caching
    244   Slow Subscriber Detection (Suicidal Snail Pattern)
    247   High-Speed Subscribers (Black Box Pattern)
    249   Reliable Pub-Sub (Clone Pattern)

311   Postface

    311   Tales from Out There
    312   How This Book Happened
    314   Removing Friction
    315   Licensing
    316   Code Connected Volume 2

Preface

ØMQ in a Hundred Words

ØMQ (also known as ZeroMQ, ØMQ, or zmq) looks like an embeddable networking library but acts like a concurrency framework. It gives you sockets that carry atomic messages across various transports like in-process, inter-process, TCP, and multicast. You can connect sockets N-to-N with patterns like fan-out, pub-sub, task distribution, and request-reply. It's fast enough to be the fabric for clustered products. Its asynchronous I/O model gives you scalable multicore applications, built as asynchronous message-processing tasks. It has a score of language APIs and runs on most operating systems. ØMQ is from iMatix[1] and is LGPLv3 open source.

How It Began

We took a normal TCP socket, injected it with a mix of radioactive isotopes stolen from a secret Soviet atomic research project, bombarded it with 1950-era cosmic rays, and put it into the hands of a drug-addled comic book author with a badly-disguised fetish for bulging muscles clad in spandex (see figure 1). Yes, ØMQ sockets are the world-saving superheroes of the networking world.

The Zen of Zero

The Ø in ØMQ is all about tradeoffs. On the one hand this strange name lowers ØMQ's visibility on Google and Twitter. On the other hand it annoys the heck out of some Danish folk who write us things like "ØMG røtfl", and "Ø is not a funny looking zero!" and "*Rødgrød med Fløde!*", which is apparently an insult that means "may your neighbours be the direct descendants of Grendel!" Seems like a fair trade.

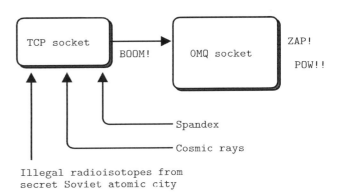

Figure 1. A terrible accident...

---

1   http://www.imatix.com

Originally the zero in ØMQ was meant as "zero broker" and (as close to) "zero latency" (as possible). Since then, it has come to encompass different goals: zero administration, zero cost, zero waste. More generally, "zero" refers to the culture of minimalism that permeates the project. We add power by removing complexity rather than by exposing new functionality.

How This Book Came To Be

In the summer of 2010, ØMQ was still a little-known niche library described by its rather terse reference manual and a living but sparse wiki. Martin Sustrik and myself were sitting in the bar of the Hotel Kyjev in Bratislava plotting how to make ØMQ more widely popular. Martin had written most of the ØMQ code, and I'd put up the funding and organized the community. Over some Zlaty Bazants, we agreed that ØMQ needed a new, simpler web site and a basic guide for new users.

Martin collected some ideas for topics to explain. I'd never written a line of ØMQ code before this, so it became a live learning documentary. As I worked through simple examples to more complex ones, I tried to answer many of the questions I'd seen on the mailing list. Because I'd been building large-scale architectures for 30 years, there were a lot of problems at which I was keen to throw ØMQ. Amazingly the results were mostly simple and elegant, even when working in C. I felt a pure joy learning ØMQ and using it to solve real problems, which brought me back to programming after a few years' pause. And often, not knowing how it was "supposed" to be done, we improved ØMQ as we went along.

From the start, I wanted the ØMQ guide to be a community project, so I put it onto GitHub and let others contribute with pull requests. This was considered a radical, even vulgar approach by some. We came to a division of labor: I'd do the writing and make the original C examples, and others would help fix the text and translate the examples into other languages.

This worked better than I dared hope. You can now find all the examples in several languages and many in a dozen languages. It's a kind of programming language Rosetta stone and a valuable outcome in itself. We set up a high score: reach 80% translation and your language got its own Guide. PHP, Python, Lua, and Haxe reached this goal. People asked for PDFs, and we created those. People asked for ebooks, and got those. About a hundred people contributed to the examples to date.

The book, in its on-line version "The Guide", achieved its goal of popularizing ØMQ. The style pleases most and annoys some, which is how it should be. In December 2010, my work on ØMQ and this guide stopped, as I found myself going through late-stage cancer, heavy surgery, and six months of chemotherapy. When I picked up work again in mid-2011, it was to start using ØMQ in anger for one of the largest use cases imaginable: on the mobile phones and tablets of the world's biggest electronics company.

But the goal of the ØMQ book was, from the start, a printed work. So it was exciting to get an email from Bill Lubanovic in January 2012 introducing me to his editor, Andy

Oram, at O'Reilly, suggesting a ØMQ book. Of course! Where do I sign? How much do I have to pay? Oh, I *get money* for this? All I have to do is finish it?

Of course as soon as O'Reilly announced a ØMQ book, other publishers started sending out emails to potential authors. You'll probably see a rash of ØMQ books coming out next year. That's good. Our niche library has hit the mainstream and deserves its six inches of shelf space. My apologies to the other ØMQ authors. We've set the bar horribly high, and my advice is to make your books complementary. Perhaps focus on a specific language, platform, or pattern.

This is the magic and power of communities: be the first community in a space, stay healthy, and you own that space for ever.

Audience

This book is written for professional programmers who want to learn how to make the massively distributed software that will dominate the future of computing. We assume you can read C code, because most of the examples here are in C even though ØMQ is used in many languages. We assume you care about scale, because ØMQ solves that problem above all others. We assume you need the best possible results with the least possible cost, because otherwise you won't appreciate the trade-offs that ØMQ makes. Other than that basic background, we try to present all the concepts in networking and distributed computing you will need to use ØMQ.

Code Connected

This book, "Code Connected Volume 1", is the first volume covering the theme of how to build distributed software over ØMQ. In this book, you'll learn how to use the ØMQ library. We'll cover the basics, the API, the different socket types and how they work, reliability, and a host of patterns you can use in your applications. You'll get the best results by working through the examples and text from start to end.

This is the Professional Edition for C/C++ developers. But whatever your programming language, the patterns and techniques that Code Connected explains are relevant to you. Get the examples online in C, C++, C#, Clojure, Delphi, Erlang, Go, Haskell, Haxe, Java, Lisp, Lua, Node.js, Objective-C, Perl, PHP, Python, Ruby, Scala, and Tcl.

Chapter 1. Basics

Fixing the World

How to explain ØMQ? Some of us start by saying all the wonderful things it does. *It's sockets on steroids. It's like mailboxes with routing. It's fast!* Others try to share their moment of enlightenment, that zap-pow-kaboom satori paradigm-shift moment when it all became obvious. *Things just become simpler. Complexity goes away. It opens the mind.* Others try to explain by comparison. *It's smaller, simpler, but still looks familiar.* Personally, I like to remember why we made ØMQ at all, because that's most likely where you, the reader, still are today.

Programming is science dressed up as art because most of us don't understand the physics of software and it's rarely, if ever, taught. The physics of software is not algorithms, data structures, languages and abstractions. These are just tools we make, use, throw away. The real physics of software is the physics of people—specifically, our limitations when it comes to complexity, and our desire to work together to solve large problems in pieces. This is the science of programming: make building blocks that people can understand and use *easily*, and people will work together to solve the very largest problems.

We live in a connected world, and modern software has to navigate this world. So the building blocks for tomorrow's very largest solutions are connected and massively parallel. It's not enough for code to be "strong and silent" any more. Code has to talk to code. Code has to be chatty, sociable, well-connected. Code has to run like the human brain, trillions of individual neurons firing off messages to each other, a massively parallel network with no central control, no single point of failure, yet able to solve immensely difficult problems. And it's no accident that the future of code looks like the human brain, because the endpoints of every network are, at some level, human brains.

If you've done any work with threads, protocols, or networks, you'll realize this is pretty much impossible. It's a dream. Even connecting a few programs across a few sockets is plain nasty when you start to handle real life situations. Trillions? The cost would be unimaginable. Connecting computers is so difficult that software and services to do this is a multi-billion dollar business.

So we live in a world where the wiring is years ahead of our ability to use it. We had a software crisis in the 1980s, when leading software engineers like Fred Brooks believed there was no "Silver Bullet"[2] to "promise even one order of magnitude of improvement in productivity, reliability, or simplicity".

---

2   http://en.wikipedia.org/wiki/No_Silver_Bullet

Brooks missed free and open source software, which solved that crisis, enabling us to share knowledge efficiently. Today we face another software crisis, but it's one we don't talk about much. Only the largest, richest firms can afford to create connected applications. There is a cloud, but it's proprietary. Our data and our knowledge is disappearing from our personal computers into clouds that we cannot access and with which we cannot compete. Who owns our social networks? It is like the mainframe-PC revolution in reverse.

We can leave the political philosophy for another book[3]. The point is that while the Internet offers the potential of massively connected code, the reality is that this is out of reach for most of us, and so large interesting problems (in health, education, economics, transport, and so on) remain unsolved because there is no way to connect the code, and thus no way to connect the brains that could work together to solve these problems.

There have been many attempts to solve the challenge of connected code. There are thousands of IETF specifications, each solving part of the puzzle. For application developers, HTTP is perhaps the one solution to have been simple enough to work, but it arguably makes the problem worse by encouraging developers and architects to think in terms of big servers and thin, stupid clients.

So today people are still connecting applications using raw UDP and TCP, proprietary protocols, HTTP, and Websockets. It remains painful, slow, hard to scale, and essentially centralized. Distributed P2P architectures are mostly for play, not work. How many applications use Skype or Bittorrent to exchange data?

Which brings us back to the science of programming. To fix the world, we needed to do two things. One, to solve the general problem of "how to connect any code to any code, anywhere". Two, to wrap that up in the simplest possible building blocks that people could understand and use *easily*.

It sounds ridiculously simple. And maybe it is. That's kind of the whole point.

Starting Assumptions

We assume you are using at least version 3.2 of ØMQ. We assume you are using a Linux box or something similar. We assume you can read C code, more or less, as that's the default language for the examples. We assume that when we write constants like PUSH or SUBSCRIBE, you can imagine they are really called `ZMQ_PUSH` or `ZMQ_SUBSCRIBE` if the programming language needs it.

---

[3] http://swsi.info

Getting the Examples

The examples live in a public GitHub repository[4]. The simplest way to get all the examples is to clone this repository:

```
git clone --depth=1 git://github.com/imatix/zguide.git
```

Next, browse the examples subdirectory. You'll find examples by language. If there are examples missing in a language you use, you're encouraged to submit a translation[5]. This is how this text became so useful, thanks to the work of many people. All examples are licensed under MIT/X11.

Ask and Ye Shall Receive

So let's start with some code. We start of course with a Hello World example. We'll make a client and a server. The client sends "Hello" to the server, which replies with "World" (see figure 2). Here's the server in C, which opens a ØMQ socket on port 5555, reads requests on it, and replies with "World" to each request:

Example 1. Hello World server (hwserver.c)

```c
//  Hello World server

#include <zmq.h>
#include <stdio.h>
#include <unistd.h>
#include <string.h>
#include <assert.h>

int main (void)
{
    //  Socket to talk to clients
    void *context = zmq_ctx_new ();
    void *responder = zmq_socket (context, ZMQ_REP);
    int rc = zmq_bind (responder, "tcp://*:5555");
    assert (rc == 0);

    while (1) {
        char buffer [10];
        zmq_recv (responder, buffer, 10, 0);
        printf ("Received Hello\n");
        zmq_send (responder, "World", 5, 0);
        sleep (1);          //  Do some 'work'
    }
    return 0;
}
```

---

4   https://github.com/imatix/zguide
5   http://zguide.zeromq.org/main:translate

The REQ-REP socket pair is in lockstep. The client issues zmq_send() and then zmq_recv(), in a loop (or once if that's all it needs). Doing any other sequence (e.g., sending two messages in a row) will result in a return code of -1 from the send or recv call. Similarly, the service issues zmq_recv() and then zmq_send() in that order, as often as it needs to.

ØMQ uses C as its reference language and this is the main language we'll use for examples. If you're reading this online, the link below the example takes you to translations into other programming languages. Let's compare the same server in C++:

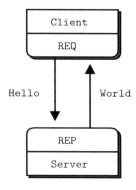

Figure 2. Request-Reply

Example 2. Hello World server (hwserver.cpp)

```
//
//  Hello World server in C++
//  Binds REP socket to tcp://*:5555
//  Expects "Hello" from client, replies with "World"
//
#include <zmq.hpp>
#include <string>
#include <iostream>
#include <unistd.h>

int main () {
    //  Prepare our context and socket
    zmq::context_t context (1);
    zmq::socket_t socket (context, ZMQ_REP);
    socket.bind ("tcp://*:5555");

    while (true) {
        zmq::message_t request;

        //  Wait for next request from client
        socket.recv (&request);
        std::cout << "Received Hello" << std::endl;

        //  Do some 'work'
        sleep (1);

        //  Send reply back to client
        zmq::message_t reply (5);
        memcpy ((void *) reply.data (), "World", 5);
        socket.send (reply);
    }
    return 0;
}
```

You can see that the ØMQ API is similar in C and C++. In a language like PHP, we can hide even more and the code becomes even easier to read:

Example 3. Hello World server (hwserver.php)

```php
<?php
/*
 *  Hello World server
 *  Binds REP socket to tcp://*:5555
 *  Expects "Hello" from client, replies with "World"
 *  @author Ian Barber <ian(dot)barber(at)gmail(dot)com>
 */

$context = new ZMQContext(1);

// Socket to talk to clients
$responder = new ZMQSocket($context, ZMQ::SOCKET_REP);
$responder->bind("tcp://*:5555");

while (true) {
    // Wait for next request from client
    $request = $responder->recv();
    printf ("Received request: [%s]\n", $request);

    // Do some 'work'
    sleep (1);

    // Send reply back to client
    $responder->send("World");
}
```

Here's the client code:

Example 4. Hello World client (hwclient.c)

```c
//  Hello World client
#include <zmq.h>
#include <string.h>
#include <stdio.h>
#include <unistd.h>

int main (void)
{
    printf ("Connecting to hello world server...\n");
    void *context = zmq_ctx_new ();
    void *requester = zmq_socket (context, ZMQ_REQ);
    zmq_connect (requester, "tcp://localhost:5555");

    int request_nbr;
    for (request_nbr = 0; request_nbr != 10; request_nbr++) {
        char buffer [10];
```

```
            printf ("Sending Hello %d...\n", request_nbr);
            zmq_send (requester, "Hello", 5, 0);
            zmq_recv (requester, buffer, 10, 0);
            printf ("Received World %d\n", request_nbr);
        }
        zmq_close (requester);
        zmq_ctx_destroy (context);
        return 0;
    }
```

Now this looks too simple to be realistic, but ØMQ sockets have, as we already learned, superpowers. You could throw thousands of clients at this server, all at once, and it would continue to work happily and quickly. For fun, try starting the client and *then* starting the server, see how it all still works, then think for a second what this means.

Let us explain briefly what these two programs are actually doing. They create a ØMQ context to work with, and a socket. Don't worry what the words mean. You'll pick it up. The server binds its REP (reply) socket to port 5555. The server waits for a request in a loop, and responds each time with a reply. The client sends a request and reads the reply back from the server.

If you kill the server (Ctrl-C) and restart it, the client won't recover properly. Recovering from crashing processes isn't quite that easy. Making a reliable request-reply flow is complex enough that we won't cover it until "Reliable Request-Reply Patterns".

There is a lot happening behind the scenes but what matters to us programmers is how short and sweet the code is, and how often it doesn't crash, even under a heavy load. This is the request-reply pattern, probably the simplest way to use ØMQ. It maps to RPC and the classic client/server model.

A Minor Note on Strings

ØMQ doesn't know anything about the data you send except its size in bytes. That means you are responsible for formatting it safely so that applications can read it back. Doing this for objects and complex data types is a job for specialized libraries like Protocol Buffers. But even for strings, you need to take care.

In C and some other languages, strings are terminated with a null byte. We could send a string like "HELLO" with that extra null byte:

```
    zmq_send (requester, "Hello", 6, 0);
```

However, if you send a string from another language, it probably will not include that null byte. For example, when we send that same string in Python, we do this:

```
    socket.send ("Hello")
```

Then what goes onto the wire is a length (one byte for shorter strings) and the string contents as individual characters (see figure 3).

And if you read this from a C
program, you will get something that
looks like a string, and might by
accident act like a string (if by luck
the five bytes find themselves followed

Figure 3. A ØMQ string

by an innocently lurking null), but isn't a proper string. When your client and server don't agree on the string format, you will get weird results.

When you receive string data from ØMQ in C, you simply cannot trust that it's safely terminated. Every single time you read a string, you should allocate a new buffer with space for an extra byte, copy the string, and terminate it properly with a null.

So let's establish the rule that **ØMQ strings are length-specified and are sent on the wire** *without* **a trailing null**. In the simplest case (and we'll do this in our examples), a ØMQ string maps neatly to a ØMQ message frame, which looks like the above figure—a length and some bytes.

Here is what we need to do, in C, to receive a ØMQ string and deliver it to the application as a valid C string:

```
// Receive OMQ string from socket and convert into C string
// Chops string at 255 chars, if it's longer
static char *
s_recv (void *socket) {
    char buffer [256];
    int size = zmq_recv (socket, buffer, 255, 0);
    if (size == -1)
        return NULL;
    if (size > 255)
        size = 255;
    buffer [size] = 0;
    return strdup (buffer);
}
```

This makes a handy helper function and in the spirit of making things we can reuse profitably, let's write a similar `s_send` function that sends strings in the correct ØMQ format, and package this into a header file we can reuse.

The result is `zhelpers.h`, which lets us write sweeter and shorter ØMQ applications in C. It is a fairly long source, and only fun for C developers, so read it at leisure[6].

Version Reporting

ØMQ does come in several versions and quite often, if you hit a problem, it'll be something that's been fixed in a later version. So it's a useful trick to know *exactly* what version of ØMQ you're actually linking with.

---

6   https://github.com/imatix/zguide/blob/master/examples/C/zhelpers.h

Here is a tiny program that does that:

Example 5. ØMQ version reporting (version.c)

```
//  Report OMQ version

#include <zmq.h>

int main (void)
{
    int major, minor, patch;
    zmq_version (&major, &minor, &patch);
    printf ("Current OMQ version is %d.%d.%d\n", major, minor, patch);
    return 0;
}
```

Getting the Message Out

The second classic pattern is one-way data distribution, in which a server pushes updates to a set of clients. Let's see an example that pushes out weather updates consisting of a zip code, temperature, and relative humidity. We'll generate random values, just like the real weather stations do.

Here's the server. We'll use port 5556 for this application:

Example 6. Weather update server (wuserver.c)

```
//  Weather update server
//  Binds PUB socket to tcp://*:5556
//  Publishes random weather updates

#include "zhelpers.h"

int main (void)
{
    //  Prepare our context and publisher
    void *context = zmq_ctx_new ();
    void *publisher = zmq_socket (context, ZMQ_PUB);
    int rc = zmq_bind (publisher, "tcp://*:5556");
    assert (rc == 0);
    rc = zmq_bind (publisher, "ipc://weather.ipc");
    assert (rc == 0);

    //  Initialize random number generator
    srandom ((unsigned) time (NULL));
    while (1) {
        //  Get values that will fool the boss
        int zipcode, temperature, relhumidity;
        zipcode     = randof (100000);
        temperature = randof (215) - 80;
```

```
            relhumidity = randof (50) + 10;

            //  Send message to all subscribers
            char update [20];
            sprintf (update, "%05d %d %d", zipcode, temperature, relhumidity);
            s_send (publisher, update);
        }
        zmq_close (publisher);
        zmq_ctx_destroy (context);
        return 0;
    }
```

There's no start and no end to this stream of updates, it's like a never ending broadcast (see figure 4).

Here is the client application, which listens to the stream of updates and grabs anything to do with a specified zip code, by default New York City because that's a great place to start any adventure:

Example 7. Weather update client (wuclient.c)

```
//  Weather update client
//  Connects SUB socket to tcp://localhost:5556
//  Collects weather updates and finds avg temp in zipcode

#include "zhelpers.h"

int main (int argc, char *argv [])
{
    //  Socket to talk to server
    printf ("Collecting updates from weather server...\n");
    void *context = zmq_ctx_new ();
    void *subscriber = zmq_socket (context, ZMQ_SUB);
    int rc = zmq_connect (subscriber, "tcp://localhost:5556");
    assert (rc == 0);

    //  Subscribe to zipcode, default is NYC, 10001
    char *filter = (argc > 1)? argv [1]: "10001 ";
    rc = zmq_setsockopt (subscriber, ZMQ_SUBSCRIBE,
                         filter, strlen (filter));
    assert (rc == 0);

    //  Process 100 updates
    int update_nbr;
    long total_temp = 0;
    for (update_nbr = 0; update_nbr < 100; update_nbr++) {
        char *string = s_recv (subscriber);

        int zipcode, temperature, relhumidity;
        sscanf (string, "%d %d %d",
            &zipcode, &temperature, &relhumidity);
```

```
            total_temp += temperature;
            free (string);
        }
        printf ("Average temperature for zipcode '%s' was %dF\n",
            filter, (int) (total_temp / update_nbr));

        zmq_close (subscriber);
        zmq_ctx_destroy (context);
        return 0;
    }
```

Note that when you use a SUB socket you **must** set a subscription using `zmq_setsockopt()` and SUBSCRIBE, as in this code. If you don't set any subscription, you won't get any messages. It's a common mistake for beginners. The subscriber can set many subscriptions, which are added together. That is, if an update matches ANY subscription, the subscriber receives it. The subscriber can also cancel specific subscriptions. A subscription is often, but not necessarily a printable string. See `zmq_setsockopt()` for how this works.

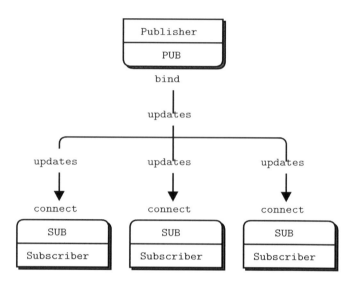

Figure 4. Publish-Subscribe

The PUB-SUB socket pair is asynchronous. The client does `zmq_recv()`, in a loop (or once if that's all it needs). Trying to send a message to a SUB socket will cause an error. Similarly, the service does `zmq_send()` as often as it needs to, but must not do `zmq_recv()` on a PUB socket.

In theory with ØMQ sockets, it does not matter which end connects and which end binds. However, in practice there are undocumented differences that I'll come to later. For now, bind the PUB and connect the SUB, unless your network design makes that impossible.

There is one more important thing to know about PUB-SUB sockets: you do not know precisely when a subscriber starts to get messages. Even if you start a subscriber, wait a while, and then start the publisher, **the subscriber will always miss the first messages that the publisher sends**. This is because as the subscriber connects to the publisher (something that takes a small but non-zero time), the publisher may already be sending messages out.

This "slow joiner" symptom hits enough people often enough that we're going to explain it in detail. Remember that ØMQ does asynchronous I/O, i.e., in the background. Say you have two nodes doing this, in this order:

- Subscriber connects to an endpoint and receives and counts messages.
- Publisher binds to an endpoint and immediately sends 1,000 messages.

Then the subscriber will most likely not receive anything. You'll blink, check that you set a correct filter and try again, and the subscriber will still not receive anything.

Making a TCP connection involves to and from handshaking that takes several milliseconds depending on your network and the number of hops between peers. In that time, ØMQ can send many messages. For sake of argument assume it takes 5 msecs to establish a connection, and that same link can handle 1M messages per second. During the 5 msecs that the subscriber is connecting to the publisher, it takes the publisher only 1 msec to send out those 1K messages.

In "Sockets and Patterns" we'll explain how to synchronize a publisher and subscribers so that you don't start to publish data until the subscribers really are connected and ready. There is a simple and stupid way to delay the publisher, which is to sleep. Don't do this in a real application, though, because it is extremely fragile as well as inelegant and slow. Use sleeps to prove to yourself what's happening, and then wait for "Sockets and Patterns" to see how to do this right.

The alternative to synchronization is to simply assume that the published data stream is infinite and has no start and no end. One also assumes that the subscriber doesn't care what transpired before it started up. This is how we built our weather client example.

So the client subscribes to its chosen zip code and collects a thousand updates for that zip code. That means about ten million updates from the server, if zip codes are randomly distributed. You can start the client, and then the server, and the client will keep working. You can stop and restart the server as often as you like, and the client will keep working. When the client has collected its thousand updates, it calculates the average, prints it, and exits.

Some points about the publish-subscribe (pub-sub) pattern:

- A subscriber can connect to more than one publisher, using one connect call each time. Data will then arrive and be interleaved ("fair-queued") so that no single publisher drowns out the others.
- If a publisher has no connected subscribers, then it will simply drop all messages.
- If you're using TCP and a subscriber is slow, messages will queue up on the publisher. We'll look at how to protect publishers against this using the "high-water mark" later.
- From ØMQ v3.x, filtering happens at the publisher side when using a connected protocol (`tcp://` or `ipc://`). Using the `epgm://` protocol, filtering happens at the subscriber side. In ØMQ v2.x, all filtering happened at the subscriber side.

This is how long it takes to receive and filter 10M messages on my laptop, which is an 2011-era Intel i5, decent but nothing special:

```
$ time wuclient
Collecting updates from weather server...
Average temperature for zipcode '10001 ' was 28F

real    0m4.470s
user    0m0.000s
sys     0m0.008s
```

Divide and Conquer

As a final example (you are surely getting tired of juicy code and want to delve back into philological discussions about comparative abstractive norms), let's do a little supercomputing. Then coffee. Our supercomputing application is a fairly typical parallel processing model (see figure 5). We have:

- A ventilator that produces tasks that can be done in parallel
- A set of workers that process tasks
- A sink that collects results back from the worker processes

In reality, workers run on superfast boxes, perhaps using GPUs (graphic processing units) to do the hard math. Here is the ventilator. It

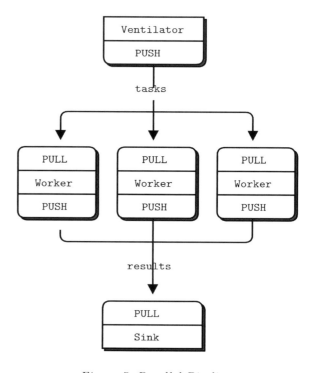

Figure 5. Parallel Pipeline

generates 100 tasks, each one is a message telling the worker to sleep for some number of milliseconds:

Example 8. Parallel task ventilator (taskvent.c)

```
//  Task ventilator
//  Binds PUSH socket to tcp://localhost:5557
//  Sends batch of tasks to workers via that socket

#include "zhelpers.h"
```

```
int main (void)
{
    void *context = zmq_ctx_new ();

    //  Socket to send messages on
    void *sender = zmq_socket (context, ZMQ_PUSH);
    zmq_bind (sender, "tcp://*:5557");

    //  Socket to send start of batch message on
    void *sink = zmq_socket (context, ZMQ_PUSH);
    zmq_connect (sink, "tcp://localhost:5558");

    printf ("Press Enter when the workers are ready: ");
    getchar ();
    printf ("Sending tasks to workers...\n");

    //  The first message is "0" and signals start of batch
    s_send (sink, "0");

    //  Initialize random number generator
    srandom ((unsigned) time (NULL));

    //  Send 100 tasks
    int task_nbr;
    int total_msec = 0;     //  Total expected cost in msecs
    for (task_nbr = 0; task_nbr < 100; task_nbr++) {
        int workload;
        //  Random workload from 1 to 100msecs
        workload = randof (100) + 1;
        total_msec += workload;
        char string [10];
        sprintf (string, "%d", workload);
        s_send (sender, string);
    }
    printf ("Total expected cost: %d msec\n", total_msec);
    sleep (1);              //  Give 0MQ time to deliver

    zmq_close (sink);
    zmq_close (sender);
    zmq_ctx_destroy (context);
    return 0;
}
```

Here is the worker application. It receives a message, sleeps for that number of seconds, and then signals that it's finished:

Example 9. Parallel task worker (taskwork.c)

```
//  Task worker
//  Connects PULL socket to tcp://localhost:5557
//  Collects workloads from ventilator via that socket
```

```
//  Connects PUSH socket to tcp://localhost:5558
//  Sends results to sink via that socket

#include "zhelpers.h"

int main (void)
{
    //  Socket to receive messages on
    void *context = zmq_ctx_new ();
    void *receiver = zmq_socket (context, ZMQ_PULL);
    zmq_connect (receiver, "tcp://localhost:5557");

    //  Socket to send messages to
    void *sender = zmq_socket (context, ZMQ_PUSH);
    zmq_connect (sender, "tcp://localhost:5558");

    //  Process tasks forever
    while (1) {
        char *string = s_recv (receiver);
        printf ("%s.", string);       //  Show progress
        fflush (stdout);
        s_sleep (atoi (string));      //  Do the work
        free (string);
        s_send (sender, "");          //  Send results to sink
    }
    zmq_close (receiver);
    zmq_close (sender);
    zmq_ctx_destroy (context);
    return 0;
}
```

Here is the sink application. It collects the 100 tasks, then calculates how long the overall processing took, so we can confirm that the workers really were running in parallel if there are more than one of them:

Example 10. Parallel task sink (tasksink.c)

```
//  Task sink
//  Binds PULL socket to tcp://localhost:5558
//  Collects results from workers via that socket

#include "zhelpers.h"

int main (void)
{
    //  Prepare our context and socket
    void *context = zmq_ctx_new ();
    void *receiver = zmq_socket (context, ZMQ_PULL);
    zmq_bind (receiver, "tcp://*:5558");

    //  Wait for start of batch
```

```c
            char *string = s_recv (receiver);
            free (string);

            //  Start our clock now
            int64_t start_time = s_clock ();

            //  Process 100 confirmations
            int task_nbr;
            for (task_nbr = 0; task_nbr < 100; task_nbr++) {
                char *string = s_recv (receiver);
                free (string);
                if ((task_nbr / 10) * 10 == task_nbr)
                    printf (":");
                else
                    printf (".");
                fflush (stdout);
            }
            //  Calculate and report duration of batch
            printf ("Total elapsed time: %d msec\n",
                (int) (s_clock () - start_time));

            zmq_close (receiver);
            zmq_ctx_destroy (context);
            return 0;
}
```

The average cost of a batch is 5 seconds. When we start 1, 2, or 4 workers we get results like this from the sink:

- 1 worker: total elapsed time: 5034 msecs.
- 2 workers: total elapsed time: 2421 msecs.
- 4 workers: total elapsed time: 1018 msecs.

Let's look at some aspects of this code in more detail:

- The workers connect upstream to the ventilator, and downstream to the sink. This means you can add workers arbitrarily. If the workers bound to their endpoints, you would need (a) more endpoints and (b) to modify the ventilator and/or the sink each time you added a worker. We say that the ventilator and sink are *stable* parts of our architecture and the workers are *dynamic* parts of it.

- We have to synchronize the start of the batch with all workers being up and running. This is a fairly common gotcha in ØMQ and there is no easy solution. The zmq_connect method takes a certain time. So when a set of workers connect to the ventilator, the first one to successfully connect will get a whole load of messages in that short time while the others are also connecting. If you don't synchronize the start of the batch somehow, the system won't run in parallel at all. Try removing the wait in the ventilator, and see what happens.

- The ventilator's PUSH socket distributes tasks to workers (assuming they are all connected *before* the batch starts going out) evenly. This is called *load balancing* and it's something we'll look at again in more detail.
- The sink's PULL socket collects results from workers evenly. This is called *fair-queuing* (see figure 6).

The pipeline pattern also exhibits the "slow joiner" syndrome, leading to accusations that PUSH sockets don't load balance properly. If you are using PUSH and PULL, and one of your workers gets way more messages than the others, it's because that PULL socket has joined faster than the others, and grabs a lot of messages before the others manage to connect. If you want proper load balancing, you probably want to look at the The load balancing pattern in "Advanced Request-Reply Patterns".

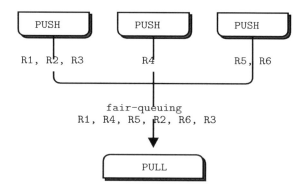

Figure 6. Fair Queuing

Programming with ØMQ

Having seen some examples, you must be eager to start using ØMQ in some apps. Before you start that, take a deep breath, chillax, and reflect on some basic advice that will save you much stress and confusion.

- Learn ØMQ step-by-step. It's just one simple API, but it hides a world of possibilities. Take the possibilities slowly and master each one.
- Write nice code. Ugly code hides problems and makes it hard for others to help you. You might get used to meaningless variable names, but people reading your code won't. Use names that are real words, that say something other than "I'm too careless to tell you what this variable is really for". Use consistent indentation and clean layout. Write nice code and your world will be more comfortable.
- Test what you make as you make it. When your program doesn't work, you should know what five lines are to blame. This is especially true when you do ØMQ magic, which just *won't* work the first few times you try it.
- When you find that things don't work as expected, break your code into pieces, test each one, see which one is not working. ØMQ lets you make essentially modular code; use that to your advantage.
- Make abstractions (classes, methods, whatever) as you need them. If you copy/paste a lot of code, you're going to copy/paste errors, too.

Getting the Context Right

ØMQ applications always start by creating a *context*, and then using that for creating sockets. In C, it's the `zmq_ctx_new()` call. You should create and use exactly one context in your process. Technically, the context is the container for all sockets in a single process, and acts as the transport for `inproc` sockets, which are the fastest way to connect threads in one process. If at runtime a process has two contexts, these are like separate ØMQ instances. If that's explicitly what you want, OK, but otherwise remember:

Do one `zmq_ctx_new()` at the start of your main line code, and one `zmq_ctx_destroy()` at the end.

If you're using the `fork()` system call, each process needs its own context. If you do `zmq_ctx_new()` in the main process before calling `fork()`, the child processes get their own contexts. In general, you want to do the interesting stuff in the child processes and just manage these from the parent process.

Making a Clean Exit

Classy programmers share the same motto as classy hit men: always clean-up when you finish the job. When you use ØMQ in a language like Python, stuff gets automatically freed for you. But when using C, you have to carefully free objects when you're finished with them or else you get memory leaks, unstable applications, and generally bad karma.

Memory leaks are one thing, but ØMQ is quite finicky about how you exit an application. The reasons are technical and painful, but the upshot is that if you leave any sockets open, the `zmq_ctx_destroy()` function will hang forever. And even if you close all sockets, `zmq_ctx_destroy()` will by default wait forever if there are pending connects or sends unless you set the LINGER to zero on those sockets before closing them.

The ØMQ objects we need to worry about are messages, sockets, and contexts. Luckily it's quite simple, at least in simple programs:

- Use `zmq_send()` and `zmq_recv()` when you can, it avoids the need to work with zmq_msg_t objects.
- If you do use `zmq_msg_recv()`, always release the received message as soon as you're done with it, by calling `zmq_msg_close()`.
- If you are opening and closing a lot of sockets, that's probably a sign that you need to redesign your application. In some cases socket handles won't be freed until you destroy the context.
- When you exit the program, close your sockets and then call `zmq_ctx_destroy()`. This destroys the context.

This is at least the case for C development. In a language with automatic object destruction, sockets and contexts will be destroyed as you leave the scope. If you use exceptions you'll have to do the clean-up in something like a "final" block, the same as for any resource.

If you're doing multithreaded work, it gets rather more complex than this. We'll get to multithreading in the next chapter, but because some of you will, despite warnings, try to run before you can safely walk, below is the quick and dirty guide to making a clean exit in a *multithreaded* ØMQ application.

First, do not try to use the same socket from multiple threads. Please don't explain why you think this would be excellent fun, just please don't do it. Next, you need to shut down each socket that has ongoing requests. The proper way is to set a low LINGER value (1 second), and then close the socket. If your language binding doesn't do this for you automatically when you destroy a context, I'd suggest sending a patch.

Finally, destroy the context. This will cause any blocking receives or polls or sends in attached threads (i.e., which share the same context) to return with an error. Catch that error, and then set linger on, and close sockets in *that* thread, and exit. Do not destroy the same context twice. The `zmq_ctx_destroy` in the main thread will block until all sockets it knows about are safely closed.

Voila! It's complex and painful enough that any language binding author worth his or her salt will do this automatically and make the socket closing dance unnecessary.

Why We Needed ØMQ

Now that you've seen ØMQ in action, let's go back to the "why".

Many applications these days consist of components that stretch across some kind of network, either a LAN or the Internet. So many application developers end up doing some kind of messaging. Some developers use message queuing products, but most of the time they do it themselves, using TCP or UDP. These protocols are not hard to use, but there is a great difference between sending a few bytes from A to B, and doing messaging in any kind of reliable way.

Let's look at the typical problems we face when we start to connect pieces using raw TCP. Any reusable messaging layer would need to solve all or most of these:

- How do we handle I/O? Does our application block, or do we handle I/O in the background? This is a key design decision. Blocking I/O creates architectures that do not scale well. But background I/O can be very hard to do right.

- How do we handle dynamic components, i.e., pieces that go away temporarily? Do we formally split components into "clients" and "servers" and mandate that servers cannot disappear? What then if we want to connect servers to servers? Do we try to reconnect every few seconds?

- How do we represent a message on the wire? How do we frame data so it's easy to write and read, safe from buffer overflows, efficient for small messages, yet adequate for the very largest videos of dancing cats wearing party hats?

- How do we handle messages that we can't deliver immediately? Particularly, if we're waiting for a component to come back online? Do we discard messages, put them into a database, or into a memory queue?
- Where do we store message queues? What happens if the component reading from a queue is very slow and causes our queues to build up? What's our strategy then?
- How do we handle lost messages? Do we wait for fresh data, request a resend, or do we build some kind of reliability layer that ensures messages cannot be lost? What if that layer itself crashes?
- What if we need to use a different network transport. Say, multicast instead of TCP unicast? Or IPv6? Do we need to rewrite the applications, or is the transport abstracted in some layer?
- How do we route messages? Can we send the same message to multiple peers? Can we send replies back to an original requester?
- How do we write an API for another language? Do we re-implement a wire-level protocol or do we repackage a library? If the former, how can we guarantee efficient and stable stacks? If the latter, how can we guarantee interoperability?
- How do we represent data so that it can be read between different architectures? Do we enforce a particular encoding for data types? How far is this the job of the messaging system rather than a higher layer?
- How do we handle network errors? Do we wait and retry, ignore them silently, or abort?

Take a typical open source project like Hadoop Zookeeper[7] and read the C API code in `src/c/src/zookeeper.c`[8]. When I read this code, in January 2013, it was 4,200 lines of mystery and in there is an undocumented, client/server network communication protocol. I see it's efficient because it uses `poll` instead of `select`. But really, Zookeeper should be using a generic messaging layer and an explicitly documented wire level protocol. It is incredibly wasteful for teams to be building this particular wheel over and over.

But how to make a reusable messaging layer? Why, when so many projects need this technology, are people still doing it the hard way by driving TCP sockets in their code, and solving the problems in that long list over and over (see figure 7)?

It turns out that building reusable messaging systems is really difficult, which is why few FOSS projects ever tried, and why commercial messaging products are complex, expensive, inflexible, and brittle. In 2006, iMatix designed AMQP[9] which started to give FOSS developers perhaps the first reusable recipe for a messaging system. AMQP works better than many other designs, but remains relatively complex, expensive, and brittle[10].

---

[7] http://hadoop.apache.org/zookeeper/
[8] http://github.com/apache/zookeeper/blob/trunk/src/c/src/zookeeper.c
[9] http://www.amqp.org
[10] http://www.imatix.com/articles:whats-wrong-with-amqp

It takes weeks to learn to use, and months to create stable architectures that don't crash when things get hairy.

Most messaging projects, like AMQP, that try to solve this long list of problems in a reusable way do so by inventing a new concept, the "broker", that does addressing, routing, and queuing. This results in a client/server protocol or a set of APIs on top of some undocumented protocol that allows applications to speak to this broker. Brokers are an excellent thing in reducing the complexity of large networks. But adding broker-based messaging to a product like Zookeeper would make it worse, not better. It would mean adding an additional big box, and a new single point of failure. A broker rapidly becomes a bottleneck and a new risk to manage. If the software supports it, we can add a second, third, and fourth broker and make some failover scheme. People do this. It creates more moving pieces, more complexity, and more things to break.

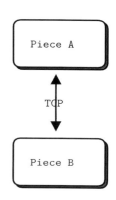

Figure 7. Messaging as it Starts

And a broker-centric setup needs its own operations team. You literally need to watch the brokers day and night, and beat them with a stick when they start misbehaving. You need boxes, and you need backup boxes, and you need people to manage those boxes. It is only worth doing for large applications with many moving pieces, built by several teams of people over several years.

So small to medium application developers are trapped. Either they avoid network programming and make monolithic applications that do not scale. Or they jump into network programming and make brittle, complex applications that are hard to maintain. Or they bet on a messaging product, and end up with scalable applications that depend on expensive, easily broken technology. There has been no really good choice, which is maybe why messaging is largely stuck in the last century and stirs strong emotions: negative ones for users, gleeful joy for those selling support and licenses (see figure 8).

What we need is something that does the job of messaging, but does it in such a simple and cheap way that it can work in any application, with close to zero cost. It should

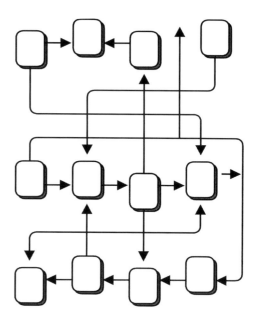

Figure 8. Messaging as it Becomes

be a library which which you just link, without any other dependencies. No additional moving pieces, so no additional risk. It should run on any OS and work with any programming language.

And this is ØMQ: an efficient, embeddable library that solves most of the problems an application needs to become nicely elastic across a network, without much cost.

Specifically:

- It handles I/O asynchronously, in background threads. These communicate with application threads using lock-free data structures, so concurrent ØMQ applications need no locks, semaphores, or other wait states.
- Components can come and go dynamically and ØMQ will automatically reconnect. This means you can start components in any order. You can create "service-oriented architectures" (SOAs) where services can join and leave the network at any time.
- It queues messages automatically when needed. It does this intelligently, pushing messages as close as possible to the receiver before queuing them.
- It has ways of dealing with over-full queues (called "high water mark"). When a queue is full, ØMQ automatically blocks senders, or throws away messages, depending on the kind of messaging you are doing (the so-called "pattern").
- It lets your applications talk to each other over arbitrary transports: TCP, multicast, in-process, inter-process. You don't need to change your code to use a different transport.
- It handles slow/blocked readers safely, using different strategies that depend on the messaging pattern.
- It lets you route messages using a variety of patterns such as request-reply and pub-sub. These patterns are how you create the topology, the structure of your network.
- It lets you create proxies to queue, forward, or capture messages with a single call. Proxies can reduce the interconnection complexity of a network.
- It delivers whole messages exactly as they were sent, using a simple framing on the wire. If you write a 10k message, you will receive a 10k message.
- It does not impose any format on messages. They are blobs of zero to gigabytes large. When you want to represent data you choose some other product on top, such as msgpack, Google's protocol buffers, and others.
- It handles network errors intelligently, by retrying automatically in cases where it makes sense.
- It reduces your carbon footprint. Doing more with less CPU means your boxes use less power, and you can keep your old boxes in use for longer. Al Gore would love ØMQ.

Actually ØMQ does rather more than this. It has a subversive effect on how you develop network-capable applications. Superficially, it's a socket-inspired API on which you do `zmq_recv()` and `zmq_send()`. But message processing rapidly becomes the central loop, and your application soon breaks down into a set of message processing tasks. It is elegant and natural. And it scales: each of these tasks maps to a node, and the nodes talk to each other across arbitrary transports. Two nodes in one process (node is a thread), two nodes on one box (node is a process), or two boxes on one network (node is a box)—it's all the same, with no application code changes.

Socket Scalability

Let's see ØMQ's scalability in action. Here is a shell script that starts the weather server and then a bunch of clients in parallel:

```
wuserver &
wuclient 12345 &
wuclient 23456 &
wuclient 34567 &
wuclient 45678 &
wuclient 56789 &
```

As the clients run, we take a look at the active processes using the `top` command', and we see something like (on a 4-core box):

```
PID    USER   PR   NI   VIRT    RES    SHR    S   %CPU   %MEM   TIME+       COMMAND
7136   ph     20    0   1040m   959m   1156   R   157    12.0   16:25.47    wuserver
7966   ph     20    0   98608   1804   1372   S    33     0.0    0:03.94    wuclient
7963   ph     20    0   33116   1748   1372   S    14     0.0    0:00.76    wuclient
7965   ph     20    0   33116   1784   1372   S     6     0.0    0:00.47    wuclient
7964   ph     20    0   33116   1788   1372   S     5     0.0    0:00.25    wuclient
7967   ph     20    0   33072   1740   1372   S     5     0.0    0:00.35    wuclient
```

Let's think for a second about what is happening here. The weather server has a single socket, and yet here we have it sending data to five clients in parallel. We could have thousands of concurrent clients. The server application doesn't see them, doesn't talk to them directly. So the ØMQ socket is acting like a little server, silently accepting client requests and shoving data out to them as fast as the network can handle it. And it's a multithreaded server, squeezing more juice out of your CPU.

Upgrading from ØMQ v2.2 to ØMQ v3.2

Compatible Changes

These changes don't impact existing application code directly:
- Pub-sub filtering is now done at the publisher side instead of subscriber side. This improves performance significantly in many pub-sub use cases. You can mix v3.2 and v2.1/v2.2 publishers and subscribers safely.
- ØMQ v3.2 has many new API methods (`zmq_disconnect()`, `zmq_unbind()`, `zmq_monitor()`, `zmq_ctx_set()`, etc.)

Incompatible Changes

These are the main areas of impact on applications and language bindings:

- Changed send/recv methods: `zmq_send()` and `zmq_recv()` have a different, simpler interface, and the old functionality is now provided by `zmq_msg_send()` and `zmq_msg_recv()`. Symptom: compile errors. Solution: fix up your code.
- These two methods return positive values on success, and -1 on error. In v2.x they always returned zero on success. Symptom: apparent errors when things actually work fine. Solution: test strictly for return code = -1, not non-zero.
- `zmq_poll()` now waits for milliseconds, not microseconds. Symptom: application stops responding (in fact responds 1000 times slower). Solution: use the `ZMQ_POLL_MSEC` macro defined below, in all `zmq_poll` calls.
- `ZMQ_NOBLOCK` is now called `ZMQ_DONTWAIT`. Symptom: compile failures on the `ZMQ_NOBLOCK` macro.
- The `ZMQ_HWM` socket option is now broken into `ZMQ_SNDHWM` and `ZMQ_RCVHWM`. Symptom: compile failures on the `ZMQ_HWM` macro.
- Most but not all `zmq_getsockopt()` options are now integer values. Symptom: runtime error returns on `zmq_setsockopt` and `zmq_getsockopt`.
- The `ZMQ_SWAP` option has been removed. Symptom: compile failures on `ZMQ_SWAP`. Solution: redesign any code that uses this functionality.

Suggested Shim Macros

For applications that want to run on both v2.x and v3.2, such as language bindings, our advice is to emulate c3.2 as far as possible. Here are C macro definitions that help your C/C++ code to work across both versions (taken from CZMQ[11]):

```
#ifndef ZMQ_DONTWAIT
#   define ZMQ_DONTWAIT     ZMQ_NOBLOCK
#endif
#if ZMQ_VERSION_MAJOR == 2
#   define zmq_msg_send(msg,sock,opt) zmq_send (sock, msg, opt)
#   define zmq_msg_recv(msg,sock,opt) zmq_recv (sock, msg, opt)
#   define zmq_ctx_destroy(context) zmq_term(context)
#   define ZMQ_POLL_MSEC    1000        //  zmq_poll is usec
#   define ZMQ_SNDHWM ZMQ_HWM
#   define ZMQ_RCVHWM ZMQ_HWM
#elif ZMQ_VERSION_MAJOR == 3
#   define ZMQ_POLL_MSEC    1           //  zmq_poll is msec
#endif
```

---

11 http://czmq.zeromq.org

Warning: Unstable Paradigms!

Traditional network programming is built on the general assumption that one socket talks to one connection, one peer. There are multicast protocols, but these are exotic. When we assume "one socket = one connection", we scale our architectures in certain ways. We create threads of logic where each thread work with one socket, one peer. We place intelligence and state in these threads.

In the ØMQ universe, sockets are doorways to fast little background communications engines that manage a whole set of connections automagically for you. You can't see, work with, open, close, or attach state to these connections. Whether you use blocking send or receive, or poll, all you can talk to is the socket, not the connections it manages for you. The connections are private and invisible, and this is the key to ØMQ's scalability.

This is because your code, talking to a socket, can then handle any number of connections across whatever network protocols are around, without change. A messaging pattern sitting in ØMQ scales more cheaply than a messaging pattern sitting in your application code.

So the general assumption no longer applies. As you read the code examples, your brain will try to map them to what you know. You will read "socket" and think "ah, that represents a connection to another node". That is wrong. You will read "thread" and your brain will again think, "ah, a thread represents a connection to another node", and again your brain will be wrong.

If you're reading this Guide for the first time, realize that until you actually write ØMQ code for a day or two (and maybe three or four days), you may feel confused, especially by how simple ØMQ makes things for you, and you may try to impose that general assumption on ØMQ, and it won't work. And then you will experience your moment of enlightenment and trust, that *zap-pow-kaboom* satori paradigm-shift moment when it all becomes clear.

Chapter 2. Sockets and Patterns

In "Basics" we took ØMQ for a drive, with some basic examples of the main ØMQ patterns: request-reply, pub-sub, and pipeline. In this chapter, we're going to get our hands dirty and start to learn how to use these tools in real programs.

We'll cover:

- How to create and work with ØMQ sockets.
- How to send and receive messages on sockets.
- How to build your apps around ØMQ's asynchronous I/O model.
- How to handle multiple sockets in one thread.
- How to handle fatal and nonfatal errors properly.
- How to handle interrupt signals like Ctrl-C.
- How to shut down a ØMQ application cleanly.
- How to check a ØMQ application for memory leaks.
- How to send and receive multipart messages.
- How to forward messages across networks.
- How to build a simple message queuing broker.
- How to write multithreaded applications with ØMQ.
- How to use ØMQ to signal between threads.
- How to use ØMQ to coordinate a network of nodes.
- How to create and use message envelopes for pub-sub.
- Using the HWM (high-water mark) to protect against memory overflows.

The Socket API

To be perfectly honest, ØMQ does a kind of switch-and-bait on you, for which we we don't apologize. It's for your own good and it hurts us more than it hurts you. ØMQ presents a familiar socket-based API, which requires great effort for us to hide a bunch of message-processing engines. However, the result will slowly fix your world view about how to design and write distributed software.

Sockets are the de facto standard API for network programming, as well as being useful for stopping your eyes from falling onto your cheeks. One thing that makes ØMQ especially tasty to developers is that it uses sockets and messages instead of some other arbitrary set of concepts. Kudos to Martin Sustrik for pulling this off. It turns "Message Oriented Middleware", a phrase guaranteed to send the whole room off to Catatonia, into "Extra Spicy Sockets!", which leaves us with a strange craving for pizza and a desire to know more.

Like a favorite dish, ØMQ sockets are easy to digest. Sockets have a life in four parts, just like BSD sockets:

- Creating and destroying sockets, which go together to form a karmic circle of socket life (see `zmq_socket()`, `zmq_close()`).
- Configuring sockets by setting options on them and checking them if necessary (see `zmq_setsockopt()`, `zmq_getsockopt()`).
- Plugging sockets onto the network topology by creating ØMQ connections to and from them (see `zmq_bind()`, `zmq_connect()`).
- Using the sockets to carry data by writing and receiving messages on them (see `zmq_send()`, `zmq_recv()`).

Note that sockets are always void pointers, and messages (which we'll come to very soon) are structures. So in C you pass sockets as-such, but you pass addresses of messages in all functions that work with messages, like `zmq_send()` and `zmq_recv()`. As a mnemonic, realize that "in ØMQ, all your sockets are belong to us", but messages are things you actually own in your code.

Creating, destroying, and configuring sockets works as you'd expect for any object. But remember that ØMQ is an asynchronous, elastic fabric. This has some impact on how we plug sockets into the network topology and how we use the sockets after that.

Plugging Sockets into the Topology

To create a connection between two nodes, you use `zmq_bind()` in one node and `zmq_connect()` in the other. As a general rule of thumb, the node that does `zmq_bind()` is a "server", sitting on a well-known network address, and the node which does `zmq_connect()` is a "client", with unknown or arbitrary network addresses. Thus we say that we "bind a socket to an endpoint" and "connect a socket to an endpoint", the endpoint being that well-known network address.

ØMQ connections are somewhat different from classic TCP connections. The main notable differences are:

- They go across an arbitrary transport (`inproc`, `ipc`, `tcp`, `pgm`, or `epgm`). See `zmq_inproc()`, `zmq_ipc()`, `zmq_tcp()`, `zmq_pgm()`, and `zmq_epgm()`.
- One socket may have many outgoing and many incoming connections.
- There is no `zmq_accept()` method. When a socket is bound to an endpoint it automatically starts accepting connections.
- The network connection itself happens in the background, and ØMQ will automatically reconnect if the network connection is broken (e.g., if the peer disappears and then comes back).
- Your application code cannot work with these connections directly; they are encapsulated under the socket.

Many architectures follow some kind of client/server model, where the server is the component that is most static, and the clients are the components that are most dynamic, i.e., they come and go the most. There are sometimes issues of addressing: servers will be visible to clients, but not necessarily vice versa. So mostly it's obvious which node should be doing `zmq_bind()` (the server) and which should be doing `zmq_connect()` (the client). It also depends on the kind of sockets you're using, with some exceptions for unusual network architectures. We'll look at socket types later.

Now, imagine we start the client *before* we start the server. In traditional networking, we get a big red Fail flag. But ØMQ lets us start and stop pieces arbitrarily. As soon as the client node does `zmq_connect()`, the connection exists and that node can start to write messages to the socket. At some stage (hopefully before messages queue up so much that they start to get discarded, or the client blocks), the server comes alive, does a `zmq_bind()`, and ØMQ starts to deliver messages.

A server node can bind to many endpoints (that is, a combination of protocol and address) and it can do this using a single socket. This means it will accept connections across different transports:

```
zmq_bind (socket, "tcp://*:5555");
zmq_bind (socket, "tcp://*:9999");
zmq_bind (socket, "inproc://somename");
```

With most transports, you cannot bind to the same endpoint twice, unlike for example in UDP. The `ipc` transport does, however, let one process bind to an endpoint already used by a first process. It's meant to allow a process to recover after a crash.

Although ØMQ tries to be neutral about which side binds and which side connects, there are differences. We'll see these in more detail later. The upshot is that you should usually think in terms of "servers" as static parts of your topology that bind to more or less fixed endpoints, and "clients" as dynamic parts that come and go and connect to these endpoints. Then, design your application around this model. The chances that it will "just work" are much better like that.

Sockets have types. The socket type defines the semantics of the socket, its policies for routing messages inwards and outwards, queuing, etc. You can connect certain types of socket together, e.g., a publisher socket and a subscriber socket. Sockets work together in "messaging patterns". We'll look at this in more detail later.

It's the ability to connect sockets in these different ways that gives ØMQ its basic power as a message queuing system. There are layers on top of this, such as proxies, which we'll get to later. But essentially, with ØMQ you define your network architecture by plugging pieces together like a child's construction toy.

Sending and Receiving Messages

To send and receive messages you use the `zmq_msg_send()` and `zmq_msg_recv()` methods. The names are conventional, but ØMQ's I/O model is different enough from the classic TCP model (see figure 9) that you will need time to get your head around it.

Let's look at the main differences between TCP sockets and ØMQ sockets when it comes to working with data:

- ØMQ sockets carry messages, like UDP, rather than a stream of bytes as TCP does. A ØMQ message is length-specified binary data. We'll come to messages shortly, their design is optimized for performance and so a little tricky.

- ØMQ sockets do their I/O in a background thread. This means that messages arrive in local input queues and are sent from local output queues, no matter what your application is busy doing.

- ØMQ sockets have one-to-N routing behavior built-in, according to the socket type.

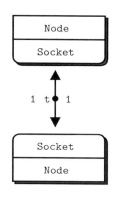

Figure 9. TCP sockets are 1 to 1

The zmq_send() method does not actually send the message to the socket connection(s). It queues the message so that the I/O thread can send it asynchronously. It does not block except in some exception cases. So the message is not necessarily sent when zmq_send() returns to your application.

Unicast Transports

ØMQ provides a set of unicast transports (inproc, ipc, and tcp) and multicast transports (epgm, pgm). Multicast is an advanced technique that we'll come to later. Don't even start using it unless you know that your fan-out ratios will make 1-to-N unicast impossible.

For most common cases, use **tcp**, which is a *disconnected TCP* transport. It is elastic, portable, and fast enough for most cases. We call this disconnected because ØMQ's tcp transport doesn't require that the endpoint exists before you connect to it. Clients and servers can connect and bind at any time, can go and come back, and it remains transparent to applications.

The inter-process ipc transport is disconnected, like tcp. It has one limitation: it does not yet work on Windows. By convention we use endpoint names with an ".ipc" extension to avoid potential conflict with other file names. On UNIX systems, if you use ipc endpoints you need to create these with appropriate permissions otherwise they may not be shareable between processes running under different user IDs. You must also make sure all processes can access the files, e.g., by running in the same working directory.

The inter-thread transport, **inproc**, is a connected signaling transport. It is much faster than tcp or ipc. This transport has a specific limitation compared to tpc and icp: **the server must issue a bind before any client issues a connect**. This is something future versions of ØMQ may fix, but at present this defines how you use inproc sockets. We create and bind one socket and start the child threads, which create and connect the other sockets.

ØMQ is Not a Neutral Carrier

A common question that newcomers to ØMQ ask (it's one I've asked myself) is, "how do I write an XYZ server in ØMQ?" For example, "how do I write an HTTP server in ØMQ?" The implication is that if we use normal sockets to carry HTTP requests and responses, we should be able to use ØMQ sockets to do the same, only much faster and better.

The answer used to be "this is not how it works". ØMQ is not a neutral carrier, it imposes a framing on the transport protocols it uses. This framing is not compatible with existing protocols, which tend to use their own framing. For example, compare an HTTP request and a ØMQ request, both over TCP/IP.

The HTTP request uses CR-LF as its simplest framing delimiter (see figure 10), whereas ØMQ uses a length-specified frame (see figure 11). So you could write an HTTP-like protocol using ØMQ, using for example the request-reply socket pattern. But it would not be HTTP.

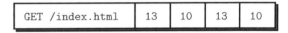

Figure 10. HTTP on the Wire

Since v3.3, however, ØMQ has a socket option called `ZMQ_ROUTER_RAW` that lets you read and write data without the ØMQ framing. You could use this to read and write proper HTTP requests and responses. Hardeep Singh contributed this change so that he could connect to Telnet servers from his ØMQ application. At time of writing this is still somewhat experimental, but it shows how ØMQ keeps evolving to solve new problems. Maybe the next patch will be yours.

Figure 11. ØMQ on the Wire

I/O Threads

We said that ØMQ does I/O in a background thread. One I/O thread (for all sockets) is sufficient for all but the most extreme applications. When you create a new context, it starts with one I/O thread. The general rule of thumb is to allow one I/O thread per gigabyte of data in or out per second. To raise the number of I/O threads, use the `zmq_ctx_set()` call *before* creating any sockets:

```
int io-threads = 4;
void *context = zmq_ctx_new ();
zmq_ctx_set (context, ZMQ_IO_THREADS, io_threads);
assert (zmq_ctx_get (context, ZMQ_IO_THREADS) == io_threads);
```

We've seen that one socket can handle dozens, even thousands of connections at once. This has a fundamental impact on how you write applications. A traditional networked application has one process or one thread per remote connection, and that process or thread handles one socket. ØMQ lets you collapse this entire structure into a single process and then break it up as necessary for scaling.

If you are using ØMQ for inter-thread communications only (i.e., a multithreaded application that does no external socket I/O) you can set the I/O threads to zero. It's not a significant optimization though, more of a curiosity.

Messaging Patterns

Underneath the brown paper wrapping of ØMQ's socket API lies the world of messaging patterns. If you have a background in enterprise messaging, or know UDP well, these will be vaguely familiar. But to most ØMQ newcomers, they are a surprise. We're so used to the TCP paradigm where a socket maps one-to-one to another node.

Let's recap briefly what ØMQ does for you. It delivers blobs of data (messages) to nodes, quickly and efficiently. You can map nodes to threads, processes, or nodes. ØMQ gives your applications a single socket API to work with, no matter what the actual transport (like in-process, inter-process, TCP, or multicast). It automatically reconnects to peers as they come and go. It queues messages at both sender and receiver, as needed. It manages these queues carefully to ensure processes don't run out of memory, overflowing to disk when appropriate. It handles socket errors. It does all I/O in background threads. It uses lock-free techniques for talking between nodes, so there are never locks, waits, semaphores, or deadlocks.

But cutting through that, it routes and queues messages according to precise recipes called *patterns*. It is these patterns that provide ØMQ's intelligence. They encapsulate our hard-earned experience of the best ways to distribute data and work. ØMQ's patterns are hard-coded but future versions may allow user-definable patterns.

ØMQ patterns are implemented by pairs of sockets with matching types. In other words, to understand ØMQ patterns you need to understand socket types and how they work together. Mostly, this just takes study; there is little that is obvious at this level.

The built-in core ØMQ patterns are:

- **Request-reply**, which connects a set of clients to a set of services. This is a remote procedure call and task distribution pattern.
- **Pub-sub**, which connects a set of publishers to a set of subscribers. This is a data distribution pattern.
- **Pipeline**, which connects nodes in a fan-out/fan-in pattern that can have multiple steps and loops. This is a parallel task distribution and collection pattern.
- **Exclusive pair**, which connects two sockets exclusively. This is a pattern for connecting two threads in a process, not to be confused with "normal" pairs of sockets.

We looked at the first three of these in "Basics", and we'll see the exclusive pair pattern later in this chapter. The `zmq_socket()` man page is fairly clear about the patterns, it's worth reading several times until it starts to make sense. These are the socket combinations that are valid for a connect-bind pair (either side can bind):

- PUB and SUB

- REQ and REP
- REQ and ROUTER
- DEALER and REP
- DEALER and ROUTER
- DEALER and DEALER
- ROUTER and ROUTER
- PUSH and PULL
- PAIR and PAIR

You'll also see references to XPUB and XSUB sockets, which we'll come to later (they're like raw versions of PUB and SUB). Any other combination will produce undocumented and unreliable results, and future versions of ØMQ will probably return errors if you try them. You can and will, of course, bridge other socket types via code, i.e., read from one socket type and write to another.

High-Level Messaging Patterns

These four core patterns are cooked into ØMQ. They are part of the ØMQ API, implemented in the core C++ library, and are guaranteed to be available in all fine retail stores.

On top of those, we add *high-level messaging patterns*. We build these high-level patterns on top of ØMQ and implement them in whatever language we're using for our application. They are not part of the core library, do not come with the ØMQ package, and exist in their own space as part of the ØMQ community. For example the Majordomo pattern, which we explore in "Reliable Request-Reply Patterns", sits in the GitHub Majordomo project in the ZeroMQ organization.

One of the things we aim to provide you with in this guide are a set of such high-level patterns, both small (how to handle messages sanely) and large (how to make a reliable pub-sub architecture).

Working with Messages

The libzmq core library has in fact two APIs to send and receive messages. The `zmq_send()` and `zmq_recv()` methods that we've already seen and used are simple one-liners. We will use these often, but `zmq_recv()` is bad at dealing with arbitrary message sizes: it truncates messages to whatever buffer size you provide. So there's a second API that works with zmq_msg_t structures, with a richer but more difficult API:

- Initialise a message: `zmq_msg_init()`, `zmq_msg_init_size()`, `zmq_msg_init_data()`.
- Sending and receiving a message: `zmq_msg_send()`, `zmq_msg_recv()`.
- Release a message: `zmq_msg_close()`.
- Access message content: `zmq_msg_data()`, `zmq_msg_size()`, `zmq_msg_more()`.
- Work with message properties: `zmq_msg_get()`, `zmq_msg_set()`.
- Message manipulation: `zmq_msg_copy()`, `zmq_msg_move()`.

On the wire, ØMQ messages are blobs of any size from zero upwards that fit in memory. You do your own serialization using protocol buffers, msgpack, JSON, or whatever else your applications need to speak. It's wise to choose a data representation that is portable, but you can make your own decisions about trade-offs.

In memory, ØMQ messages are `zmq_msg_t` structures (or classes depending on your language). Here are the basic ground rules for using ØMQ messages in C:

- You create and pass around `zmq_msg_t` objects, not blocks of data.
- To read a message, you use `zmq_msg_init()` to create an empty message, and then you pass that to `zmq_msg_recv()`.
- To write a message from new data, you use `zmq_msg_init_size()` to create a message and at the same time allocate a block of data of some size. You then fill that data using `memcpy`, and pass the message to `zmq_msg_send()`.
- To release (not destroy) a message, you call `zmq_msg_close()`. This drops a reference, and eventually ØMQ will destroy the message.
- To access the message content, you use `zmq_msg_data()`. To know how much data the message contains, use `zmq_msg_size()`.
- Do not use `zmq_msg_move()`, `zmq_msg_copy()`, or `zmq_msg_init_data()` unless you read the man pages and know precisely why you need these.
- After you pass a message to `zmq_msg_send()`, ØMQ will clear the message, i.e., set the size to zero. You cannot send the same message twice, and you cannot access the message data after sending it.
- These rules don't apply if you use `zmq_send()` and `zmq_recv()`, to which you pass byte arrays, not message structures.

If you want to send the same message more than once, and it's sizable, create a second message, initialize it using `zmq_msg_init()`, and then use `zmq_msg_copy()` to create a copy of the first message. This does not copy the data but copies a reference. You can then send the message twice (or more, if you create more copies) and the message will only be finally destroyed when the last copy is sent or closed.

ØMQ also supports *multipart* messages, which let you send or receive a list of frames as a single on-the-wire message. This is widely used in real applications and we'll look at that later in this chapter and in "Advanced Request-Reply Patterns".

Frames (also called "message parts" in the ØMQ reference manual pages) are the basic wire format for ØMQ messages. A frame is a length-specified block of data. The length can be zero upwards. If you've done any TCP programming you'll appreciate why frames are a useful answer to the question "how much data am I supposed to read of this network socket now?"

There is a wire-level protocol called ZMTP[12] that defines how ØMQ reads and writes frames on a TCP connection. If you're interested in how this works, the spec is quite short.

---

12 http://rfc.zeromq.org/spec:15

Originally, a ØMQ message was one frame, like UDP. We later extended this with multipart messages, which are quite simply series of frames with a "more" bit set to one, followed by one with that bit set to zero. The ØMQ API then lets you write messages with a "more" flag and when you read messages, it lets you check if there's "more".

In the low-level ØMQ API and the reference manual, therefore, there's some fuzziness about messages versus frames. So here's a useful lexicon:

- A message can be one or more parts.
- These parts are also called "frames".
- Each part is a `zmq_msg_t` object.
- You send and receive each part separately, in the low-level API.
- Higher-level APIs provide wrappers to send entire multipart messages.

Some other things that are worth knowing about messages:

- You may send zero-length messages, e.g., for sending a signal from one thread to another.
- ØMQ guarantees to deliver all the parts (one or more) for a message, or none of them.
- ØMQ does not send the message (single or multipart) right away, but at some indeterminate later time. A multipart message must therefore fit in memory.
- A message (single or multipart) must fit in memory. If you want to send files of arbitrary sizes, you should break them into pieces and send each piece as separate single-part messages. *Using multipart data will not reduce memory consumption.*
- You must call `zmq_msg_close()` when finished with a received message, in languages that don't automatically destroy objects when a scope closes. You don't call this method after sending a message.

And to be repetitive, do not use `zmq_msg_init_data()` yet. This is a zero-copy method and is guaranteed to create trouble for you. There are far more important things to learn about ØMQ before you start to worry about shaving off microseconds.

This rich API can be tiresome to work with. The methods are optimized for performance, not simplicity. If you start using these you will almost definitely get them wrong until you've read the man pages with some care. So one of the main jobs of a good language binding is to wrap this API up in classes that are easier to use.

Handling Multiple Sockets

In all the examples so far, the main loop of most examples has been:

1. Wait for message on socket.
2. Process message.
3. Repeat.

What if we want to read from multiple endpoints at the same time? The simplest way is to connect one socket to all the endpoints and get ØMQ to do the fan-in for us. This is legal if the remote endpoints are in the same pattern, but it would be wrong to connect a PULL socket to a PUB endpoint.

To actually read from multiple sockets all at once, use zmq_poll(). An even better way might be to wrap zmq_poll() in a framework that turns it into a nice event-driven *reactor*, but it's significantly more work than we want to cover here.

Let's start with a dirty hack, partly for the fun of not doing it right, but mainly because it lets me show you how to do non-blocking socket reads. Here is a simple example of reading from two sockets using non-blocking reads. This rather confused program acts both as a subscriber to weather updates, and a worker for parallel tasks:

Example 11. Multiple socket reader (msreader.c)

```
//  Reading from multiple sockets
//  This version uses a simple recv loop

#include "zhelpers.h"

int main (void)
{
    //  Connect to task ventilator
    void *context = zmq_ctx_new ();
    void *receiver = zmq_socket (context, ZMQ_PULL);
    zmq_connect (receiver, "tcp://localhost:5557");

    //  Connect to weather server
    void *subscriber = zmq_socket (context, ZMQ_SUB);
    zmq_connect (subscriber, "tcp://localhost:5556");
    zmq_setsockopt (subscriber, ZMQ_SUBSCRIBE, "10001 ", 6);

    //  Process messages from both sockets
    //  We prioritize traffic from the task ventilator
    while (1) {
        char msg [256];
        while (1) {
            int size = zmq_recv (receiver, msg, 255, ZMQ_DONTWAIT);
            if (size != -1) {
                //  Process task
            }
            else
                break;
        }
        while (1) {
            int size = zmq_recv (subscriber, msg, 255, ZMQ_DONTWAIT);
            if (size != -1) {
                //  Process weather update
            }
            else
```

```
                break;
        }
        //  No activity, so sleep for 1 msec
        s_sleep (1);
    }
    zmq_close (receiver);
    zmq_close (subscriber);
    zmq_ctx_destroy (context);
    return 0;
}
```

The cost of this approach is some additional latency on the first message (the sleep at the end of the loop, when there are no waiting messages to process). This would be a problem in applications where submillisecond latency was vital. Also, you need to check the documentation for nanosleep() or whatever function you use to make sure it does not busy-loop.

You can treat the sockets fairly by reading first from one, then the second rather than prioritizing them as we did in this example.

Now let's see the same senseless little application done right, using `zmq_poll()`:

Example 12. Multiple socket poller (mspoller.c)

```
//  Reading from multiple sockets
//  This version uses zmq_poll()

#include "zhelpers.h"

int main (void)
{
    //  Connect to task ventilator
    void *context = zmq_ctx_new ();
    void *receiver = zmq_socket (context, ZMQ_PULL);
    zmq_connect (receiver, "tcp://localhost:5557");

    //  Connect to weather server
    void *subscriber = zmq_socket (context, ZMQ_SUB);
    zmq_connect (subscriber, "tcp://localhost:5556");
    zmq_setsockopt (subscriber, ZMQ_SUBSCRIBE, "10001 ", 6);

    //  Process messages from both sockets
    while (1) {
        char msg [256];
        zmq_pollitem_t items [] = {
            { receiver,   0, ZMQ_POLLIN, 0 },
            { subscriber, 0, ZMQ_POLLIN, 0 }
        };
        zmq_poll (items, 2, -1);
        if (items [0].revents & ZMQ_POLLIN) {
            int size = zmq_recv (receiver, msg, 255, 0);
            if (size != -1) {
```

```
                // Process task
            }
        }
        if (items [1].revents & ZMQ_POLLIN) {
            int size = zmq_recv (subscriber, msg, 255, 0);
            if (size != -1) {
                // Process weather update
            }
        }
    }
    zmq_close (subscriber);
    zmq_ctx_destroy (context);
    return 0;
}
```

The items structure has these four members:

```
typedef struct {
    void *socket;       //  OMQ socket to poll on
    int fd;             //  OR, native file handle to poll on
    short events;       //  Events to poll on
    short revents;      //  Events returned after poll
} zmq_pollitem_t;
```

Multipart Messages

ØMQ lets us compose a message out of several frames, giving us a "multipart message". Realistic applications use multipart messages heavily, both for wrapping messages with address information and for simple serialization. We'll look at reply envelopes later.

What we'll learn now is simply how to blindly and safely read and write multipart messages in any application (such as a proxy) that needs to forward messages without inspecting them.

When you work with multipart messages, each part is a `zmq_msg` item. E.g., if you are sending a message with five parts, you must construct, send, and destroy five `zmq_msg` items. You can do this in advance (and store the `zmq_msg` items in an array or other structure), or as you send them, one-by-one.

Here is how we send the frames in a multipart message (we receive each frame into a message object):

```
zmq_msg_send (socket, &message, ZMQ_SNDMORE);
...
zmq_msg_send (socket, &message, ZMQ_SNDMORE);
...
zmq_msg_send (socket, &message, 0);
```

Here is how we receive and process all the parts in a message, be it single part or multipart:

```
while (1) {
    zmq_msg_t message;
    zmq_msg_init (&message);
    zmq_msg_recv (socket, &message, 0);
    //  Process the message frame
    ...
    zmq_msg_close (&message);
    if (!zmq_msg_more (&message))
        break;      //  Last message frame
}
```

Some things to know about multipart messages:
- When you send a multipart message, the first part (and all following parts) are only actually sent on the wire when you send the final part.
- If you are using zmq_poll(), when you receive the first part of a message, all the rest has also arrived.
- You will receive all parts of a message, or none at all.
- Each part of a message is a separate zmq_msg item.
- You will receive all parts of a message whether or not you check the more property.
- On sending, ØMQ queues message frames in memory until the last is received, then sends them all.
- There is no way to cancel a partially sent message, except by closing the socket.

Intermediaries and Proxies

ØMQ aims for decentralized intelligence, but that doesn't mean your network is empty space in the middle. It's filled with message-aware infrastructure and quite often, we build that infrastructure with ØMQ. The ØMQ plumbing can range from tiny pipes to full-blown service-oriented brokers. The messaging industry calls this *intermediation*, meaning that the stuff in the middle deals with either side. In ØMQ, we call these proxies, queues, forwarders, device, or brokers, depending on the context.

This pattern is extremely common in the real world and is why our societies and economies are filled with intermediaries who have no other real function than to reduce the complexity and scaling costs of larger networks. Real-world intermediaries are typically called wholesalers, distributors, managers, and so on.

The Dynamic Discovery Problem

One of the problems you will hit as you design larger distributed architectures is discovery. That is, how do pieces know about each other? It's especially difficult if pieces come and go, thus we can call this the "dynamic discovery problem".

There are several solutions to dynamic discovery. The simplest is to entirely avoid it by hard-coding (or configuring) the network architecture so discovery is done by hand. That is, when you add a new piece, you reconfigure the network to know about it.

In practice, this leads to increasingly fragile and unwieldy architectures. Let's say you have one publisher and a hundred subscribers. You connect each subscriber to the publisher by configuring a publisher endpoint in each subscriber. That's easy (see figure 12). Subscribers are dynamic; the publisher is static. Now say you add more publishers. Suddenly, it's not so easy any more. If you continue to connect each subscriber to each publisher, the cost of avoiding dynamic discovery gets higher and higher.

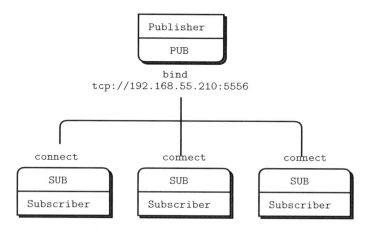

Figure 12. Small-Scale Pub-Sub Network

There are quite a few answers to this, but the very simplest answer is to add an intermediary; that is, a static point in the network to which all other nodes connect. In classic messaging, this is the job of the message broker. ØMQ doesn't come with a message broker as such, but it lets us build intermediaries quite easily.

You might wonder, if all networks eventually get large enough to need intermediaries, why don't we simply have a message broker in place for all applications? For beginners, it's a fair compromise. Just always use a star topology, forget about performance, and things will usually work. However, message brokers are greedy things; in their role as central intermediaries, they become too complex, too stateful, and eventually a problem.

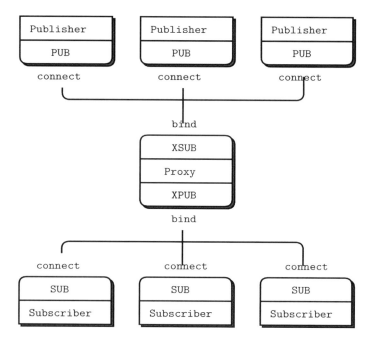

Figure 13. Pub-Sub Network with a Proxy

It's better to think of intermediaries as simple stateless message switches. A good analogy is an HTTP proxy; it's there, but doesn't have any special role. Adding a pub-sub proxy solves the dynamic discovery problem in our example. We set the proxy in the "middle" of the network (see figure 13). The proxy opens an XSUB socket, an XPUB socket, and binds each to well-known IP addresses and ports. Then, all other processes connect to the proxy, instead of to each other. It becomes trivial to add more subscribers or publishers.

We need XPUB and XSUB sockets because ØMQ does subscription forwarding from subscribers to publishers. XSUB and XPUB are exactly like SUB and PUB except they expose subscriptions as special messages. The proxy has to forward these subscription messages from subscriber side to publisher side, by reading them from the XPUB socket and writing them to the XSUB socket. This is the main use case for XSUB and XPUB (see figure 14).

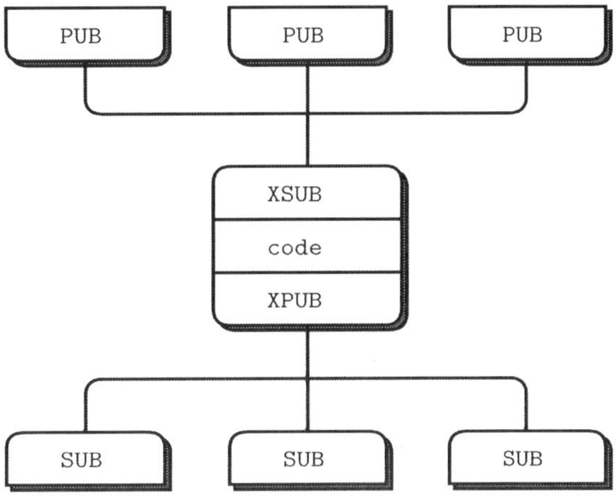

Figure 14. Extended Pub-Sub

Shared Queue (DEALER and ROUTER sockets)

In the Hello World client/server application, we have one client that talks to one service. However, in real cases we usually need to allow multiple services as well as multiple clients. This lets us scale up the power of the service (many threads or processes or nodes rather than just one). The only constraint is that services must be stateless, all state being in the request or in some shared storage such as a database.

There are two ways to connect multiple clients to multiple servers. The brute force way is to connect each client socket to multiple service endpoints. One client socket can connect to multiple service sockets, and the REQ socket will then distribute requests among these services. Let's say you connect a client socket to three service endpoints; A, B, and C. The client makes requests R1, R2, R3, R4. R1 and R4 go to service A, R2 goes to B, and R3 goes to service C (see figure 15).

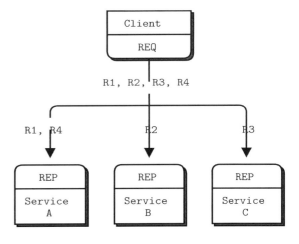

Figure 15. Request Distribution

This design lets you add more clients cheaply. You can also add more services. Each client will distribute its requests to the services. But each client has to know the service topology. If you have 100 clients and then you decide to add three more services, you need to reconfigure and restart 100 clients in order for the clients to know about the three new services.

That's clearly not the kind of thing we want to be doing at 3 a.m. when our supercomputing cluster has run out of resources and we desperately need to add a couple of hundred of new service nodes. Too many static pieces are like liquid concrete: knowledge is distributed and the more static pieces you have, the more effort it is to change the topology. What we want is something sitting in between clients and services that centralizes all knowledge of the topology. Ideally, we should be able to add and remove services or clients at any time without touching any other part of the topology.

So we'll write a little message queuing broker that gives us this flexibility. The broker binds to two endpoints, a frontend for clients and a backend for services. It then uses `zmq_poll()` to monitor these two sockets for activity and when it has some, it shuttles messages between its two sockets. It doesn't actually manage any queues explicitly—ØMQ does that automatically on each socket.

When you use REQ to talk to REP, you get a strictly synchronous request-reply dialog. The client sends a request. The service reads the request and sends a reply. The client then reads the reply. If either the client or the service try to do anything else (e.g., sending two requests in a row without waiting for a response), they will get an error.

But our broker has to be non-blocking. Obviously, we can use `zmq_poll()` to wait for activity on either socket, but we can't use REP and REQ.

Luckily, there are two sockets called DEALER and ROUTER that let you do non-blocking request-response. You'll see in "Advanced Request-Reply Patterns" how DEALER and ROUTER sockets let you build all kinds of asynchronous request-reply flows. For now, we're just going to see how DEALER and ROUTER let us extend REQ-REP across an intermediary, that is, our little broker.

In this simple extended request-reply pattern, REQ talks to ROUTER and DEALER talks to REP. In between the DEALER and ROUTER, we have to have code (like our broker) that pulls messages off the one socket and shoves them onto the other (see figure 16).

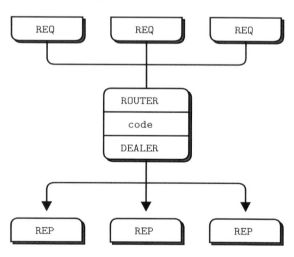

Figure 16. Extended Request-Reply

Code Connected Volume 1 - Chapter 2. Sockets and Patterns   51

The request-reply broker binds to two endpoints, one for clients to connect to (the
frontend socket) and one for workers to connect to (the backend). To test this broker,
you will want to change your workers so they connect to the backend socket. Here is a
client that shows what I mean:

Example 13. Request-reply client (rrclient.c)

```
//  Hello World client
//  Connects REQ socket to tcp://localhost:5559
//  Sends "Hello" to server, expects "World" back

#include "zhelpers.h"

int main (void)
{
    void *context = zmq_ctx_new ();

    //  Socket to talk to server
    void *requester = zmq_socket (context, ZMQ_REQ);
    zmq_connect (requester, "tcp://localhost:5559");

    int request_nbr;
    for (request_nbr = 0; request_nbr != 10; request_nbr++) {
        s_send (requester, "Hello");
        char *string = s_recv (requester);
        printf ("Received reply %d [%s]\n", request_nbr, string);
        free (string);
    }
    zmq_close (requester);
    zmq_ctx_destroy (context);
    return 0;
}
```

Here is the worker:

Example 14. Request-reply worker (rrworker.c)

```
//  Hello World worker
//  Connects REP socket to tcp://*:5560
//  Expects "Hello" from client, replies with "World"

#include "zhelpers.h"

int main (void)
{
    void *context = zmq_ctx_new ();

    //  Socket to talk to clients
    void *responder = zmq_socket (context, ZMQ_REP);
    zmq_connect (responder, "tcp://localhost:5560");
```

```
    while (1) {
        //  Wait for next request from client
        char *string = s_recv (responder);
        printf ("Received request: [%s]\n", string);
        free (string);

        //  Do some 'work'
        sleep (1);

        //  Send reply back to client
        s_send (responder, "World");
    }
    //  We never get here, but clean up anyhow
    zmq_close (responder);
    zmq_ctx_destroy (context);
    return 0;
}
```

And here is the broker, which properly handles multipart messages:

Example 15. Request-reply broker (rrbroker.c)

```
//  Simple request-reply broker

#include "zhelpers.h"

int main (void)
{
    //  Prepare our context and sockets
    void *context = zmq_ctx_new ();
    void *frontend = zmq_socket (context, ZMQ_ROUTER);
    void *backend  = zmq_socket (context, ZMQ_DEALER);
    zmq_bind (frontend, "tcp://*:5559");
    zmq_bind (backend,  "tcp://*:5560");

    //  Initialize poll set
    zmq_pollitem_t items [] = {
        { frontend, 0, ZMQ_POLLIN, 0 },
        { backend,  0, ZMQ_POLLIN, 0 }
    };
    //  Switch messages between sockets
    while (1) {
        zmq_msg_t message;
        zmq_poll (items, 2, -1);
        if (items [0].revents & ZMQ_POLLIN) {
            while (1) {
                //  Process all parts of the message
                zmq_msg_init (&message);
                zmq_msg_recv (&message, frontend, 0);
                zmq_msg_send (&message, backend,
                    zmq_msg_more (&message)? ZMQ_SNDMORE: 0);
```

```
                    zmq_msg_close (&message);
                    if (!zmq_msg_more (&message))
                        break;      //  Last message part
                }
            }
            if (items [1].revents & ZMQ_POLLIN) {
                while (1) {
                    //  Process all parts of the message
                    zmq_msg_init (&message);
                    zmq_msg_recv (&message, backend, 0);
                    zmq_msg_send (&message, frontend,
                        zmq_msg_more (&message)? ZMQ_SNDMORE: 0);
                    zmq_msg_close (&message);
                    if (!zmq_msg_more (&message))
                        break;      //  Last message part
                }
            }
        }
        //  We never get here, but clean up anyhow
        zmq_close (frontend);
        zmq_close (backend);
        zmq_ctx_destroy (context);
        return 0;
    }
```

Using a request-reply broker makes your client/server architectures easier to scale because clients don't see workers, and workers don't see clients. The only static node is the broker in the middle (see figure 17).

ØMQ's Built-In Proxy Function

It turns out that the core loop in the previous section's rrbroker is very useful, and reusable. It lets us build pub-sub forwarders and shared queues and other little intermediaries with very little effort. ØMQ wraps this up in a single method, zmq_proxy():

```
zmq_proxy (frontend, backend,
    capture);
```

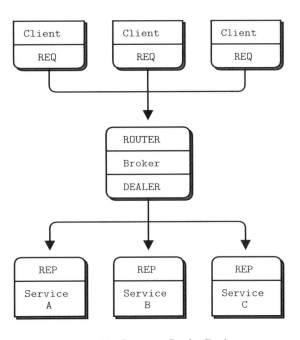

Figure 17. Request-Reply Broker

The two (or three sockets, if we want to capture data) must be properly connected, bound, and configured. When we call the zmq_proxy, method it's exactly like starting the main loop of rrbroker. Let's rewrite the request-reply broker to call zmq_proxy, and re-badge this as an expensive-sounding "message queue" (people have charged houses for code that did less):

Example 16. Message queue broker (msgqueue.c)

```c
//  Simple message queuing broker
//  Same as request-reply broker but using QUEUE device

#include "zhelpers.h"

int main (void)
{
    void *context = zmq_ctx_new ();

    //  Socket facing clients
    void *frontend = zmq_socket (context, ZMQ_ROUTER);
    int rc = zmq_bind (frontend, "tcp://*:5559");
    assert (rc == 0);

    //  Socket facing services
    void *backend = zmq_socket (context, ZMQ_DEALER);
    rc = zmq_bind (backend, "tcp://*:5560");
    assert (rc == 0);

    //  Start the proxy
    zmq_proxy (frontend, backend, NULL);

    //  We never get here...
    zmq_close (frontend);
    zmq_close (backend);
    zmq_ctx_destroy (context);
    return 0;
}
```

If you're like most ØMQ users, at this stage your mind is starting to think, "What kind of evil stuff can I do if I plug random socket types into the proxy?" The short answer is: try it and work out what is happening. In practice, you would usually stick to ROUTER/DEALER, XSUB/XPUB, or PULL/PUSH.

Transport Bridging

A frequent request from ØMQ users is, "How do I connect my ØMQ network with technology X?" where X is some other networking or messaging technology.

The simple answer is to build a *bridge*. A bridge is a small application that speaks one protocol at one socket, and converts to/from a second protocol at another socket. A protocol interpreter, if you like. A common bridging problem in ØMQ is to bridge two transports or networks.

As an example, we're going to write a little proxy that sits in between a publisher and a set of subscribers, bridging two networks. The frontend socket (SUB) faces the internal network where the weather server is sitting, and the backend

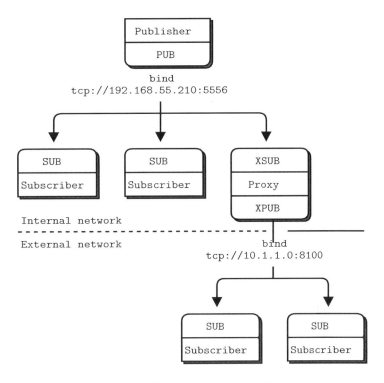

Figure 18. Pub-Sub Forwarder Proxy

(PUB) faces subscribers on the external network. It subscribes to the weather service on the frontend socket, and republishes its data on the backend socket.

Example 17. Weather update proxy (wuproxy.c)

```
//  Weather proxy device

#include "zhelpers.h"

int main (void)
{
    void *context = zmq_ctx_new ();

    //  This is where the weather server sits
    void *frontend = zmq_socket (context, ZMQ_XSUB);
    zmq_connect (frontend, "tcp://192.168.55.210:5556");

    //  This is our public endpoint for subscribers
    void *backend = zmq_socket (context, ZMQ_XPUB);
    zmq_bind (backend, "tcp://10.1.1.0:8100");

    //  Run the proxy until the user interrupts us
    zmq_proxy (frontend, backend, NULL);

    zmq_close (frontend);
    zmq_close (backend);
```

```
        zmq_ctx_destroy (context);
        return 0;
}
```

It looks very similar to the earlier proxy example, but the key part is that the frontend and backend sockets are on two different networks (see figure 18). We can use this model for example to connect a multicast network (pgm transport) to a tcp publisher.

Handling Errors and ETERM

ØMQ's error handling philosophy is a mix of fail-fast and resilience. Processes, we believe, should be as vulnerable as possible to internal errors, and as robust as possible against external attacks and errors. To give an analogy, a living cell will self-destruct if it detects a single internal error, yet it will resist attack from the outside by all means possible.

Assertions, which pepper the ØMQ code, are absolutely vital to robust code; they just have to be on the right side of the cellular wall. And there should be such a wall. If it is unclear whether a fault is internal or external, that is a design flaw to be fixed. In C/C++, assertions stop the application immediately with an error. In other languages, you may get exceptions or halts.

When ØMQ detects an external fault it returns an error to the calling code. In some rare cases, it drops messages silently if there is no obvious strategy for recovering from the error.

In most of the C examples we've seen so far there's been no error handling. **Real code should do error handling on every single ØMQ call**. If you're using a language binding other than C, the binding may handle errors for you. In C, you do need to do this yourself. There are some simple rules, starting with POSIX conventions:

- Methods that create objects return NULL if they fail.
- Methods that process data may return the number of bytes processed, or -1 on an error or failure.
- Other methods return 0 on success and -1 on an error or failure.
- The error code is provided in errno or zmq_errno().
- A descriptive error text for logging is provided by zmq_strerror().

For example:

```
void *context = zmq_ctx_new ();
assert (context);
void *socket = zmq_socket (context, ZMQ_REP);
assert (socket);
int rc = zmq_bind (socket, "tcp://*:5555");
if (rc == -1) {
    printf ("E: bind failed: %s\n", strerror (errno));
    return -1;
}
```

There are two main exceptional conditions that you should handle as nonfatal:

- When your code receives a message with the `ZMQ_DONTWAIT` option and there is no waiting data, ØMQ will return -1 and set `errno` to `EAGAIN`.
- When one thread calls `zmq_ctx_destroy()`, and other threads are still doing blocking work, the `zmq_ctx_destroy()` call closes the context and all blocking calls exit with -1, and `errno` set to `ETERM`.

In C/C++, asserts can be removed entirely in optimized code, so don't make the mistake of wrapping the whole ØMQ call in an `assert()`. It looks neat; then the optimizer removes all the asserts and the calls you want to make, and your application breaks in impressive ways.

Let's see how to shut down a process cleanly. We'll take the parallel pipeline example from the previous section. If we've started a whole lot of workers in the background, we now want to kill them when the batch is finished. Let's do this by sending a kill message to the workers. The best place to do this is the sink because it really knows when the batch is done.

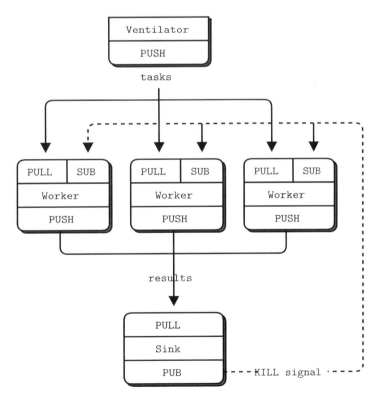

Figure 19. Parallel Pipeline with Kill Signaling

How do we connect the sink to the workers? The PUSH/PULL sockets are one-way only. We could switch to another socket type, or we could mix multiple socket flows. Let's try the latter: using a pub-sub model to send kill messages to the workers (see figure 19):

- The sink creates a PUB socket on a new endpoint.
- Workers bind their input socket to this endpoint.
- When the sink detects the end of the batch, it sends a kill to its PUB socket.
- When a worker detects this kill message, it exits.

It doesn't take much new code in the sink:

```
void *control = zmq_socket (context, ZMQ_PUB);
zmq_bind (control, "tcp://*:5559");
...
//  Send kill signal to workers
s_send (controller, "KILL");
```

Here is the worker process, which manages two sockets (a PULL socket getting tasks, and a SUB socket getting control commands), using the zmq_poll() technique we saw earlier:

Example 18. Parallel task worker with kill signaling (taskwork2.c)

```
//  Task worker - design 2
//  Adds pub-sub flow to receive and respond to kill signal

#include "zhelpers.h"

int main (void)
{
    //  Socket to receive messages on
    void *context = zmq_ctx_new ();
    void *receiver = zmq_socket (context, ZMQ_PULL);
    zmq_connect (receiver, "tcp://localhost:5557");

    //  Socket to send messages to
    void *sender = zmq_socket (context, ZMQ_PUSH);
    zmq_connect (sender, "tcp://localhost:5558");

    //  Socket for control input
    void *controller = zmq_socket (context, ZMQ_SUB);
    zmq_connect (controller, "tcp://localhost:5559");
    zmq_setsockopt (controller, ZMQ_SUBSCRIBE, "", 0);

    //  Process messages from either socket
    while (1) {
        zmq_pollitem_t items [] = {
            { receiver, 0, ZMQ_POLLIN, 0 },
            { controller, 0, ZMQ_POLLIN, 0 }
```

Code Connected Volume 1 - Chapter 2. Sockets and Patterns

```
            };
            zmq_poll (items, 2, -1);
            if (items [0].revents & ZMQ_POLLIN) {
                char *string = s_recv (receiver);
                printf ("%s.", string);      //  Show progress
                fflush (stdout);
                s_sleep (atoi (string));     //  Do the work
                free (string);
                s_send (sender, "");         //  Send results to sink
            }
            //  Any waiting controller command acts as 'KILL'
            if (items [1].revents & ZMQ_POLLIN)
                break;                       //  Exit loop
        }
        zmq_close (receiver);
        zmq_close (sender);
        zmq_close (controller);
        zmq_ctx_destroy (context);
        return 0;
    }
```

Here is the modified sink application. When it's finished collecting results, it broadcasts a kill message to all workers:

Example 19. Parallel task sink with kill signaling (tasksink2.c)

```
//  Task sink - design 2
//  Adds pub-sub flow to send kill signal to workers

#include "zhelpers.h"

int main (void)
{
    //  Socket to receive messages on
    void *context = zmq_ctx_new ();
    void *receiver = zmq_socket (context, ZMQ_PULL);
    zmq_bind (receiver, "tcp://*:5558");

    //  Socket for worker control
    void *controller = zmq_socket (context, ZMQ_PUB);
    zmq_bind (controller, "tcp://*:5559");

    //  Wait for start of batch
    char *string = s_recv (receiver);
    free (string);

    //  Start our clock now
    int64_t start_time = s_clock ();

    //  Process 100 confirmations
    int task_nbr;
```

```
        for (task_nbr = 0; task_nbr < 100; task_nbr++) {
            char *string = s_recv (receiver);
            free (string);
            if ((task_nbr / 10) * 10 == task_nbr)
                printf (":");
            else
                printf (".");
            fflush (stdout);
        }
        printf ("Total elapsed time: %d msec\n",
            (int) (s_clock () - start_time));

        //  Send kill signal to workers
        s_send (controller, "KILL");
        sleep (1);              //  Give 0MQ time to deliver

        zmq_close (receiver);
        zmq_close (controller);
        zmq_ctx_destroy (context);
        return 0;
}
```

Handling Interrupt Signals

Realistic applications need to shut down cleanly when interrupted with Ctrl-C or another signal such as SIGTERM. By default, these simply kill the process, meaning messages won't be flushed, files won't be closed cleanly, and so on.

Here is how we handle a signal in various languages:

Example 20. Handling Ctrl-C cleanly (interrupt.c)

```
//  Shows how to handle Ctrl-C

#include <zmq.h>
#include <stdio.h>
#include <signal.h>

//  Signal handling
//
//  Call s_catch_signals() in your application at startup, and then
//  exit your main loop if s_interrupted is ever 1. Works especially
//  well with zmq_poll.

static int s_interrupted = 0;
static void s_signal_handler (int signal_value)
{
    s_interrupted = 1;
}
```

```
static void s_catch_signals (void)
{
    struct sigaction action;
    action.sa_handler = s_signal_handler;
    action.sa_flags = 0;
    sigemptyset (&action.sa_mask);
    sigaction (SIGINT, &action, NULL);
    sigaction (SIGTERM, &action, NULL);
}

int main (void)
{
    void *context = zmq_ctx_new ();
    void *socket = zmq_socket (context, ZMQ_REP);
    zmq_bind (socket, "tcp://*:5555");

    s_catch_signals ();
    while (1) {
        //  Blocking read will exit on a signal
        char buffer [255];
        zmq_recv (socket, buffer, 255, 0);
        if (s_interrupted) {
            printf ("W: interrupt received, killing server...\n");
            break;
        }
    }
    zmq_close (socket);
    zmq_ctx_destroy (context);
    return 0;
}
```

The program provides s_catch_signals(), which traps Ctrl-C (SIGINT) and SIGTERM. When either of these signals arrive, the s_catch_signals() handler sets the global variable s_interrupted. Thanks to your signal handler, your application will not die automatically. Instead, you have a chance to clean up and exit gracefully. You have to now explicitly check for an interrupt and handle it properly. Do this by calling s_catch_signals() (copy this from interrupt.c) at the start of your main code. This sets up the signal handling. The interrupt will affect ØMQ calls as follows:

- If your code is blocking in a blocking call (sending a message, receiving a message, or polling), then when a signal arrives, the call will return with EINTR.
- Wrappers like s_recv() return NULL if they are interrupted.

So check for an EINTR return code, a NULL return, and/or s_interrupted.

Here is a typical code fragment:

```
s_catch_signals ();
client = zmq_socket (...);
while (!s_interrupted) {
    char *message = s_recv (client);
```

```
        if (!message)
            break;              //  Ctrl-C used
    }
    zmq_close (client);
```

If you call `s_catch_signals()` and don't test for interrupts, then your application will become immune to Ctrl-C and SIGTERM, which may be useful, but is usually not.

Detecting Memory Leaks

Any long-running application has to manage memory correctly, or eventually it'll use up all available memory and crash. If you use a language that handles this automatically for you, congratulations. If you program in C or C++ or any other language where you're responsible for memory management, here's a short tutorial on using valgrind, which among other things will report on any leaks your programs have.

- To install valgrind, e.g., on Ubuntu or Debian, issue this command:

```
sudo apt-get install valgrind
```

- By default, ØMQ will cause valgrind to complain a lot. To remove these warnings, create a file called vg.supp that contains this:

```
{
    <socketcall_sendto>
    Memcheck:Param
    socketcall.sendto(msg)
    fun:send
    ...
}
{
    <socketcall_sendto>
    Memcheck:Param
    socketcall.send(msg)
    fun:send
    ...
}
```

- Fix your applications to exit cleanly after Ctrl-C. For any application that exits by itself, that's not needed, but for long-running applications, this is essential, otherwise valgrind will complain about all currently allocated memory.
- Build your application with -DDEBUG if it's not your default setting. That ensures valgrind can tell you exactly where memory is being leaked.
- Finally, run valgrind thus:

```
valgrind --tool=memcheck --leak-check=full --suppressions=vg.supp
someprog
```

And after fixing any errors it reported, you should get the pleasant message:

```
==30536== ERROR SUMMARY: 0 errors from 0 contexts...
```

Multithreading with ØMQ

ØMQ is perhaps the nicest way ever to write multithreaded (MT) applications. Whereas ØMQ sockets require some readjustment if you are used to traditional sockets, ØMQ multithreading will take everything you know about writing MT applications, throw it into a heap in the garden, pour gasoline over it, and set it alight. It's a rare book that deserves burning, but most books on concurrent programming do.

To make utterly perfect MT programs (and I mean that literally), **we don't need mutexes, locks, or any other form of inter-thread communication except messages sent across ØMQ sockets.**

By "perfect MT programs", I mean code that's easy to write and understand, that works with the same design approach in any programming language, and on any operating system, and that scales across any number of CPUs with zero wait states and no point of diminishing returns.

If you've spent years learning tricks to make your MT code work at all, let alone rapidly, with locks and semaphores and critical sections, you will be disgusted when you realize it was all for nothing. If there's one lesson we've learned from 30+ years of concurrent programming, it is: *just don't share state*. It's like two drunkards trying to share a beer. It doesn't matter if they're good buddies. Sooner or later, they're going to get into a fight. And the more drunkards you add to the table, the more they fight each other over the beer. The tragic majority of MT applications look like drunken bar fights.

The list of weird problems that you need to fight as you write classic shared-state MT code would be hilarious if it didn't translate directly into stress and risk, as code that seems to work suddenly fails under pressure. A large firm with world-beating experience in buggy code released its list of "11 Likely Problems In Your Multithreaded Code", which covers forgotten synchronization, incorrect granularity, read and write tearing, lock-free reordering, lock convoys, two-step dance, and priority inversion.

Yeah, we counted seven problems, not eleven. That's not the point though. The point is, do you really want that code running the power grid or stock market to start getting two-step lock convoys at 3 p.m. on a busy Thursday? Who cares what the terms actually mean? This is not what turned us on to programming, fighting ever more complex side effects with ever more complex hacks.

Some widely used models, despite being the basis for entire industries, are fundamentally broken, and shared state concurrency is one of them. Code that wants to scale without limit does it like the Internet does, by sending messages and sharing nothing except a common contempt for broken programming models.

You should follow some rules to write happy multithreaded code with ØMQ:

- Isolate data privately within its thread and never share data in multiple threads. The only exception to this are ØMQ contexts, which are threadsafe.
- Stay away from the classic concurrency mechanisms like as mutexes, critical sections, semaphores, etc. These are an anti-pattern in ØMQ applications.
- Create one ØMQ context at the start of your process, and pass that to all threads that you want to connect via `inproc` sockets.
- Use *attached* threads to create structure within your application, and connect these to their parent threads using PAIR sockets over `inproc`. The pattern is: bind parent socket, then create child thread which connects its socket.
- Use *detached* threads to simulate independent tasks, with their own contexts. Connect these over `tcp`. Later you can move these to stand-alone processes without changing the code significantly.
- All interaction between threads happens as ØMQ messages, which you can define more or less formally.
- Don't share ØMQ sockets between threads. ØMQ sockets are not threadsafe. Technically it's possible to migrate a socket from one thread to another but it demands skill. The only place where it's remotely sane to share sockets between threads are in language bindings that need to do magic like garbage collection on sockets.

If you need to start more than one proxy in an application, for example, you will want to run each in their own thread. It is easy to make the error of creating the proxy frontend and backend sockets in one thread, and then passing the sockets to the proxy in another thread. This may appear to work at first but will fail randomly in real use. Remember: *Do not use or close sockets except in the thread that created them.*

If you follow these rules, you can quite easily build elegant multithreaded applications, and later split off threads into separate processes as you need to. Application logic can sit in threads, processes, or nodes: whatever your scale needs.

ØMQ uses native OS threads rather than virtual "green" threads. The advantage is that you don't need to learn any new threading API, and that ØMQ threads map cleanly to your operating system. You can use standard tools like Intel's ThreadChecker to see what your application is doing. The disadvantages are that native threading APIs are not always portable, and that if you have a huge number of threads (in the thousands), some operating systems will get stressed.

Let's see how this works in practice. We'll turn our old Hello World server into something more capable. The original server ran in a single thread. If the work per request is low, that's fine: one ØMQ thread can run at full speed on a CPU core, with no waits, doing an awful lot of work. But realistic servers have to do nontrivial work per request. A single core may not be enough when 10,000 clients hit the server all at once. So a realistic server will start multiple worker threads. It then accepts requests as fast as it can and distributes these to its worker threads. The worker threads grind through the work and eventually send their replies back.

You can, of course, do all this using a proxy broker and external worker processes, but often it's easier to start one process that gobbles up sixteen cores than sixteen processes, each gobbling up one core. Further, running workers as threads will cut out a network hop, latency, and network traffic.

The MT version of the Hello World service basically collapses the broker and workers into a single process:

Example 21. Multithreaded service (mtserver.c)

```c
//  Multithreaded Hello World server

#include "zhelpers.h"
#include <pthread.h>

static void *
worker_routine (void *context) {
    //  Socket to talk to dispatcher
    void *receiver = zmq_socket (context, ZMQ_REP);
    zmq_connect (receiver, "inproc://workers");

    while (1) {
        char *string = s_recv (receiver);
        printf ("Received request: [%s]\n", string);
        free (string);
        //  Do some 'work'
        sleep (1);
        //  Send reply back to client
        s_send (receiver, "World");
    }
    zmq_close (receiver);
    return NULL;
}

int main (void)
{
    void *context = zmq_ctx_new ();

    //  Socket to talk to clients
    void *clients = zmq_socket (context, ZMQ_ROUTER);
    zmq_bind (clients, "tcp://*:5555");

    //  Socket to talk to workers
    void *workers = zmq_socket (context, ZMQ_DEALER);
    zmq_bind (workers, "inproc://workers");

    //  Launch pool of worker threads
    int thread_nbr;
    for (thread_nbr = 0; thread_nbr < 5; thread_nbr++) {
        pthread_t worker;
        pthread_create (&worker, NULL, worker_routine, context);
```

```
    }
    //  Connect work threads to client threads via a queue proxy
    zmq_proxy (clients, workers, NULL);

    //  We never get here, but clean up anyhow
    zmq_close (clients);
    zmq_close (workers);
    zmq_ctx_destroy (context);
    return 0;
}
```

All the code should be recognizable to you by now. How it works:

- The server starts a set of worker threads. Each worker thread creates a REP socket and then processes requests on this socket. Worker threads are just like single-threaded servers. The only differences are the transport (inproc instead of tcp), and the bind-connect direction.
- The server creates a ROUTER socket to talk to clients and binds this to its external interface (over tcp).
- The server creates a DEALER socket to talk to the workers and binds this to its internal interface (over inproc).
- The server starts a proxy that connects the two sockets. The proxy pulls incoming requests fairly from all clients, and distributes those out to workers. It also routes replies back to their origin.

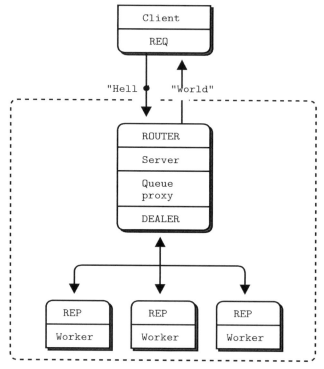

Figure 20. Multithreaded Server

Note that creating threads is not portable in most programming languages. The POSIX library is pthreads, but on Windows you have to use a different API. In our example, the pthread_create call starts up a new thread running the worker_routine function we defined. We'll see in "Advanced Request-Reply Patterns" how to wrap this in a portable API.

Here the "work" is just a one-second pause. We could do anything in the workers, including talking to other nodes. This is what the MT server looks like in terms of

ØMQ sockets and nodes. Note how the request-reply chain is REQ-ROUTER-queue-DEALER-REP (see figure 20).

Signaling Between Threads (PAIR Sockets)

When you start making multithreaded applications with ØMQ, you'll encounter the question of how to coordinate your threads. Though you might be tempted to insert "sleep" statements, or use multithreading techniques such as semaphores or mutexes, **the only mechanism that you should use are ØMQ messages**. Remember the story of The Drunkards and The Beer Bottle.

Let's make three threads that signal each other when they are ready (see figure 21). In this example, we use PAIR sockets over the inproc transport:

Example 22. Multithreaded relay (mtrelay.c)

```c
//  Multithreaded relay

#include "zhelpers.h"
#include <pthread.h>

static void *
step1 (void *context) {
    //  Connect to step2 and tell it we're ready
    void *xmitter = zmq_socket (context, ZMQ_PAIR);
    zmq_connect (xmitter, "inproc://step2");
    printf ("Step 1 ready, signaling step 2\n");
    s_send (xmitter, "READY");
    zmq_close (xmitter);

    return NULL;
}

static void *
step2 (void *context) {
    //  Bind inproc socket before starting step1
    void *receiver = zmq_socket (context, ZMQ_PAIR);
    zmq_bind (receiver, "inproc://step2");
    pthread_t thread;
    pthread_create (&thread, NULL, step1, context);

    //  Wait for signal and pass it on
    char *string = s_recv (receiver);
    free (string);
    zmq_close (receiver);

    //  Connect to step3 and tell it we're ready
    void *xmitter = zmq_socket (context, ZMQ_PAIR);
    zmq_connect (xmitter, "inproc://step3");
    printf ("Step 2 ready, signaling step 3\n");
```

```
    s_send (xmitter, "READY");
    zmq_close (xmitter);

    return NULL;
}

int main (void)
{
    void *context = zmq_ctx_new ();

    //  Bind inproc socket before starting step2
    void *receiver = zmq_socket (context, ZMQ_PAIR);
    zmq_bind (receiver, "inproc://step3");
    pthread_t thread;
    pthread_create (&thread, NULL, step2, context);

    //  Wait for signal
    char *string = s_recv (receiver);
    free (string);
    zmq_close (receiver);

    printf ("Test successful!\n");
    zmq_ctx_destroy (context);
    return 0;
}
```

This is a classic pattern for multithreading with ØMQ:

1. Two threads communicate over inproc, using a shared context.

2. The parent thread creates one socket, binds it to an inproc:// endpoint, and *then* starts the child thread, passing the context to it.

3. The child thread creates the second socket, connects it to that inproc:// endpoint, and *then* signals to the parent thread that it's ready.

Note that multithreading code using this pattern is not scalable out to processes. If you use inproc and socket pairs, you are building a tightly-bound application, i.e., one where your threads are structurally interdependent. Do this when low latency is really vital. The other design pattern is a loosely bound application, where threads have their own context and communicate over ipc or tcp. You can easily break loosely bound threads into separate processes.

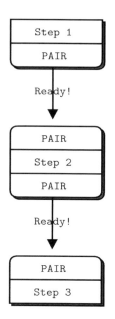

Figure 21. The Relay Race

This is the first time we've shown an example using PAIR sockets. Why use PAIR? Other socket combinations might seem to work, but they all have side effects that could interfere with signaling:

- You can use PUSH for the sender and PULL for the receiver. This looks simple and will work, but remember that PUSH will distribute messages to all available receivers. If you by accident start two receivers (e.g., you already have one running and you start a second), you'll "lose" half of your signals. PAIR has the advantage of refusing more than one connection; the pair is *exclusive*.

- You can use DEALER for the sender and ROUTER for the receiver. ROUTER, however, wraps your message in an "envelope", meaning your zero-size signal turns into a multipart message. If you don't care about the data and treat anything as a valid signal, and if you don't read more than once from the socket, that won't matter. If, however, you decide to send real data, you will suddenly find ROUTER providing you with "wrong" messages. DEALER also distributes outgoing messages, giving the same risk as PUSH.

- You can use PUB for the sender and SUB for the receiver. This will correctly deliver your messages exactly as you sent them and PUB does not distribute as PUSH or DEALER do. However, you need to configure the subscriber with an empty subscription, which is annoying.

For these reasons, PAIR makes the best choice for coordination between pairs of threads.

Node Coordination

When you want to coordinate a set of nodes on a network, PAIR sockets won't work well any more. This is one of the few areas where the strategies for threads and nodes are different. Principally, nodes come and go whereas threads are usually static. PAIR sockets do not automatically reconnect if the remote node goes away and comes back.

The second significant difference between threads and nodes is that you typically have a fixed number of threads but a more variable number of nodes. Let's take one of our earlier scenarios (the weather server and clients) and use node coordination to ensure that subscribers don't lose data when starting up.

This is how the application will work:

- The publisher knows in advance how many subscribers it expects. This is just a magic number it gets from somewhere.

- The publisher starts up and waits for all subscribers to connect. This is the node coordination part. Each subscriber subscribes and then tells the publisher it's ready via another socket.

- When the publisher has all subscribers connected, it starts to publish data.

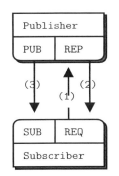

Figure 22. Pub-Sub Synchronization

In this case, we'll use a REQ-REP socket flow to synchronize subscribers and publisher (see figure 22). Here is the publisher:

Example 23. Synchronized publisher (syncpub.c)

```c
//  Synchronized publisher

#include "zhelpers.h"
#define SUBSCRIBERS_EXPECTED  10   //  We wait for 10 subscribers

int main (void)
{
    void *context = zmq_ctx_new ();

    //  Socket to talk to clients
    void *publisher = zmq_socket (context, ZMQ_PUB);
    zmq_bind (publisher, "tcp://*:5561");

    //  Socket to receive signals
    void *syncservice = zmq_socket (context, ZMQ_REP);
    zmq_bind (syncservice, "tcp://*:5562");

    //  Get synchronization from subscribers
    printf ("Waiting for subscribers\n");
    int subscribers = 0;
    while (subscribers < SUBSCRIBERS_EXPECTED) {
        //  - wait for synchronization request
        char *string = s_recv (syncservice);
        free (string);
        //  - send synchronization reply
        s_send (syncservice, "");
        subscribers++;
    }
    //  Now broadcast exactly 1M updates followed by END
    printf ("Broadcasting messages\n");
    int update_nbr;
    for (update_nbr = 0; update_nbr < 1000000; update_nbr++)
        s_send (publisher, "Rhubarb");

    s_send (publisher, "END");

    zmq_close (publisher);
    zmq_close (syncservice);
    zmq_ctx_destroy (context);
    return 0;
}
```

And here is the subscriber:

Example 24. Synchronized subscriber (syncsub.c)

```c
//  Synchronized subscriber

#include "zhelpers.h"

int main (void)
{
    void *context = zmq_ctx_new ();

    //  First, connect our subscriber socket
    void *subscriber = zmq_socket (context, ZMQ_SUB);
    zmq_connect (subscriber, "tcp://localhost:5561");
    zmq_setsockopt (subscriber, ZMQ_SUBSCRIBE, "", 0);

    //  0MQ is so fast, we need to wait a while...
    sleep (1);

    //  Second, synchronize with publisher
    void *syncclient = zmq_socket (context, ZMQ_REQ);
    zmq_connect (syncclient, "tcp://localhost:5562");

    //  - send a synchronization request
    s_send (syncclient, "");

    //  - wait for synchronization reply
    char *string = s_recv (syncclient);
    free (string);

    //  Third, get our updates and report how many we got
    int update_nbr = 0;
    while (1) {
        char *string = s_recv (subscriber);
        if (strcmp (string, "END") == 0) {
            free (string);
            break;
        }
        free (string);
        update_nbr++;
    }
    printf ("Received %d updates\n", update_nbr);

    zmq_close (subscriber);
    zmq_close (syncclient);
    zmq_ctx_destroy (context);
    return 0;
}
```

This Bash shell script will start ten subscribers and then the publisher:

```
echo "Starting subscribers..."
for ((a=0; a<10; a++)); do
    syncsub &
done
echo "Starting publisher..."
syncpub
```

Which gives us this satisfying output:

```
Starting subscribers...
Starting publisher...
Received 1000000 updates
Received 1000000 updates
...
Received 1000000 updates
Received 1000000 updates
```

We can't assume that the SUB connect will be finished by the time the REQ/REP dialog is complete. There are no guarantees that outbound connects will finish in any order whatsoever, if you're using any transport except `inproc`. So, the example does a brute force sleep of one second between subscribing, and sending the REQ/REP synchronization.

A more robust model could be:

- Publisher opens PUB socket and starts sending "Hello" messages (not data).
- Subscribers connect SUB socket and when they receive a Hello message they tell the publisher via a REQ/REP socket pair.
- When the publisher has had all the necessary confirmations, it starts to send real data.

Zero-Copy

ØMQ's message API lets you can send and receive messages directly from and to application buffers without copying data. We call *zero-copy*, and it can improve performance in some applications.

You should think about using zero-copy in the specific case where you are sending large blocks of memory (thousands of bytes), at a high frequency. For short messages, or for lower message rates, using zero-copy will make your code messier and more complex with no measurable benefit. Like all optimizations, use this when you know it helps, and *measure* before and after.

To do zero-copy, you use `zmq_msg_init_data()` to create a message that refers to a block of data already allocated with `malloc()` or some other allocator, and then you pass that to `zmq_msg_send()`. When you create the message, you also pass a function that ØMQ will call to free the block of data, when it has finished sending the message. This is the simplest example, assuming `buffer` is a block of 1,000 bytes allocated on the heap:

```
void my_free (void *data, void *hint) {
    free (data);
}
// Send message from buffer, which we allocate and OMQ will free for us
zmq_msg_t message;
zmq_msg_init_data (&message, buffer, 1000, my_free, NULL);
zmq_msg_send (socket, &message, 0);
```

Note that you don't call `zmq_msg_close()` after sending a message—libzmq will do this automatically when it's actually done sending the message.

There is no way to do zero-copy on receive: ØMQ delivers you a buffer that you can store as long as you wish, but it will not write data directly into application buffers.

On writing, ØMQ's multipart messages work nicely together with zero-copy. In traditional messaging, you need to marshal different buffers together into one buffer that you can send. That means copying data. With ØMQ, you can send multiple buffers coming from different sources as individual message frames. Send each field as a length-delimited frame. To the application, it looks like a series of send and receive calls. But internally, the multiple parts get written to the network and read back with single system calls, so it's very efficient.

Pub-Sub Message Envelopes

In the pub-sub pattern, we can split the key into a separate message frame that we call an *envelope* (see figure 23). If you want to use pub-sub envelopes, make them yourself. It's optional, and in previous pub-sub examples we didn't do this. Using a pub-sub envelope is a little more work for simple cases, but it's cleaner especially for real cases, where the key and the data are naturally separate things.

Recall that subscriptions do a prefix match. That is, they look for "all messages starting with XYZ". The obvious question is: how to delimit keys from data so that the prefix match doesn't accidentally match data. The best answer is to use an envelope because the match won't cross a frame boundary. Here is a minimalist example of how pub-sub envelopes look in code. This publisher sends messages of two types, A and B.

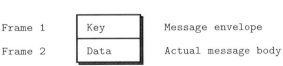

Figure 23. Pub-Sub Envelope with Separate Key

The envelope holds the message type:

Example 25. Pub-Sub envelope publisher (psenvpub.c)

```
//  Pubsub envelope publisher
//  Note that the zhelpers.h file also provides s_sendmore

#include "zhelpers.h"

int main (void)
{
    //  Prepare our context and publisher
    void *context = zmq_ctx_new ();
    void *publisher = zmq_socket (context, ZMQ_PUB);
    zmq_bind (publisher, "tcp://*:5563");

    while (1) {
        //  Write two messages, each with an envelope and content
        s_sendmore (publisher, "A");
        s_send (publisher, "We don't want to see this");
        s_sendmore (publisher, "B");
        s_send (publisher, "We would like to see this");
        sleep (1);
    }
    //  We never get here, but clean up anyhow
    zmq_close (publisher);
    zmq_ctx_destroy (context);
    return 0;
}
```

The subscriber wants only messages of type B:

Example 26. Pub-Sub envelope subscriber (psenvsub.c)

```
//  Pubsub envelope subscriber

#include "zhelpers.h"

int main (void)
{
    //  Prepare our context and subscriber
    void *context = zmq_ctx_new ();
    void *subscriber = zmq_socket (context, ZMQ_SUB);
    zmq_connect (subscriber, "tcp://localhost:5563");
    zmq_setsockopt (subscriber, ZMQ_SUBSCRIBE, "B", 1);

    while (1) {
        //  Read envelope with address
        char *address = s_recv (subscriber);
        //  Read message contents
        char *contents = s_recv (subscriber);
```

```
                printf ("[%s] %s\n", address, contents);
                free (address);
                free (contents);
        }
        //  We never get here, but clean up anyhow
        zmq_close (subscriber);
        zmq_ctx_destroy (context);
        return 0;
}
```

When you run the two programs, the subscriber should show you this:

```
[B] We would like to see this
[B] We would like to see this
[B] We would like to see this
...
```

This example shows that the subscription filter rejects or accepts the entire multipart message (key plus data). You won't get part of a multipart message, ever. If you subscribe to multiple publishers and you want to know their address so that you can send them data via another socket (and this is a typical use case), create a three-part message (see figure 24).

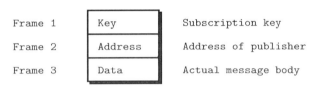

Figure 24. Pub-Sub Envelope with Sender Address

High-Water Marks

When you can send messages rapidly from process to process, you soon discover that memory is a precious resource, and one that can be trivially filled up. A few seconds of delay somewhere in a process can turn into a backlog that blows up a server unless you understand the problem and take precautions.

The problem is this: imagine you have process A sending messages at high frequency to process B, which is processing them. Suddenly B gets very busy (garbage collection, CPU overload, whatever), and can't process the messages for a short period. It could be a few seconds for some heavy garbage collection, or it could be much longer, if there's a more serious problem. What happens to the messages that process A is still trying to send frantically? Some will sit in B's network buffers. Some will sit on the Ethernet wire itself. Some will sit in A's network buffers. And the rest will accumulate in A's memory, as rapidly as the application behind A sends them. If you don't take some precaution, A can easily run out of memory and crash.

It is a consistent, classic problem with message brokers. What makes it hurt more is that it's B's fault, superficially, and B is typically a user-written application which A has no control over.

What are the answers? One is to pass the problem upstream. A is getting the messages from somewhere else. So tell that process, "Stop!" And so on. This is called *flow control*. It sounds plausible, but what if you're sending out a Twitter feed? Do you tell the whole world to stop tweeting while B gets its act together?

Flow control works in some cases, but not in others. The transport layer can't tell the application layer to "stop" any more than a subway system can tell a large business, "please keep your staff at work for another half an hour. I'm too busy". The answer for messaging is to set limits on the size of buffers, and then when we reach those limits, to take some sensible action. In some cases (not for a subway system, though), the answer is to throw away messages. In a others, the best strategy is to wait.

ØMQ uses the concept of HWM (high-water mark) to define the capacity of its internal pipes. Each connection out of a socket or into a socket has its own pipe, and HWM for sending, and/or receiving, depending on the socket type. Some sockets (PUB, PUSH) only have send buffers. Some (SUB, PULL, REQ, REP) only have receive buffers. Some (DEALER, ROUTER, PAIR) have both send and receive buffers.

In ØMQ v2.x, the HWM was infinite by default. This was easy but also typically fatal for high-volume publishers. In ØMQ v3.x, it's set to 1,000 by default, which is more sensible. If you're still using ØMQ v2.x, you should always set a HWM on your sockets, be it 1,000 to match ØMQ v3.x or another figure that takes into account your message sizes and expected subscriber performance.

When your socket reaches its HWM, it will either block or drop data depending on the socket type. PUB and ROUTER sockets will drop data if they reach their HWM, while other socket types will block. Over the `inproc` transport, the sender and receiver share the same buffers, so the real HWM is the sum of the HWM set by both sides.

Lastly, the HWMs are not exact; while you may get *up to* 1,000 messages by default, the real buffer size may be much lower (as little as half), due to the way libzmq implements its queues.

Missing Message Problem Solver

As you build applications with ØMQ, you will come across this problem more than once: losing messages that you expect to receive. We have put together a diagram (see figure 25) that walks through the most common causes for this.

Code Connected Volume 1 - Chapter 2. Sockets and Patterns

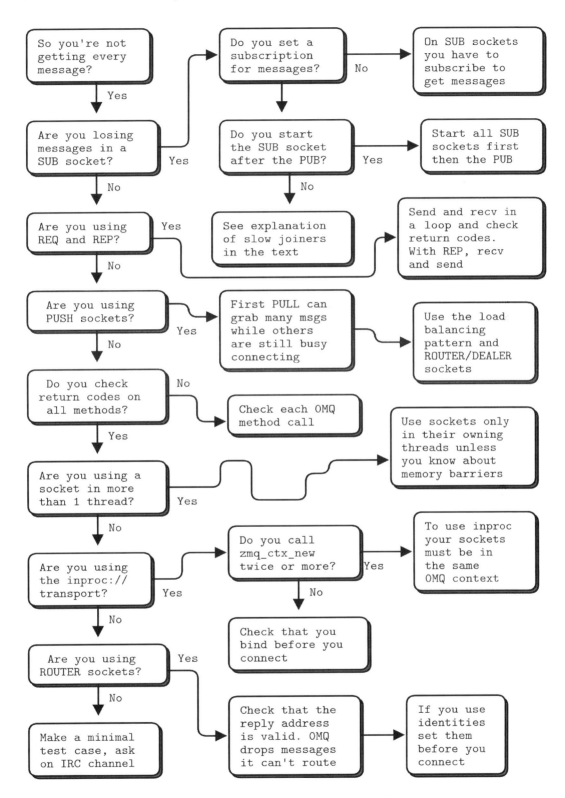

Figure 25. Missing Message Problem Solver

Here's a summary of what the graphic says:

- On SUB sockets, set a subscription using `zmq_setsockopt()` with `ZMQ_SUBSCRIBE`, or you won't get messages. Because you subscribe to messages by prefix, if you subscribe to "" (an empty subscription), you will get everything.

- If you start the SUB socket (i.e., establish a connection to a PUB socket) *after* the PUB socket has started sending out data, you will lose whatever it published before the connection was made. If this is a problem, set up your architecture so the SUB socket starts first, then the PUB socket starts publishing.

- Even if you synchronize a SUB and PUB socket, you may still lose messages. It's due to the fact that internal queues aren't created until a connection is actually created. If you can switch the bind/connect direction so the SUB socket binds, and the PUB socket connects, you may find it works more as you'd expect.

- If you're using REP and REQ sockets, and you're not sticking to the synchronous send/recv/send/recv order, ØMQ will report errors, which you might ignore. Then, it would look like you're losing messages. If you use REQ or REP, stick to the send/recv order, and always, in real code, check for errors on ØMQ calls.

- If you're using PUSH sockets, you'll find that the first PULL socket to connect will grab an unfair share of messages. The accurate rotation of messages only happens when all PULL sockets are successfully connected, which can take some milliseconds. As an alternative to PUSH/PULL, for lower data rates, consider using ROUTER/DEALER and the load balancing pattern.

- If you're sharing sockets across threads, don't. It will lead to random weirdness, and crashes.

- If you're using `inproc`, make sure both sockets are in the same context. Otherwise the connecting side will in fact fail. Also, bind first, then connect. `inproc` is not a disconnected transport like `tcp`.

- If you're using ROUTER sockets, it's remarkably easy to lose messages by accident, by sending malformed identity frames (or forgetting to send an identity frame). In general setting the `ZMQ_ROUTER_MANDATORY` option on ROUTER sockets is a good idea, but do also check the return code on every send call.

- Lastly, if you really can't figure out what's going wrong, make a *minimal* test case that reproduces the problem, and ask for help from the ØMQ community.

Chapter 3. Advanced Request-Reply Patterns

In "Sockets and Patterns" we worked through the basics of using ØMQ by developing a series of small applications, each time exploring new aspects of ØMQ. We'll continue this approach in this chapter as we explore advanced patterns built on top of ØMQ's core request-reply pattern.

We'll cover:

- How the request-reply mechanisms work.
- How to combine REQ, REP, DEALER, and ROUTER sockets.
- How ROUTER sockets work, in detail.
- The load balancing pattern.
- Building a simple load balancing message broker.
- Designing a high-level API for ØMQ.
- Building an asynchronous request-reply server.
- A detailed inter-broker routing example.

The Request-Reply Mechanisms

We already looked briefly at multipart messages. Let's now look at a major use case, which is *reply message envelopes*. An envelope is a way of safely packaging up data with an address, without touching the data itself. By separating reply addresses into an envelope we make it possible to write general purpose intermediaries such as APIs and proxies that create, read, and remove addresses no matter what the message payload or structure.

In the request-reply pattern, the envelope holds the return address for replies. It is how a ØMQ network with no state can create round-trip request-reply dialogs.

When you use REQ and REP sockets you don't even see envelopes; these sockets deal with them automatically. But for most of the interesting request-reply patterns, you'll want to understand envelopes and particularly ROUTER sockets. We'll work through this step-by-step.

The Simple Reply Envelope

A request-reply exchange consists of a *request* message, and an eventual *reply* message. In the simple request-reply pattern, there's one reply for each request. In more advanced patterns, requests and replies can flow asynchronously. However, the reply envelope always works the same way.

The ØMQ reply envelope formally consists of zero or more reply addresses, followed by an empty frame (the envelope delimiter), followed by the message body (zero or more frames). The envelope is created by multiple sockets working together in a chain. We'll break this down.

We'll start by sending "Hello" through a REQ socket. The REQ socket creates the simplest possible reply envelope, which has no addresses, just an empty delimiter frame and the message frame containing the "Hello" string. This is a two-frame message (see figure 26).

The REP socket does the matching work: it strips off the envelope, up to and including the delimiter frame, saves the whole envelope, and passes the

Figure 26. Request with Minimal Envelope

"Hello" string up the application. Thus our original Hello World example used request-reply envelopes internally, but the application never saw them.

If you spy on the network data flowing between `hwclient` and `hwserver`, this is what you'll see: every request and every reply is in fact two frames, an empty frame and then the body. It doesn't seem to make much sense for a simple REQ-REP dialog. However you'll see the reason when we explore how ROUTER and DEALER handle envelopes.

The Extended Reply Envelope

Now let's extend the REQ-REP pair with a ROUTER-DEALER proxy in the middle and see how this affects the reply envelope. This is the *extended request-reply pattern* we already saw in "Sockets and Patterns". We can, in fact, insert any number of proxy steps (see figure 27). The mechanics are the same.

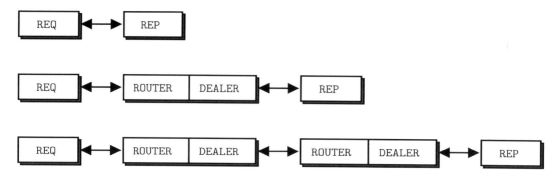

Figure 27. Extended Request-Reply Pattern

The proxy does this, in pseudo-code:

```
prepare context, frontend and backend sockets
while true:
    poll on both sockets
    if frontend had input:
        read all frames from frontend
        send to backend
    if backend had input:
        read all frames from backend
        send to frontend
```

The ROUTER socket, unlike other sockets, tracks every connection it has, and tells the caller about these. The way it tells the caller is to stick the connection *identity* in front of each message received. An identity, sometimes called an *address*, is just a binary string with no meaning except "this is a unique handle to the connection". Then, when you send a message via a ROUTER socket, you first send an identity frame.

The zmq_socket() man page describes it thus:

When receiving messages a ZMQ_ROUTER socket shall prepend a message part containing the identity of the originating peer to the message before passing it to the application. Messages received are fair-queued from among all connected peers. When sending messages a ZMQ_ROUTER socket shall remove the first part of the message and use it to determine the identity of the peer the message shall be routed to.

As a historical note, ØMQ v2.2 and earlier use UUIDs as identities, and ØMQ v3.0 and later use short integers. There's some impact on network performance, but only when you use multiple proxy hops, which is rare. Mostly the change was to simplify building libzmq by removing the dependency on a UUID library.

Identies are a difficult concept to understand, but it's essential if you want to become a ØMQ expert. The ROUTER socket *invents* a random identity for each connection with which it works. If there are three REQ sockets connected to a ROUTER socket, it will invent three random identities, one for each REQ socket.

So if we continue our worked example, let's say the REQ socket has a 3-byte identity ABC". Internally, this means the ROUTER socket keeps a hash table where it can search for ABC and find the TCP connection for the REQ socket.

When we receive the message off the ROUTER socket, we get three frames (see figure 28).

The core of the proxy loop is "read from one socket, write to the other", so we literally send these three frames out on the DEALER socket. If you

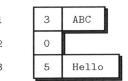

Figure 28. Request with One Address

now sniffed the network traffic, you would see these three frames flying from the DEALER socket to the REP socket. The REP socket does as before, strips off the whole envelope including the new reply address, and once again delivers the "Hello" to the caller.

Incidentally the REP socket can only deal with one request-reply exchange at a time, which is why if you try to read multiple requests or send multiple replies without sticking to a strict recv-send cycle, it gives an error.

You should now be able to visualize the return path. When hwserver sends "World" back, the REP socket wraps that with the envelope it saved, and sends a three-frame reply message across the wire to the DEALER socket (see figure 29).

Now the DEALER reads these three frames, and sends all three out via the ROUTER socket. The ROUTER takes the first frame for the message, which is the ABC identity, and looks up the connection for this. If it finds that, it then pumps the next two frames out onto the wire (see figure 30).

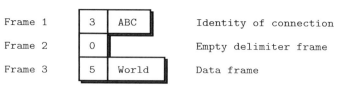

Figure 29. Reply with one Address

The REQ socket picks this message up, and checks that the first frame is the empty delimiter, which it is. The REQ socket discards that frame and passes

Figure 30. Reply with Minimal Envelope

"World" to the calling application, which prints it out to the amazement of the younger us looking at ØMQ for the first time.

What's This Good For?

To be honest, the use cases for strict request-reply or extended request-reply are somewhat limited. For one thing, there's no easy way to recover from common failures like the server crashing due to buggy application code. We'll see more about this in "Reliable Request-Reply Patterns". However once you grasp the way these four sockets deal with envelopes, and how they talk to each other, you can do very useful things. We saw how ROUTER uses the reply envelope to decide which client REQ socket to route a reply back to. Now let's express this another way:

- Each time ROUTER gives you a message, it tells you what peer that came from, as an identity.
- You can use this with a hash table (with the identity as key) to track new peers as they arrive.
- ROUTER will route messages asynchronously to any peer connected to it, if you prefix the identity as the first frame of the message.

ROUTER sockets don't care about the whole envelope. They don't know anything about the empty delimiter. All they care about is that one identity frame that lets them figure out which connection to send a message to.

Recap of Request-Reply Sockets

Let's recap this:

- The REQ socket sends, to the network, an empty delimiter frame in front of the message data. REQ sockets are synchronous. REQ sockets always send one request and then wait for one reply. REQ sockets talk to one peer at a time. If you connect a REQ socket to multiple peers, requests are distributed to and replies expected from each peer one turn at a time.

- The REP socket reads and saves all identity frames up to and including the empty delimiter, then passes the following frame or frames to the caller. REP sockets are synchronous and talk to one peer at a time. If you connect a REP socket to multiple peers, requests are read from peers in fair fashion, and replies are always sent to the same peer that made the last request.

- The DEALER socket is oblivious to the reply envelope and handles this like any multipart message. DEALER sockets are asynchronous and like PUSH and PULL combined. They distribute sent messages among all connections, and fair-queue received messages from all connections.

- The ROUTER socket is oblivious to the reply envelope, like DEALER. It creates identities for its connections, and passes these identities to the caller as a first frame in any received message. Conversely, when the caller sends a message, it use the first message frame as an identity to look up the connection to send to. ROUTERS are asynchronous.

Request-Reply Combinations

We have four request-reply sockets, each with a certain behavior. We've seen how they connect in simple and extended request-reply patterns. But these sockets are building blocks that you can use to solve many problems.

These are the legal combinations:

- REQ to REP
- DEALER to REP
- REQ to ROUTER
- DEALER to ROUTER
- DEALER to DEALER
- ROUTER to ROUTER

And these combinations are invalid (and I'll explain why):

- REQ to REQ
- REQ to DEALER

- REP to REP
- REP to ROUTER

Here are some tips for remembering the semantics. DEALER is like an asynchronous REQ socket, and ROUTER is like an asynchronous REP socket. Where we use a REQ socket, we can use a DEALER; we just have to read and write the envelope ourselves. Where we use a REP socket, we can stick a ROUTER; we just need to manage the identities ourselves.

Think of REQ and DEALER sockets as "clients" and REP and ROUTER sockets as "servers". Mostly, you'll want to bind REP and ROUTER sockets, and connect REQ and DEALER sockets to them. It's not always going to be this simple, but it is a clean and memorable place to start.

The REQ to REP Combination

We've already covered a REQ client talking to a REP server but let's take one aspect: the REQ client *must* initiate the message flow. A REP server cannot talk to a REQ client that hasn't first sent it a request. Technically, it's not even possible, and the API also returns an EFSM error if you try it.

The DEALER to REP Combination

Now, let's replace the REQ client with a DEALER. This gives us an asynchronous client that can talk to multiple REP servers. If we rewrote the "Hello World" client using DEALER, we'd be able to send off any number of "Hello" requests without waiting for replies.

When we use a DEALER to talk to a REP socket, we *must* accurately emulate the envelope that the REQ socket would have sent, otherwise the REP socket will discard the message as invalid. So, to send a message, we:

- Send an empty message frame with the MORE flag set; then
- Send the message body.

And when we receive a message, we:

- Receive the first frame and if it's not empty, discard the whole message;
- Receive the next frame and pass that to the application.

The REQ to ROUTER Combination

In the same way that we can replace REQ with DEALER, we can replace REP with ROUTER. This gives us an asynchronous server that can talk to multiple REQ clients at the same time. If we rewrote the "Hello World" server using ROUTER, we'd be able to process any number of "Hello" requests in parallel. We saw this in the "Sockets and Patterns" mtserver example.

We can use ROUTER in two distinct ways:

- As a proxy that switches messages between frontend and backend sockets.

- As an application that reads the message and acts on it.

In the first case, the ROUTER simply reads all frames, including the artificial identity frame, and passes them on blindly. In the second case the ROUTER *must* know the format of the reply envelope it's being sent. As the other peer is a REQ socket, the ROUTER gets the identity frame, an empty frame, and then the data frame.

The DEALER to ROUTER Combination

Now we can switch out both REQ and REP with DEALER and ROUTER to get the most powerful socket combination, which is DEALER talking to ROUTER. It gives us asynchronous clients talking to asynchronous servers, where both sides have full control over the message formats.

Because both DEALER and ROUTER can work with arbitrary message formats, if you hope to use these safely, you have to become a little bit of a protocol designer. At the very least you must decide whether you wish to emulate the REQ/REP reply envelope. It depends on whether you actually need to send replies or not.

The DEALER to DEALER Combination

You can swap a REP with a ROUTER, but you can also swap a REP with a DEALER, if the DEALER is talking to one and only one peer.

When you replace a REP with a DEALER, your worker can suddenly go full asynchronous, sending any number of replies back. The cost is that you have to manage the reply envelopes yourself, and get them right, or nothing at all will work. We'll see a worked example later. Let's just say for now that DEALER to DEALER is one of the trickier patterns to get right, and happily it's rare that we need it.

The ROUTER to ROUTER Combination

This sounds perfect for N-to-N connections, but it's the most difficult combination to use. You should avoid it until you are well advanced with ØMQ. We'll see one example it in the Freelance pattern in "Reliable Request-Reply Patterns", and an alternative DEALER to ROUTER design for peer-to-peer work in Code Connected Volume 2.

Invalid Combinations

Mostly, trying to connect clients to clients, or servers to servers is a bad idea and won't work. However, rather than give general vague warnings, I'll explain in detail:
- REQ to REQ: both sides want to start by sending messages to each other, and this could only work if you timed things so that both peers exchanged messages at the same time. It hurts my brain to even think about it.
- REQ to DEALER: you could in theory do this, but it would break if you added a second REQ because DEALER has no way of sending a reply to the original peer. Thus the REQ socket would get confused, and/or return messages meant for another client.

- REP to REP: both sides would wait for the other to send the first message.
- REP to ROUTER: the ROUTER socket can in theory initiate the dialog and send a properly-formatted request, if it knows the REP socket has connected *and* it knows the identity of that connection. It's messy and adds nothing over DEALER to ROUTER.

The common thread in this valid versus invalid breakdown is that a ØMQ socket connection is always biased towards one peer that binds to an endpoint, and another that connects to that. Further, that which side binds and which side connects is not arbitrary, but follows natural patterns. The side which we expect to "be there" binds: it'll be a server, a broker, a publisher, a collector. The side that "comes and goes" connects: it'll be clients and workers. Remembering this will help you design better ØMQ architectures.

Exploring ROUTER Sockets

Identities and Addresses

The *identity* concept in ØMQ refers specifically to ROUTER sockets and how they identify the connections they have to other sockets. More broadly, identities are used as addresses in the reply envelope. In most cases, the identity is arbitrary and local to the ROUTER socket: it's a lookup key in a hash table. Independently, a peer can have an address that is physical (a network endpoint like "tcp://192.168.55.117:5670") or logical (a UUID or email address or other unique key).

An application that uses a ROUTER socket to talk to specific peers can convert a logical address to an identity if it has built the necessary hash table. Because ROUTER sockets only announce the identity of a connection (to a specific peer) when that peer sends a message, you can only really reply to a message, not spontaneously talk to a peer.

This is true even if you flip the rules and make the ROUTER connect to the peer rather than wait for the peer to connect to the ROUTER. However you can force the ROUTER socket to use a logical address in place of its identity. The `zmq_setsockopt` reference page calls this *setting the socket identity*. It works as follows:

- The peer application sets the `ZMQ_IDENTITY` option of its peer socket (DEALER or REQ) *before* binding or connecting.
- Usually the peer then connects to the already-bound ROUTER socket. But the ROUTER can also connect to the peer.
- At connection time, the peer socket tells the router socket, "please use this identity for this connection".
- If the peer socket doesn't say that, the router generates its usual arbitrary random identity for the connection.
- The ROUTER socket now provides this logical address to the application as a prefix identity frame for any messages coming in from that peer.

- The ROUTER also expects the logical address as the prefix identity frame for any outgoing messages.

Here is a simple example of two peers that connect to a ROUTER socket, one that imposes a logical address "PEER2":

Example 27. Identity check (identity.c)

```c
//  Demonstrate request-reply identities

#include "zhelpers.h"

int main (void)
{
    void *context = zmq_ctx_new ();
    void *sink = zmq_socket (context, ZMQ_ROUTER);
    zmq_bind (sink, "inproc://example");

    //  First allow 0MQ to set the identity
    void *anonymous = zmq_socket (context, ZMQ_REQ);
    zmq_connect (anonymous, "inproc://example");
    s_send (anonymous, "ROUTER uses a generated UUID");
    s_dump (sink);

    //  Then set the identity ourselves
    void *identified = zmq_socket (context, ZMQ_REQ);
    zmq_setsockopt (identified, ZMQ_IDENTITY, "PEER2", 5);
    zmq_connect (identified, "inproc://example");
    s_send (identified, "ROUTER socket uses REQ's socket identity");
    s_dump (sink);

    zmq_close (sink);
    zmq_close (anonymous);
    zmq_close (identified);
    zmq_ctx_destroy (context);
    return 0;
}
```

Here is what the program prints:

```
----------------------------------------
[005] 006B8B4567
[000]
[026] ROUTER uses a generated UUID
----------------------------------------
[005] PEER2
[000]
[038] ROUTER uses REQ's socket identity
```

ROUTER Error Handling

ROUTER sockets do have a somewhat brutal way of dealing with messages they can't send anywhere: they drop them silently. It's an attitude that makes sense in working code, but it makes debugging hard. The "send identity as first frame" approach is tricky enough that we often get this wrong when we're learning, and the ROUTER's stony silence when we mess up isn't very constructive.

Since ØMQ v3.2 there's a socket option you can set to catch this error: `ZMQ_ROUTER_MANDATORY`. Set that on the ROUTER socket and then when you provide an unroutable identity on a send call, the socket will signal an EHOSTUNREACH error.

The Load Balancing Pattern

Now let's look at some code. We'll see how to connect a ROUTER socket to a REQ socket, and then to a DEALER socket. These two examples follow the same logic, which is a *load balancing* pattern. This pattern is our first exposure to using the ROUTER socket for deliberate routing, rather than simply acting as a reply channel.

The load balancing pattern is very common and we'll see it several times in this book. It solves the main problem with simple round robin routing (as PUSH and DEALER offer) which is that round robin becomes inefficient if tasks do not all roughly take the same time.

It's the post office analogy. If you have one queue per counter, and you have some people buying stamps (a fast, simple transaction), and some people opening new accounts (a very slow transaction), then you will find stamp buyers getting unfairly stuck in queues. Just as in a post office, if your messaging architecture is unfair, people will get annoyed.

The solution in the post office is to create a single queue so that even if one or two counters get stuck with slow work, other counters will continue to serve clients on a first-come, first-serve basis.

One reason PUSH and DEALER use the simplistic approach is sheer performance. If you arrive in any major US airport, you'll find long queues of people waiting at immigration. The border patrol officials will send people in advance to queue up at each counter, rather than using a single queue. Having people walk fifty yards in advance saves a minute or two per passenger. And because every passport check takes roughly the same time, it's more or less fair. This is the strategy for PUSH and DEALER: send work loads ahead of time so that there is less travel distance.

This is a recurring theme with ØMQ: the world's problems are diverse and you can benefit from solving different problems each in the right way. The airport isn't the post office and one size fits no one, really well.

Let's return to the scenario of a worker (DEALER or REQ) connected to a broker (ROUTER). The broker has to know when the worker is ready, and keep a list of workers so that it can take the *least recently used* worker each time.

The solution is really simple, in fact: workers send a "ready" message when they start, and after they finish each task. The broker reads these messages one-by-one. Each time it reads a message, it is from the last used worker. And because we're using a ROUTER socket, we get an identity that we can then use to send a task back to the worker.

It's a twist on request-reply because the task is sent with the reply, and any response for the task is sent as a new request. The following code examples should make it clearer.

ROUTER Broker and REQ Workers

Here is an example of the load balancing pattern using a ROUTER broker talking to a set of REQ workers:

Example 28. ROUTER-to-REQ (rtreq.c)

```
//  ROUTER-to-REQ example

#include "zhelpers.h"
#include <pthread.h>
#define NBR_WORKERS 10

static void *
worker_task (void *args)
{
    void *context = zmq_ctx_new ();
    void *worker = zmq_socket (context, ZMQ_REQ);
    s_set_id (worker);          //  Set a printable identity
    zmq_connect (worker, "tcp://localhost:5671");

    int total = 0;
    while (1) {
        //  Tell the broker we're ready for work
        s_send (worker, "Hi Boss");

        //  Get workload from broker, until finished
        char *workload = s_recv (worker);
        int finished = (strcmp (workload, "Fired!") == 0);
        free (workload);
        if (finished) {
            printf ("Completed: %d tasks\n", total);
            break;
        }
        total++;

        //  Do some random work
        s_sleep (randof (500) + 1);
    }
    zmq_close (worker);
    zmq_ctx_destroy (context);
```

```
        return NULL;
}
```

While this example runs in a single process, that is only to make it easier to start and stop the example. Each thread has its own context and conceptually acts as a separate process.

Example 28-1. ROUTER-to-REQ (rtreq.c) - main task

```
int main (void)
{
    void *context = zmq_ctx_new ();
    void *broker = zmq_socket (context, ZMQ_ROUTER);

    zmq_bind (broker, "tcp://*:5671");
    srandom ((unsigned) time (NULL));

    int worker_nbr;
    for (worker_nbr = 0; worker_nbr < NBR_WORKERS; worker_nbr++) {
        pthread_t worker;
        pthread_create (&worker, NULL, worker_task, NULL);
    }
    //  Run for five seconds and then tell workers to end
    int64_t end_time = s_clock () + 5000;
    int workers_fired = 0;
    while (1) {
        //  Next message gives us least recently used worker
        char *identity = s_recv (broker);
        s_sendmore (broker, identity);
        free (identity);
        free (s_recv (broker));     //  Envelope delimiter
        free (s_recv (broker));     //  Response from worker
        s_sendmore (broker, "");

        //  Encourage workers until it's time to fire them
        if (s_clock () < end_time)
            s_send (broker, "Work harder");
        else {
            s_send (broker, "Fired!");
            if (++workers_fired == NBR_WORKERS)
                break;
        }
    }
    zmq_close (broker);
    zmq_ctx_destroy (context);
    return 0;
}
```

The example runs for five seconds and then each worker prints how many tasks they handled. If the routing worked, we'd expect a fair distribution of work:

```
Completed: 20 tasks
Completed: 18 tasks
Completed: 21 tasks
Completed: 23 tasks
Completed: 19 tasks
Completed: 21 tasks
Completed: 17 tasks
Completed: 17 tasks
Completed: 25 tasks
Completed: 19 tasks
```

To talk to the workers in this example, we have to create a REQ-friendly envelope consisting of an identity plus an empty envelope delimiter frame (see figure 31).

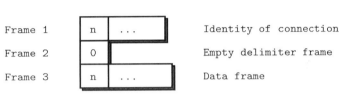

Figure 31. Routing Envelope for REQ

ROUTER Broker and DEALER Workers

Anywhere you can use REQ, you can use DEALER. There are two specific differences:

- The REQ socket always sends an empty delimiter frame before any data frames; the DEALER does not.
- The REQ socket will send only one message before it receives a reply; the DEALER is fully asynchronous.

The synchronous versus asynchronous behavior has no effect on our example because we're doing strict request-reply. It is more relevant when we address recovering from failures, which we'll come to in "Reliable Request-Reply Patterns".

Now let's look at exactly the same example but with the REQ socket replaced by a DEALER socket:

Example 29. ROUTER-to-DEALER (rtdealer.c)

```
//  ROUTER-to-DEALER example

#include "zhelpers.h"
#include <pthread.h>
#define NBR_WORKERS 10

static void *
worker_task (void *args)
{
```

```
    void *context = zmq_ctx_new ();
    void *worker = zmq_socket (context, ZMQ_DEALER);
    s_set_id (worker);          //  Set a printable identity
    zmq_connect (worker, "tcp://localhost:5671");

    int total = 0;
    while (1) {
        //  Tell the broker we're ready for work
        s_sendmore (worker, "");
        s_send (worker, "Hi Boss");

        //  Get workload from broker, until finished
        free (s_recv (worker));     //  Envelope delimiter
        char *workload = s_recv (worker);
...
```

The code is almost identical except that the worker uses a DEALER socket, and reads and writes that empty frame before the data frame. This is the approach I use when I want to keep compatibility with REQ workers.

However, remember the reason for that empty delimiter frame: it's to allow multihop extended requests that terminate in a REP socket, which uses that delimiter to split off the reply envelope so it can hand the data frames to its application.

If we never need to pass the message along to a REP socket, we can simply drop the empty delimiter frame at both sides, which makes things simpler. This is usually the design I use for pure DEALER to ROUTER protocols.

A Load Balancing Message Broker

The previous example is half-complete. It can manage a set of workers with dummy requests and replies, but it has no way to talk to clients.

If we add a second *frontend* ROUTER socket that accepts client requests, and turn our example into a proxy that can switch messages from frontend to backend, we get a useful and reusable tiny load balancing message broker (see figure 32).

This broker does the following:

- Accepts connections from a set of clients.
- Accepts connections from a set of workers.

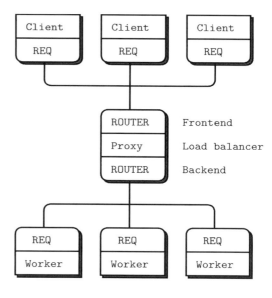

Figure 32. Load Balancing Broker

Code Connected Volume 1 - Chapter 3. Advanced Request-Reply Patterns

- Accepts requests from clients and holds these in a single queue.
- Sends these requests to workers using the load balancing pattern.
- Receives replies back from workers.
- Sends these replies back to the original requesting client.

The broker code is fairly long, but worth understanding:

Example 30. Load balancing broker (lbbroker.c)

```c
//  Load-balancing broker
//  Clients and workers are shown here in-process

#include "zhelpers.h"
#include <pthread.h>
#define NBR_CLIENTS 10
#define NBR_WORKERS 3

//  Dequeue operation for queue implemented as array of anything
#define DEQUEUE(q) memmove (&(q)[0], &(q)[1], sizeof (q) - sizeof (q [0]))

//  Basic request-reply client using REQ socket
//  Because s_send and s_recv can't handle 0MQ binary identities, we
//  set a printable text identity to allow routing.
//
static void *
client_task (void *args)
{
    void *context = zmq_ctx_new ();
    void *client = zmq_socket (context, ZMQ_REQ);
    s_set_id (client);          //  Set a printable identity
    zmq_connect (client, "ipc://frontend.ipc");

    //  Send request, get reply
    s_send (client, "HELLO");
    char *reply = s_recv (client);
    printf ("Client: %s\n", reply);
    free (reply);
    zmq_close (client);
    zmq_ctx_destroy (context);
    return NULL;
}
```

While this example runs in a single process, that is just to make it easier to start and stop the example. Each thread has its own context and conceptually acts as a separate process. This is the worker task, using a REQ socket to do load-balancing. Because s_send and s_recv can't handle ØMQ binary identities, we set a printable text identity to allow routing.

Example 30-1. Load balancing broker (lbbroker.c) - worker task

```c
static void *
worker_task (void *args)
{
    void *context = zmq_ctx_new ();
    void *worker = zmq_socket (context, ZMQ_REQ);
    s_set_id (worker);          //  Set a printable identity
    zmq_connect (worker, "ipc://backend.ipc");

    //  Tell broker we're ready for work
    s_send (worker, "READY");

    while (1) {
        //  Read and save all frames until we get an empty frame
        //  In this example there is only 1, but there could be more
        char *identity = s_recv (worker);
        char *empty = s_recv (worker);
        assert (*empty == 0);
        free (empty);

        //  Get request, send reply
        char *request = s_recv (worker);
        printf ("Worker: %s\n", request);
        free (request);

        s_sendmore (worker, identity);
        s_sendmore (worker, "");
        s_send     (worker, "OK");
        free (identity);
    }
    zmq_close (worker);
    zmq_ctx_destroy (context);
    return NULL;
}
```

This is the main task. It starts the clients and workers, and then routes requests between the two layers. Workers signal READY when they start; after that we treat them as ready when they reply with a response back to a client. The load-balancing data structure is just a queue of next available workers.

Example 30-2. Load balancing broker (lbbroker.c) - main task

```c
int main (void)
{
    //  Prepare our context and sockets
    void *context = zmq_ctx_new ();
    void *frontend = zmq_socket (context, ZMQ_ROUTER);
    void *backend  = zmq_socket (context, ZMQ_ROUTER);
    zmq_bind (frontend, "ipc://frontend.ipc");
    zmq_bind (backend,  "ipc://backend.ipc");
```

Code Connected Volume 1 - Chapter 3. Advanced Request-Reply Patterns

```
    int client_nbr;
    for (client_nbr = 0; client_nbr < NBR_CLIENTS; client_nbr++) {
        pthread_t client;
        pthread_create (&client, NULL, client_task, NULL);
    }
    int worker_nbr;
    for (worker_nbr = 0; worker_nbr < NBR_WORKERS; worker_nbr++) {
        pthread_t worker;
        pthread_create (&worker, NULL, worker_task, NULL);
    }
```

Here is the main loop for the least-recently-used queue. It has two sockets; a frontend for clients and a backend for workers. It polls the backend in all cases, and polls the frontend only when there are one or more workers ready. This is a neat way to use ØMQ's own queues to hold messages we're not ready to process yet. When we get a client reply, we pop the next available worker and send the request to it, including the originating client identity. When a worker replies, we requeue that worker and forward the reply to the original client using the reply envelope.

Example 30-3. Load balancing broker (lbbroker.c) - main task body

```
    //  Queue of available workers
    int available_workers = 0;
    char *worker_queue [10];

    while (1) {
        zmq_pollitem_t items [] = {
            { backend,  0, ZMQ_POLLIN, 0 },
            { frontend, 0, ZMQ_POLLIN, 0 }
        };
        //  Poll frontend only if we have available workers
        int rc = zmq_poll (items, available_workers ? 2 : 1, -1);
        if (rc == -1)
            break;              //  Interrupted

        //  Handle worker activity on backend
        if (items [0].revents & ZMQ_POLLIN) {
            //  Queue worker identity for load-balancing
            char *worker_id = s_recv (backend);
            assert (available_workers < NBR_WORKERS);
            worker_queue [available_workers++] = worker_id;

            //  Second frame is empty
            char *empty = s_recv (backend);
            assert (empty [0] == 0);
            free (empty);

            //  Third frame is READY or else a client reply identity
            char *client_id = s_recv (backend);
```

```c
            //  If client reply, send rest back to frontend
            if (strcmp (client_id, "READY") != 0) {
                empty = s_recv (backend);
                assert (empty [0] == 0);
                free (empty);
                char *reply = s_recv (backend);
                s_sendmore (frontend, client_id);
                s_sendmore (frontend, "");
                s_send     (frontend, reply);
                free (reply);
                if (--client_nbr == 0)
                    break;      //  Exit after N messages
            }
            free (client_id);
        }
```

Here is how we handle a client request:

Example 30-4. Load balancing broker (lbbroker.c) - handling a client request

```c
        if (items [1].revents & ZMQ_POLLIN) {
            //  Now get next client request, route to last-used worker
            //  Client request is [identity][empty][request]
            char *client_id = s_recv (frontend);
            char *empty = s_recv (frontend);
            assert (empty [0] == 0);
            free (empty);
            char *request = s_recv (frontend);

            s_sendmore (backend, worker_queue [0]);
            s_sendmore (backend, "");
            s_sendmore (backend, client_id);
            s_sendmore (backend, "");
            s_send     (backend, request);

            free (client_id);
            free (request);

            //  Dequeue and drop the next worker identity
            free (worker_queue [0]);
            DEQUEUE (worker_queue);
            available_workers--;
        }
    }
    zmq_close (frontend);
    zmq_close (backend);
    zmq_ctx_destroy (context);
    return 0;
}
```

The difficult part of this program is (a) the envelopes that each socket reads and writes, and (b) the load balancing algorithm. We'll take these in turn, starting with the message envelope formats.

Let's walk through a full request-reply chain from client to worker and back. In this code we set the identity of client and worker sockets to make it easier to trace the message frames. In reality, we'd allow the ROUTER sockets to invent identities for connections. Let's assume the client's identity is "CLIENT" and the worker's identity is "WORKER". The client application sends a single frame containing "Hello" (see figure 33).

Figure 33. Message that Client Sends

Because the REQ socket adds its empty delimiter frame and the ROUTER socket adds its connection identity, the proxy reads off the frontend ROUTER socket the client address, empty delimiter frame, and the data part (see figure 34).

Figure 34. Message Coming in on Frontend

The broker sends this to the worker, prefixed by the address of the chosen worker, plus an additional empty part to keep the REQ at the other end happy (see figure 35).

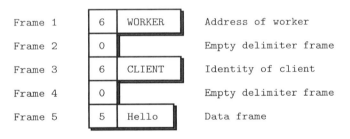

Figure 35. Message Sent to Backend

This complex envelope stack gets chewed up first by the backend ROUTER socket, which removes the first frame. Then the REQ socket in the worker removes the empty part, and provides the rest to the worker application (see figure 36).

The worker has to save the envelope (which is all the parts up to and including the empty message frame) and then it can do what's needed with the data part. Note that a REP socket would do this automatically, but we're using the REQ-ROUTER pattern so that we can get proper load balancing.

On the return path, the messages are the same as when they come in, i.e., the backend socket gives the broker a message in five parts, and the broker sends the frontend socket a message in three parts, and the client gets a message in one part.

Figure 36. Message Delivered to Worker

Now let's look at the load balancing algorithm. It requires that both clients and workers use REQ sockets, and that workers correctly store and replay the envelope on messages they get. The algorithm is:

- Create a pollset that always polls the backend, and polls the frontend only if there are one or more workers available.
- Poll for activity with infinite timeout.
- If there is activity on the backend, we either have a "ready" message or a reply for a client. In either case, we store the worker address (the first part) on our worker queue, and if the rest is a client reply, we send it back to that client via the frontend.
- If there is activity on the frontend, we take the client request, pop the next worker (which is the last used), and send the request to the backend. This means sending the worker address, empty part, and then the three parts of the client request.

You should now see that you can reuse and extend the load balancing algorithm with variations based on the information the worker provides in its initial "ready" message. For example, workers might start up and do a performance self test, then tell the broker how fast they are. The broker can then choose the fastest available worker rather than the oldest.

A High-Level API for ØMQ

Making a Detour

We're going to push request-reply onto the stack and open a different area, which is the ØMQ API itself. There's a reason for this detour: as we write more complex examples, the low-level ØMQ API starts to look increasingly clumsy. Look at the core of the worker thread from our load balancing broker:

```
while (true) {
    //  Get one address frame and empty delimiter
    char *address = s_recv (worker);
    char *empty = s_recv (worker);
    assert (*empty == 0);
    free (empty);

    //  Get request, send reply
    char *request = s_recv (worker);
    printf ("Worker: %s\n", request);
    free (request);

    s_sendmore (worker, address);
    s_sendmore (worker, "");
    s_send     (worker, "OK");
```

```
        free (address);
}
```

That code isn't even reusable because it can only handle one reply address in the envelope, and it already does some wrapping around the ØMQ API. If we used the libzmq simple message API this is what we'd have to write:

```
while (true) {
    // Get one address frame and empty delimiter
    char address [255];
    int address_size = zmq_recv (worker, address, 255, 0);
    if (address_size == -1)
        break;

    char empty [1];
    int empty_size = zmq_recv (worker, empty, 1, 0);
    zmq_recv (worker, &empty, 0);
    assert (empty_size <= 0);
    if (empty_size == -1)
        break;

    // Get request, send reply
    char request [256];
    int request_size = zmq_recv (worker, request, 255, 0);
    if (request_size == -1)
        return NULL;
    request [request_size] = 0;
    printf ("Worker: %s\n", request);

    zmq_send (worker, address, address_size, ZMQ_SNDMORE);
    zmq_send (worker, empty, 0, ZMQ_SNDMORE);
    zmq_send (worker, "OK", 2, 0);
}
```

And when code is too long to write quickly, it's also too long to understand. Up until now, I've stuck to the native API because, as ØMQ users, we need to know that intimately. But when it gets in our way, we have to treat it as a problem to solve.

We can't of course just change the ØMQ API, which is a documented public contract on which thousands of people agree and depend. Instead, we construct a higher-level API on top based on our experience so far, and most specifically, our experience from writing more complex request-reply patterns.

What we want is an API that lets us receive and send an entire message in one shot, including the reply envelope with any number of reply addresses. One that lets us do what we want with the absolute least lines of code.

Making a good message API is fairly difficult. We have a problem of terminology: ØMQ uses "message" to describe both multipart messages, and individual message frames. We have a problem of expectations: sometimes it's natural to see message content as printable string data, sometimes as binary blobs. And we have technical challenges, especially if we want to avoid copying data around too much.

The challenge of making a good API affects all languages, though my specific use case is C. Whatever language you use, think about how you could contribute to your language binding to make it as good (or better) than the C binding I'm going to describe.

Features of a Higher-Level API

My solution is to use three fairly natural and obvious concepts: *string* (already the basis for our `s_send` and `s_recv` helpers), *frame* (a message frame), and *message* (a list of one or more frames). Here is the worker code, rewritten onto an API using these concepts:

```
while (true) {
    zmsg_t *msg = zmsg_recv (worker);
    zframe_reset (zmsg_last (msg), "OK", 2);
    zmsg_send (&msg, worker);
}
```

Cutting the amount of code we need to read and write complex messages is great: the results are easy to read and understand. Let's continue this process for other aspects of working with ØMQ. Here's a wish list of things I'd like in a higher-level API, based on my experience with ØMQ so far:

- *Automatic handling of sockets.* I find it cumbersome to have to close sockets manually, and to have to explicitly define the linger timeout in some (but not all) cases. It'd be great to have a way to close sockets automatically when I close the context.

- *Portable thread management.* Every nontrivial ØMQ application uses threads, but POSIX threads aren't portable. So a decent high-level API should hide this under a portable layer.

- *Piping from parent to child threads.* It's a recurrent problem: how to signal between parent and child threads. Our API should provide a ØMQ message pipe (using PAIR sockets and `inproc` automatically.

- *Portable clocks.* Even getting the time to a millisecond resolution, or sleeping for some milliseconds, is not portable. Realistic ØMQ applications need portable clocks, so our API should provide them.

- *A reactor to replace `zmq_poll()`.* The poll loop is simple, but clumsy. Writing a lot of these, we end up doing the same work over and over: calculating timers, and calling code when sockets are ready. A simple reactor with socket readers and timers would save a lot of repeated work.

- *Proper handling of Ctrl-C.* We already saw how to catch an interrupt. It would be useful if this happened in all applications.

The CZMQ High-Level API

Turning this wish list into reality for the C language gives us CZMQ[13], a ØMQ language binding for C. This high-level binding, in fact, developed out of earlier versions of the examples. It combines nicer semantics for working with ØMQ with some portability layers, and (importantly for C, but less for other languages) containers like hashes and lists. CZMQ also uses an elegant object model that leads to frankly lovely code.

Here is the load balancing broker rewritten to use a higher-level API (CZMQ for the C case):

Example 31. Load balancing broker using high-level API (lbbroker2.c)

```c
//  Load-balancing broker
//  Demonstrates use of the CZMQ API

#include "czmq.h"

#define NBR_CLIENTS 10
#define NBR_WORKERS 3
#define WORKER_READY   "\001"      //  Signals worker is ready

//  Basic request-reply client using REQ socket
//
static void *
client_task (void *args)
{
    zctx_t *ctx = zctx_new ();
    void *client = zsocket_new (ctx, ZMQ_REQ);
    zsocket_connect (client, "ipc://frontend.ipc");

    //  Send request, get reply
    while (true) {
        zstr_send (client, "HELLO");
        char *reply = zstr_recv (client);
        if (!reply)
            break;
        printf ("Client: %s\n", reply);
        free (reply);
        sleep (1);
    }
    zctx_destroy (&ctx);
    return NULL;
}

//  Worker using REQ socket to do load-balancing
//
static void *
```

---

[13] http://zero.mq/c

```
worker_task (void *args)
{
    zctx_t *ctx = zctx_new ();
    void *worker = zsocket_new (ctx, ZMQ_REQ);
    zsocket_connect (worker, "ipc://backend.ipc");

    //  Tell broker we're ready for work
    zframe_t *frame = zframe_new (WORKER_READY, 1);
    zframe_send (&frame, worker, 0);

    //  Process messages as they arrive
    while (true) {
        zmsg_t *msg = zmsg_recv (worker);
        if (!msg)
            break;              //  Interrupted
        zframe_reset (zmsg_last (msg), "OK", 2);
        zmsg_send (&msg, worker);
    }
    zctx_destroy (&ctx);
    return NULL;
}
```

Now we come to the main task. This has the identical functionality to the previous lbbroker broker example, but uses CZMQ to start child threads, to hold the list of workers, and to read and send messages:

Example 31-1. Load balancing broker using high-level API (lbbroker2.c) - main task

```
int main (void)
{
    zctx_t *ctx = zctx_new ();
    void *frontend = zsocket_new (ctx, ZMQ_ROUTER);
    void *backend = zsocket_new (ctx, ZMQ_ROUTER);
    zsocket_bind (frontend, "ipc://frontend.ipc");
    zsocket_bind (backend, "ipc://backend.ipc");

    int client_nbr;
    for (client_nbr = 0; client_nbr < NBR_CLIENTS; client_nbr++)
        zthread_new (client_task, NULL);
    int worker_nbr;
    for (worker_nbr = 0; worker_nbr < NBR_WORKERS; worker_nbr++)
        zthread_new (worker_task, NULL);

    //  Queue of available workers
    zlist_t *workers = zlist_new ();
```

Here is the main loop for the load balancer. It works the same way as the previous example, but is a lot shorter because CZMQ gives us an API that does more with fewer calls:

Example 31-2. Load balancing broker using high-level API (lbbroker2.c) - main load-balancer loop

```
        zmq_pollitem_t items [] = {
            { backend,  0, ZMQ_POLLIN, 0 },
            { frontend, 0, ZMQ_POLLIN, 0 }
        };
        // Poll frontend only if we have available workers
        int rc = zmq_poll (items, zlist_size (workers)? 2: 1, -1);
        if (rc == -1)
            break;              // Interrupted

        // Handle worker activity on backend
        if (items [0].revents & ZMQ_POLLIN) {
            // Use worker identity for load-balancing
            zmsg_t *msg = zmsg_recv (backend);
            if (!msg)
                break;          // Interrupted
            zframe_t *identity = zmsg_unwrap (msg);
            zlist_append (workers, identity);

            // Forward message to client if it's not a READY
            zframe_t *frame = zmsg_first (msg);
            if (memcmp (zframe_data (frame), WORKER_READY, 1) == 0)
                zmsg_destroy (&msg);
            else
                zmsg_send (&msg, frontend);
        }
        if (items [1].revents & ZMQ_POLLIN) {
            // Get client request, route to first available worker
            zmsg_t *msg = zmsg_recv (frontend);
            if (msg) {
                zmsg_wrap (msg, (zframe_t *) zlist_pop (workers));
                zmsg_send (&msg, backend);
            }
        }
    }
    // When we're done, clean up properly
    while (zlist_size (workers)) {
        zframe_t *frame = (zframe_t *) zlist_pop (workers);
        zframe_destroy (&frame);
    }
    zlist_destroy (&workers);
    zctx_destroy (&ctx);
    return 0;
}
```

One thing CZMQ provides is clean interrupt handling. This means that Ctrl-C will cause any blocking ØMQ call to exit with a return code -1 and errno set to EINTR. The high-level recv methods will return NULL in such cases. So, you can cleanly exit a loop like this:

```
while (true) {
    zstr_send (client, "Hello");
    char *reply = zstr_recv (client);
    if (!reply)
        break;              // Interrupted
    printf ("Client: %s\n", reply);
    free (reply);
    sleep (1);
}
```

Or, if you're calling `zmq_poll()`, test on the return code:

```
if (zmq_poll (items, 2, 1000 * 1000) == -1)
    break;                 // Interrupted
```

The previous example still uses `zmq_poll()`. So how about reactors? The CZMQ `zloop` reactor is simple but functional. It lets you:

- Set a reader on any socket, i.e., code that is called whenever the socket has input.
- Cancel a reader on a socket.
- Set a timer that goes off once or multiple times at specific intervals.
- Cancel a timer.

`zloop` of course uses `zmq_poll()` internally. It rebuilds its poll set each time you add or remove readers, and it calculates the poll timeout to match the next timer. Then, it calls the reader and timer handlers for each socket and timer that need attention.

When we use a reactor pattern, our code turns inside out. The main logic looks like this:

```
zloop_t *reactor = zloop_new ();
zloop_reader (reactor, self->backend, s_handle_backend, self);
zloop_start (reactor);
zloop_destroy (&reactor);
```

The actual handling of messages sits inside dedicated functions or methods. You may not like the style—it's a matter of taste. What it does help with is mixing timers and socket activity. In the rest of this text, we'll use `zmq_poll()` in simpler cases, and `zloop` in more complex examples.

Here is the load balancing broker rewritten once again, this time to use `zloop`:

Example 32. Load balancing broker using zloop (lbbroker3.c)

```
//  Load-balancing broker
//  Demonstrates use of the CZMQ API and reactor style
```

```
//
// The client and worker tasks are identical from the previous example.
...
// Our load-balancer structure, passed to reactor handlers
typedef struct {
    void *frontend;             //  Listen to clients
    void *backend;              //  Listen to workers
    zlist_t *workers;           //  List of ready workers
} lbbroker_t;
```

In the reactor design, each time a message arrives on a socket, the reactor passes it to a handler function. We have two handlers; one for the frontend, one for the backend:

Example 32-1. Load balancing broker using zloop (lbbroker3.c) - reactor design

```
//  Handle input from client, on frontend
int s_handle_frontend (zloop_t *loop, zmq_pollitem_t *poller, void *arg)
{
    lbbroker_t *self = (lbbroker_t *) arg;
    zmsg_t *msg = zmsg_recv (self->frontend);
    if (msg) {
        zmsg_wrap (msg, (zframe_t *) zlist_pop (self->workers));
        zmsg_send (&msg, self->backend);

        //  Cancel reader on frontend if we went from 1 to 0 workers
        if (zlist_size (self->workers) == 0) {
            zmq_pollitem_t poller = { self->frontend, 0, ZMQ_POLLIN };
            zloop_poller_end (loop, &poller);
        }
    }
    return 0;
}

//  Handle input from worker, on backend
int s_handle_backend (zloop_t *loop, zmq_pollitem_t *poller, void *arg)
{
    //  Use worker identity for load-balancing
    lbbroker_t *self = (lbbroker_t *) arg;
    zmsg_t *msg = zmsg_recv (self->backend);
    if (msg) {
        zframe_t *identity = zmsg_unwrap (msg);
        zlist_append (self->workers, identity);

        //  Enable reader on frontend if we went from 0 to 1 workers
        if (zlist_size (self->workers) == 1) {
            zmq_pollitem_t poller = { self->frontend, 0, ZMQ_POLLIN };
            zloop_poller (loop, &poller, s_handle_frontend, self);
        }
        //  Forward message to client if it's not a READY
        zframe_t *frame = zmsg_first (msg);
        if (memcmp (zframe_data (frame), WORKER_READY, 1) == 0)
```

```
            zmsg_destroy (&msg);
        else
            zmsg_send (&msg, self->frontend);
    }
    return 0;
}
```

And the main task now sets up child tasks, then starts its reactor. If you press Ctrl-C, the reactor exits and the main task shuts down. Because the reactor is a CZMQ class, this example may not translate into all languages equally well.

Example 32-2. Load balancing broker using zloop (lbbroker3.c) - main task

```
int main (void)
{
    zctx_t *ctx = zctx_new ();
    lbbroker_t *self = (lbbroker_t *) zmalloc (sizeof (lbbroker_t));
    self->frontend = zsocket_new (ctx, ZMQ_ROUTER);
    self->backend = zsocket_new (ctx, ZMQ_ROUTER);
    zsocket_bind (self->frontend, "ipc://frontend.ipc");
    zsocket_bind (self->backend, "ipc://backend.ipc");

    int client_nbr;
    for (client_nbr = 0; client_nbr < NBR_CLIENTS; client_nbr++)
        zthread_new (client_task, NULL);
    int worker_nbr;
    for (worker_nbr = 0; worker_nbr < NBR_WORKERS; worker_nbr++)
        zthread_new (worker_task, NULL);

    //  Queue of available workers
    self->workers = zlist_new ();

    //  Prepare reactor and fire it up
    zloop_t *reactor = zloop_new ();
    zmq_pollitem_t poller = { self->backend, 0, ZMQ_POLLIN };
    zloop_poller (reactor, &poller, s_handle_backend, self);
    zloop_start  (reactor);
    zloop_destroy (&reactor);

    //  When we're done, clean up properly
    while (zlist_size (self->workers)) {
        zframe_t *frame = (zframe_t *) zlist_pop (self->workers);
        zframe_destroy (&frame);
    }
    zlist_destroy (&self->workers);
    zctx_destroy (&ctx);
    free (self);
    return 0;
}
```

Getting applications to properly shut down when you send them Ctrl-C can be tricky. If you use the zctx class it'll automatically set up signal handling, but your code still has to cooperate. You must break any loop if zmq_poll returns -1 or if any of the zstr_recv, zframe_recv, or zmsg_recv methods return NULL. If you have nested loops, it can be useful to make the outer ones conditional on !zctx_interrupted.

The Asynchronous Client/Server Pattern

In the ROUTER to DEALER example, we saw a 1-to-N use case where one server talks asynchronously to multiple workers. We can turn this upside down to get a very useful N-to-1 architecture where various clients talk to a single server, and do this asynchronously (see figure 37).

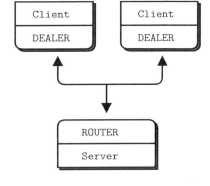

Figure 37. Asynchronous Client/Server

Here's how it works:

- Clients connect to the server and send requests.
- For each request, the server sends 0 or more replies.
- Clients can send multiple requests without waiting for a reply.
- Servers can send multiple replies without waiting for new requests.

Here's code that shows how this works:

Example 33. Asynchronous client/server (asyncsrv.c)

```
//  Asynchronous client-to-server (DEALER to ROUTER)
//
//  While this example runs in a single process, that is to make
//  it easier to start and stop the example. Each task has its own
//  context and conceptually acts as a separate process.

#include "czmq.h"

//  This is our client task
//  It connects to the server, and then sends a request once per second
//  It collects responses as they arrive, and it prints them out. We will
//  run several client tasks in parallel, each with a different random ID.

static void *
client_task (void *args)
{
    zctx_t *ctx = zctx_new ();
    void *client = zsocket_new (ctx, ZMQ_DEALER);

    //  Set random identity to make tracing easier
```

```
            char identity [10];
            sprintf (identity, "%04X-%04X", randof (0x10000), randof (0x10000));
            zsockopt_set_identity (client, identity);
            zsocket_connect (client, "tcp://localhost:5570");

            zmq_pollitem_t items [] = { { client, 0, ZMQ_POLLIN, 0 } };
            int request_nbr = 0;
            while (true) {
                //  Tick once per second, pulling in arriving messages
                int centitick;
                for (centitick = 0; centitick < 100; centitick++) {
                    zmq_poll (items, 1, 10 * ZMQ_POLL_MSEC);
                    if (items [0].revents & ZMQ_POLLIN) {
                        zmsg_t *msg = zmsg_recv (client);
                        zframe_print (zmsg_last (msg), identity);
                        zmsg_destroy (&msg);
                    }
                }
                zstr_send (client, "request #%d", ++request_nbr);
            }
            zctx_destroy (&ctx);
            return NULL;
        }
```

This is our server task. It uses the multithreaded server model to deal requests out to a pool of workers and route replies back to clients. One worker can handle one request at a time but one client can talk to multiple workers at once.

Example 33-1. Asynchronous client/server (asyncsrv.c) - server task

```
        static void server_worker (void *args, zctx_t *ctx, void *pipe);

        void *server_task (void *args)
        {
            //  Frontend socket talks to clients over TCP
            zctx_t *ctx = zctx_new ();
            void *frontend = zsocket_new (ctx, ZMQ_ROUTER);
            zsocket_bind (frontend, "tcp://*:5570");

            //  Backend socket talks to workers over inproc
            void *backend = zsocket_new (ctx, ZMQ_DEALER);
            zsocket_bind (backend, "inproc://backend");

            //  Launch pool of worker threads, precise number is not critical
            int thread_nbr;
            for (thread_nbr = 0; thread_nbr < 5; thread_nbr++)
                zthread_fork (ctx, server_worker, NULL);

            //  Connect backend to frontend via a proxy
            zmq_proxy (frontend, backend, NULL);
```

```
        zctx_destroy (&ctx);
        return NULL;
}
```

Each worker task works on one request at a time and sends a random number of replies back, with random delays between replies:

Example 33-2. Asynchronous client/server (asyncsrv.c) - worker task

```
static void
server_worker (void *args, zctx_t *ctx, void *pipe)
{
    void *worker = zsocket_new (ctx, ZMQ_DEALER);
    zsocket_connect (worker, "inproc://backend");

    while (true) {
        //  The DEALER socket gives us the reply envelope and message
        zmsg_t *msg = zmsg_recv (worker);
        zframe_t *identity = zmsg_pop (msg);
        zframe_t *content = zmsg_pop (msg);
        assert (content);
        zmsg_destroy (&msg);

        //  Send 0..4 replies back
        int reply, replies = randof (5);
        for (reply = 0; reply < replies; reply++) {
            //  Sleep for some fraction of a second
            zclock_sleep (randof (1000) + 1);
            zframe_send (&identity, worker, ZFRAME_REUSE + ZFRAME_MORE);
            zframe_send (&content, worker, ZFRAME_REUSE);
        }
        zframe_destroy (&identity);
        zframe_destroy (&content);
    }
}

//  The main thread simply starts several clients and a server, and then
//  waits for the server to finish.

int main (void)
{
    zthread_new (client_task, NULL);
    zthread_new (client_task, NULL);
    zthread_new (client_task, NULL);
    zthread_new (server_task, NULL);
    zclock_sleep (5 * 1000);     //  Run for 5 seconds then quit
    return 0;
}
```

The example runs in one process, with multiple threads simulating a real multiprocess architecture. When you run the example, you'll see three clients (each with a random

ID), printing out the replies they get from the server. Look carefully and you'll see each client task gets 0 or more replies per request.

Some comments on this code:

- The clients send a request once per second, and get zero or more replies back. To make this work using zmq_poll(), we can't simply poll with a 1-second timeout, or we'd end up sending a new request only one second *after we received the last reply*. So we poll at a high frequency (100 times at 1/100th of a second per poll), which is approximately accurate.
- The server uses a pool of worker threads, each processing one request synchronously. It connects these to its frontend socket using an internal queue (see figure 38). It connects the frontend and backend sockets using a zmq_proxy() call.

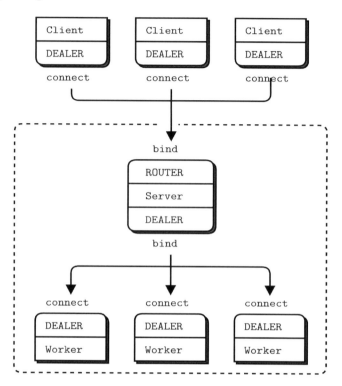

Figure 38. Detail of Asynchronous Server

Note that we're doing DEALER to ROUTER dialog between client and server, but internally between the server main thread and workers, we're doing DEALER to DEALER. If the workers were strictly synchronous, we'd use REP. However, because we want to send multiple replies, we need an async socket. We do *not* want to route replies, they always go to the single server thread that sent us the request.

Let's think about the routing envelope. The client sends a message consisting of a single frame. The server thread receives a two-frame message (original message prefixed by client identity). We send these two frames on to the worker, which treats it as a normal reply envelope, returns that to us as a two frame message. We then use the first frame as an identity to route the second frame back to the client as a reply.

It looks something like this:

```
         client            server          frontend         worker
       [ DEALER ]<---->[ ROUTER  <----> DEALER  <----> DEALER ]
               1 part           2 parts         2 parts
```

Now for the sockets: we could use the load balancing ROUTER to DEALER pattern to talk to workers, but it's extra work. In this case, a DEALER to DEALER pattern is probably fine: the trade-off is lower latency for each request, but higher risk of unbalanced work distribution. Simplicity wins in this case.

When you build servers that maintain stateful conversations with clients, you will run into a classic problem. If the server keeps some state per client, and clients keep coming and going, eventually it will run out of resources. Even if the same clients keep connecting, if you're using default identities, each connection will look like a new one.

We cheat in the above example by keeping state only for a very short time (the time it takes a worker to process a request) and then throwing away the state. But that's not practical for many cases. To properly manage client state in a stateful asynchronous server, you have to:

- Do heartbeating from client to server. In our example, we send a request once per second, which can reliably be used as a heartbeat.
- Store state using the client identity (whether generated or explicit) as key.
- Detect a stopped heartbeat. If there's no request from a client within, say, two seconds, the server can detect this and destroy any state it's holding for that client.

Worked Example: Inter-Broker Routing

Let's take everything we've seen so far, and scale things up to a real application. We'll build this step-by-step over several iterations. Our best client calls us urgently and asks for a design of a large cloud computing facility. He has this vision of a cloud that spans many data centers, each a cluster of clients and workers, and that works together as a whole. Because we're smart enough to know that practice always beats theory, we propose to make a working simulation using ØMQ. Our client, eager to lock down the budget before his own boss changes his mind, and having read great things about ØMQ on Twitter, agrees.

Establishing the Details

Several espressos later, we want to jump into writing code, but a little voice tells us to get more details before making a sensational solution to entirely the wrong problem. "What kind of work is the cloud doing?", we ask.

The client explains:

- Workers run on various kinds of hardware, but they are all able to handle any task. There are several hundred workers per cluster, and as many as a dozen clusters in total.
- Clients create tasks for workers. Each task is an independent unit of work and all the client wants is to find an available worker, and send it the task, as soon as possible. There will be a lot of clients and they'll come and go arbitrarily.

- The real difficulty is to be able to add and remove clusters at any time. A cluster can leave or join the cloud instantly, bringing all its workers and clients with it.
- If there are no workers in their own cluster, clients' tasks will go off to other available workers in the cloud.
- Clients send out one task at a time, waiting for a reply. If they don't get an answer within X seconds, they'll just send out the task again. This isn't our concern; the client API does it already.
- Workers process one task at a time; they are very simple beasts. If they crash, they get restarted by whatever script started them.

So we double-check to make sure that we understood this correctly:

- "There will be some kind of super-duper network interconnect between clusters, right?", we ask. The client says, "Yes, of course, we're not idiots."
- "What kind of volumes are we talking about?", we ask. The client replies, "Up to a thousand clients per cluster, each doing at most ten requests per second. Requests are small, and replies are also small, no more than 1K bytes each."

So we do a little calculation and see that this will work nicely over plain TCP. 2,500 clients x 10/second x 1,000 bytes x 2 directions = 50MB/sec or 400Mb/sec, not a problem for a 1Gb network.

It's a straightforward problem that requires no exotic hardware or protocols, just some clever routing algorithms and careful design. We start by designing one cluster (one data center) and then we figure out how to connect clusters together.

Architecture of a Single Cluster

Workers and clients are synchronous. We want to use the load balancing pattern to route tasks to workers. Workers are all identical; our facility has no notion of different services. Workers are anonymous; clients never address them directly. We make no attempt here to provide guaranteed delivery, retry, and so on.

For reasons we already examined, clients and workers won't speak to each other directly. It makes it impossible to add or remove nodes dynamically. So our basic model consists of the request-reply message broker we saw earlier (see figure 39).

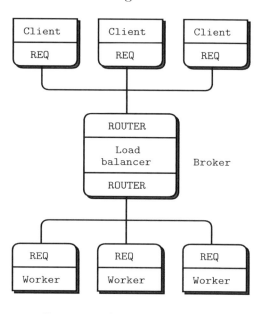

Figure 39. Cluster Architecture

Scaling to Multiple Clusters

Now we scale this out to more than one cluster. Each cluster has a set of clients and workers, and a broker that joins these together (see figure 40).

The question is: how do we get the clients of each cluster talking to the workers of the other cluster? There are a few possibilities, each with pros and cons:

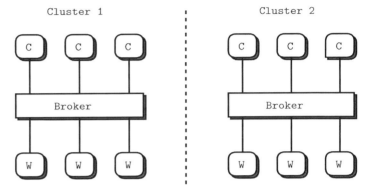

Figure 40. Multiple Clusters

- Clients could connect directly to both brokers. The advantage is that we don't need to modify brokers or workers. But clients get more complex and become aware of the overall topology. If we want to add a third or forth cluster, for example, all the clients are affected. In effect we have to move routing and failover logic into the clients and that's not nice.

- Workers might connect directly to both brokers. But REQ workers can't do that, they can only reply to one broker. We might use REPs but REPs don't give us customizable broker-to-worker routing like load balancing does, only the built-in load balancing. That's a fail; if we want to distribute work to idle workers, we precisely need load balancing. One solution would be to use ROUTER sockets for the worker nodes. Let's label this "Idea #1".

- Brokers could connect to each other. This looks neatest because it creates the fewest additional connections. We can't add clusters on the fly, but that is probably out of scope. Now clients and workers remain ignorant of the real network topology, and brokers tell each other when they have spare capacity. Let's label this "Idea #2".

Let's explore Idea #1. In this model, we have workers connecting to both brokers and accepting jobs from either one (see figure 41).

It looks feasible. However, it doesn't provide what we wanted, which was that clients get local workers if possible and remote workers only if it's better than waiting. Also workers will signal "ready" to both brokers and can get two jobs at once, while other workers remain idle. It seems this design fails because again we're putting routing logic at the edges.

So, idea #2 then. We interconnect the brokers and don't touch the clients or workers, which are REQs like we're used to (see figure 42).

This design is appealing because the problem is solved in one place, invisible to the rest of the world. Basically, brokers open secret channels to each other and whisper, like camel traders, "Hey, I've got some spare capacity. If you have too many clients, give me a shout and we'll deal".

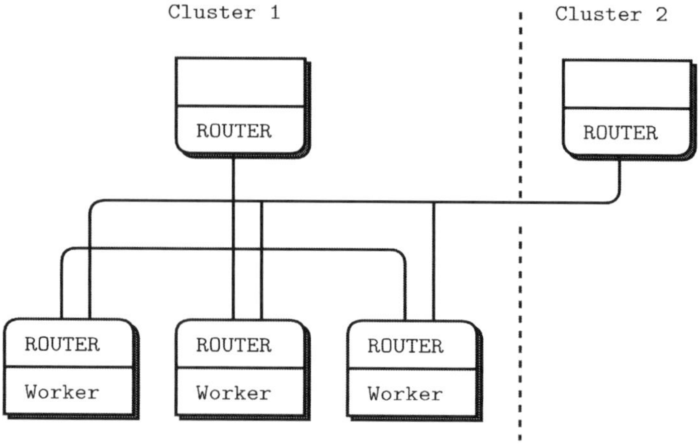

In effect it is just a more sophisticated routing algorithm: brokers become subcontractors for each other. There are other things to like about this design, even before we play with real code:

- It treats the common case (clients and workers on the same cluster) as default and does extra work for the exceptional case (shuffling jobs between clusters).
- It lets us use different message flows for the different types of work. That means we can handle them differently, e.g., using different types of network connection.
- It feels like it would scale smoothly. Interconnecting three or more brokers doesn't get overly complex. If we find this to be a problem, it's easy to solve by adding a super-broker.

Figure 41. Idea 1: Cross-connected Workers

We'll now make a worked example. We'll pack an entire cluster into one process. That is obviously not realistic, but it makes it simple to simulate, and the simulation can accurately scale to real processes. This is the beauty of ØMQ—you can design at the micro-level and scale that up to the macro-level. Threads become processes, and then become boxes and the patterns and logic remain the same. Each of our "cluster" processes contains client threads, worker threads, and a broker thread.

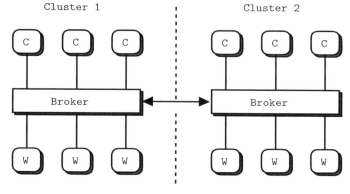

Figure 42. Idea 2: Brokers Talking to Each Other

We know the basic model well by now:

- The REQ client (REQ) threads create workloads and pass them to the broker (ROUTER).
- The REQ worker (REQ) threads process workloads and return the results to the broker (ROUTER).

- The broker queues and distributes workloads using the load balancing pattern.

Federation Versus Peering

There are several possible ways to interconnect brokers. What we want is to be able to tell other brokers, "we have capacity", and then receive multiple tasks. We also need to be able to tell other brokers, "stop, we're full". It doesn't need to be perfect; sometimes we may accept jobs we can't process immediately, then we'll do them as soon as possible.

The simplest interconnect is *federation*, in which brokers simulate clients and workers for each other. We would do this by connecting our frontend to the other broker's backend socket (see figure 43). Note that it is legal to both bind a socket to an endpoint and connect it to other endpoints.

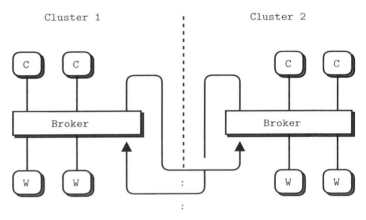

Figure 43. Cross-connected Brokers in Federation Model

This would give us simple logic in both brokers and a reasonably good mechanism: when there are no clients, tell the other broker "ready", and accept one job from it. The problem is also that it is too simple for this problem. A federated broker would be able to handle only one task at a time. If the broker emulates a lock-step client and worker, it is by definition also going to be lock-step, and if it has lots of available workers they won't be used. Our brokers need to be connected in a fully asynchronous fashion.

The federation model is perfect for other kinds of routing, especially service-oriented architectures (SOAs), which route by service name and proximity rather than load balancing or round robin. So don't dismiss it as useless, it's just not right for all use cases.

Instead of federation, let's look at a *peering* approach in which brokers are explicitly aware of each other and talk over privileged channels. Let's break this down, assuming we want to interconnect N brokers. Each broker has (N - 1) peers, and all brokers are using exactly the same code and logic. There are two distinct flows of information between brokers:

- Each broker needs to tell its peers how many workers it has available at any time. This can be fairly simple information—just a quantity that is updated regularly. The obvious (and correct) socket pattern for this is pub-sub. So every broker opens a PUB socket and publishes state information on that, and every broker also opens a SUB socket and connects that to the PUB socket of every other broker to get state information from its peers.

- Each broker needs a way to delegate tasks to a peer and get replies back, asynchronously. We'll do this using ROUTER sockets; no other combination works. Each broker has two such sockets: one for tasks it receives and one for tasks it delegates. If we didn't use two sockets, it would be more work to know whether we were reading a request or a reply each time. That would mean adding more information to the message envelope.

And there is also the flow of information between a broker and its local clients and workers.

The Naming Ceremony

Three flows x two sockets for each flow = six sockets that we have to manage in the broker. Choosing good names is vital to keeping a multisocket juggling act reasonably coherent in our minds. Sockets *do* something and what they do should form the basis for their names. It's about being able to read the code several weeks later on a cold Monday morning before coffee, and not feel any pain.

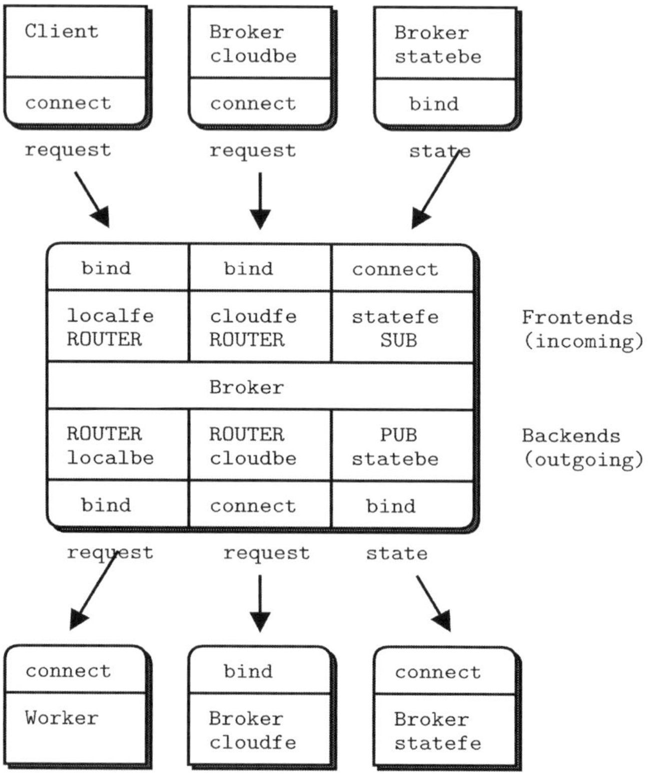

Let's do a shamanistic naming ceremony for the sockets. The three flows are:

- A *local* request-reply flow between the broker and its clients and workers.
- A *cloud* request-reply flow between the broker and its peer brokers.
- A *state* flow between the broker and its peer brokers.

Figure 44. Broker Socket Arrangement

Finding meaningful names that are all the same length means our code will align nicely. It's not a big thing, but attention to details helps. For each flow the broker has two sockets that we can orthogonally call the *frontend* and *backend*. We've used these names quite often. A frontend receives information or tasks. A backend sends those out to other peers. The conceptual flow is from front to back (with replies going in the opposite direction from back to front).

So in all the code we write for this tutorial, we will use these socket names:

- *localfe* and *localbe* for the local flow.
- *cloudfe* and *cloudbe* for the cloud flow.
- *statefe* and *statebe* for the state flow.

For our transport and because we're simulating the whole thing on one box, we'll use `ipc` for everything. This has the advantage of working like `tcp` in terms of connectivity (i.e., it's a disconnected transport, unlike `inproc`), yet we don't need IP addresses or DNS names, which would be a pain here. Instead, we will use `ipc` endpoints called *something*-local, *something*-cloud, and *something*-state, where *something* is the name of our simulated cluster.

You might be thinking that this is a lot of work for some names. Why not call them s1, s2, s3, s4, etc.? The answer is that if your brain is not a perfect machine, you need a lot of help when reading code, and we'll see that these names do help. It's easier to remember "three flows, two directions" than "six different sockets" (see figure 44).

Note that we connect the cloudbe in each broker to the cloudfe in every other broker, and likewise we connect the statebe in each broker to the statefe in every other broker.

Prototyping the State Flow

Because each socket flow has its own little traps for the unwary, we will test them in real code one-by-one, rather than try to throw the whole lot into code in one go. When we're happy with each flow, we can put them together into a full program. We'll start with the state flow (see figure 45).

Here is how this works in code:

Example 34. Prototype state flow (peering1.c)

```c
//  Broker peering simulation (part 1)
//  Prototypes the state flow

#include "czmq.h"

int main (int argc, char *argv [])
{
    //  First argument is this broker's name
    //  Other arguments are our peers' names
    //
    if (argc < 2) {
        printf ("syntax: peering1 me {you}...\n");
        return 0;
    }
    char *self = argv [1];
    printf ("I: preparing broker at %s...\n", self);
    srandom ((unsigned) time (NULL));

    zctx_t *ctx = zctx_new ();
```

```
    // Bind state backend to endpoint
    void *statebe = zsocket_new (ctx, ZMQ_PUB);
    zsocket_bind (statebe, "ipc://%s-state.ipc", self);

    // Connect statefe to all peers
    void *statefe = zsocket_new (ctx, ZMQ_SUB);
    zsockopt_set_subscribe (statefe, "");
    int argn;
    for (argn = 2; argn < argc; argn++) {
        char *peer = argv [argn];
        printf ("I: connecting to state backend at '%s'\n", peer);
        zsocket_connect (statefe, "ipc://%s-state.ipc", peer);
    }
```

The main loop sends out status messages to peers, and collects status messages back from peers. The zmq_poll timeout defines our own heartbeat:

Example 34-1. Prototype state flow (peering1.c) - main loop

```
    while (true) {
        //  Poll for activity, or 1 second timeout
        zmq_pollitem_t items [] = { { statefe, 0, ZMQ_POLLIN, 0 } };
        int rc = zmq_poll (items, 1, 1000 * ZMQ_POLL_MSEC);
        if (rc == -1)
            break;              //  Interrupted

        //  Handle incoming status messages
        if (items [0].revents & ZMQ_POLLIN) {
            char *peer_name = zstr_recv (statefe);
            char *available = zstr_recv (statefe);
            printf ("%s - %s workers free\n", peer_name, available);
            free (peer_name);
            free (available);
        }
        else {
            //  Send random values for worker availability
            zstr_sendm (statebe, self);
            zstr_send  (statebe, "%d", randof (10));
        }
    }
    zctx_destroy (&ctx);
    return EXIT_SUCCESS;
}
```

Notes about this code:

- Each broker has an identity that we use to construct `ipc` endpoint names. A real broker would need to work with TCP and a more sophisticated configuration scheme. We'll look at such schemes later in this book, but for now, using generated `ipc` names lets us ignore the problem of where to get TCP/IP addresses or names.

- We use a `zmq_poll()` loop as the core of the program. This processes incoming messages and sends out state messages. We send a state message *only* if we did not get any incoming messages *and* we waited for a second. If we send out a state message each time we get one in, we'll get message storms.

- We use a two-part pub-sub message consisting of sender address and data. Note that we will need to know the address of the publisher in order to send it tasks, and the only way is to send this explicitly as a part of the message.

- We don't set identities on subscribers because if we did then we'd get outdated state information when connecting to running brokers.

- We don't set a HWM on the publisher, but if we were using ØMQ v2.x that would be a wise idea.

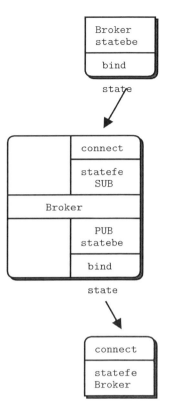

Figure 45. The State Flow

We can build this little program and run it three times to simulate three clusters. Let's call them DC1, DC2, and DC3 (the names are arbitrary). We run these three commands, each in a separate window:

```
peering1 DC1 DC2 DC3    #   Start DC1 and connect to DC2 and DC3
peering1 DC2 DC1 DC3    #   Start DC2 and connect to DC1 and DC3
peering1 DC3 DC1 DC2    #   Start DC3 and connect to DC1 and DC2
```

You'll see each cluster report the state of its peers, and after a few seconds they will all happily be printing random numbers once per second. Try this and satisfy yourself that the three brokers all match up and synchronize to per-second state updates.

In real life, we'd not send out state messages at regular intervals, but rather whenever we had a state change, i.e., whenever a worker becomes available or unavailable. That may seem like a lot of traffic, but state messages are small and we've established that the inter-cluster connections are super fast.

If we wanted to send state messages at precise intervals, we'd create a child thread and open the `statebe` socket in that thread. We'd then send irregular state updates to that child thread from our main thread and allow the child thread to conflate them into regular outgoing messages. This is more work than we need here.

Prototyping the Local and Cloud Flows

Let's now prototype at the flow of tasks via the local and cloud sockets (see figure 46). This code pulls requests from clients and then distributes them to local workers and cloud peers on a random basis.

Before we jump into the code, which is getting a little complex, let's sketch the core routing logic and break it down into a simple yet robust design.

We need two queues, one for requests from local clients and one for requests from cloud clients. One option would be to pull messages off the local and cloud frontends, and pump these onto their respective queues. But this is kind of pointless because ØMQ sockets *are* queues already. So let's use the ØMQ socket buffers as queues.

This was the technique we used in the load balancing broker, and it worked nicely. We only read from the two frontends when there is somewhere to send the requests. We can always read from the backends, as they give us replies to route back. As long as the backends aren't talking to us, there's no point in even looking at the frontends.

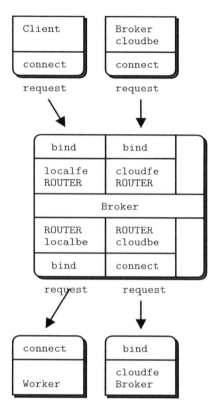

Figure 46. The Flow of Tasks

So our main loop becomes:
- Poll the backends for activity. When we get a message, it may be "ready" from a worker or it may be a reply. If it's a reply, route back via the local or cloud frontend.
- If a worker replied, it became available, so we queue it and count it.
- While there are workers available, take a request, if any, from either frontend and route to a local worker, or randomly, to a cloud peer.

Randomly sending tasks to a peer broker rather than a worker simulates work distribution across the cluster. It's dumb, but that is fine for this stage.

We use broker identities to route messages between brokers. Each broker has a name that we provide on the command line in this simple prototype. As long as these names don't overlap with the ØMQ-generated UUIDs used for client nodes, we can figure out whether to route a reply back to a client or to a broker.

Here is how this works in code. The interesting part starts around the comment "Interesting part".

Example 35. Prototype local and cloud flow (peering2.c)

```
//  Broker peering simulation (part 2)
//  Prototypes the request-reply flow

#include "czmq.h"
#define NBR_CLIENTS 10
#define NBR_WORKERS 3
#define WORKER_READY   "\001"      //  Signals worker is ready

//  Our own name; in practice this would be configured per node
static char *self;
```

The client task does a request-reply dialog using a standard synchronous REQ socket:

Example 35-1. Prototype local and cloud flow (peering2.c) - client task

```
static void *
client_task (void *args)
{
    zctx_t *ctx = zctx_new ();
    void *client = zsocket_new (ctx, ZMQ_REQ);
    zsocket_connect (client, "ipc://%s-localfe.ipc", self);

    while (true) {
        //  Send request, get reply
        zstr_send (client, "HELLO");
        char *reply = zstr_recv (client);
        if (!reply)
            break;              //  Interrupted
        printf ("Client: %s\n", reply);
        free (reply);
        sleep (1);
    }
    zctx_destroy (&ctx);
    return NULL;
}
```

The worker task plugs into the load-balancer using a REQ socket:

Example 35-2. Prototype local and cloud flow (peering2.c) - worker task

```
static void *
worker_task (void *args)
{
    zctx_t *ctx = zctx_new ();
    void *worker = zsocket_new (ctx, ZMQ_REQ);
    zsocket_connect (worker, "ipc://%s-localbe.ipc", self);

    //  Tell broker we're ready for work
    zframe_t *frame = zframe_new (WORKER_READY, 1);
    zframe_send (&frame, worker, 0);
```

```
        //  Process messages as they arrive
        while (true) {
            zmsg_t *msg = zmsg_recv (worker);
            if (!msg)
                break;              //  Interrupted

            zframe_print (zmsg_last (msg), "Worker: ");
            zframe_reset (zmsg_last (msg), "OK", 2);
            zmsg_send (&msg, worker);
        }
        zctx_destroy (&ctx);
        return NULL;
}
```

The main task begins by setting-up its frontend and backend sockets and then starting its client and worker tasks:

Example 35-3. Prototype local and cloud flow (peering2.c) - main task

```
int main (int argc, char *argv [])
{
    //  First argument is this broker's name
    //  Other arguments are our peers' names
    //
    if (argc < 2) {
        printf ("syntax: peering2 me {you}...\n");
        return 0;
    }
    self = argv [1];
    printf ("I: preparing broker at %s...\n", self);
    srandom ((unsigned) time (NULL));

    zctx_t *ctx = zctx_new ();

    //  Bind cloud frontend to endpoint
    void *cloudfe = zsocket_new (ctx, ZMQ_ROUTER);
    zsockopt_set_identity (cloudfe, self);
    zsocket_bind (cloudfe, "ipc://%s-cloud.ipc", self);

    //  Connect cloud backend to all peers
    void *cloudbe = zsocket_new (ctx, ZMQ_ROUTER);
    zsockopt_set_identity (cloudbe, self);
    int argn;
    for (argn = 2; argn < argc; argn++) {
        char *peer = argv [argn];
        printf ("I: connecting to cloud frontend at '%s'\n", peer);
        zsocket_connect (cloudbe, "ipc://%s-cloud.ipc", peer);
    }
    //  Prepare local frontend and backend
    void *localfe = zsocket_new (ctx, ZMQ_ROUTER);
```

```
zsocket_bind (localfe, "ipc://%s-localfe.ipc", self);
void *localbe = zsocket_new (ctx, ZMQ_ROUTER);
zsocket_bind (localbe, "ipc://%s-localbe.ipc", self);

// Get user to tell us when we can start...
printf ("Press Enter when all brokers are started: ");
getchar ();

// Start local workers
int worker_nbr;
for (worker_nbr = 0; worker_nbr < NBR_WORKERS; worker_nbr++)
    zthread_new (worker_task, NULL);

// Start local clients
int client_nbr;
for (client_nbr = 0; client_nbr < NBR_CLIENTS; client_nbr++)
    zthread_new (client_task, NULL);
```

Here, we handle the request-reply flow. We're using load-balancing to poll workers at all times, and clients only when there are one or more workers available.

Example 35-4. Prototype local and cloud flow (peering2.c) - request-reply handling

```
// Least recently used queue of available workers
int capacity = 0;
zlist_t *workers = zlist_new ();

while (true) {
    // First, route any waiting replies from workers
    zmq_pollitem_t backends [] = {
        { localbe, 0, ZMQ_POLLIN, 0 },
        { cloudbe, 0, ZMQ_POLLIN, 0 }
    };
    // If we have no workers, wait indefinitely
    int rc = zmq_poll (backends, 2,
        capacity? 1000 * ZMQ_POLL_MSEC: -1);
    if (rc == -1)
        break;              //  Interrupted

    // Handle reply from local worker
    zmsg_t *msg = NULL;
    if (backends [0].revents & ZMQ_POLLIN) {
        msg = zmsg_recv (localbe);
        if (!msg)
            break;          //  Interrupted
        zframe_t *identity = zmsg_unwrap (msg);
        zlist_append (workers, identity);
        capacity++;

        // If it's READY, don't route the message any further
        zframe_t *frame = zmsg_first (msg);
```

```
            if (memcmp (zframe_data (frame), WORKER_READY, 1) == 0)
                zmsg_destroy (&msg);
        }
        //  Or handle reply from peer broker
        else
        if (backends [1].revents & ZMQ_POLLIN) {
            msg = zmsg_recv (cloudbe);
            if (!msg)
                break;          //  Interrupted
            //  We don't use peer broker identity for anything
            zframe_t *identity = zmsg_unwrap (msg);
            zframe_destroy (&identity);
        }
        //  Route reply to cloud if it's addressed to a broker
        for (argn = 2; msg && argn < argc; argn++) {
            char *data = (char *) zframe_data (zmsg_first (msg));
            size_t size = zframe_size (zmsg_first (msg));
            if (size == strlen (argv [argn])
            &&  memcmp (data, argv [argn], size) == 0)
                zmsg_send (&msg, cloudfe);
        }
        //  Route reply to client if we still need to
        if (msg)
            zmsg_send (&msg, localfe);
```

Now we route as many client requests as we have worker capacity for. We may reroute requests from our local frontend, but not from the cloud frontend. We reroute randomly now, just to test things out. In the next version, we'll do this properly by calculating cloud capacity:

Example 35-5. Prototype local and cloud flow (peering2.c) - route client requests

```
        while (capacity) {
            zmq_pollitem_t frontends [] = {
                { localfe, 0, ZMQ_POLLIN, 0 },
                { cloudfe, 0, ZMQ_POLLIN, 0 }
            };
            rc = zmq_poll (frontends, 2, 0);
            assert (rc >= 0);
            int reroutable = 0;
            //  We'll do peer brokers first, to prevent starvation
            if (frontends [1].revents & ZMQ_POLLIN) {
                msg = zmsg_recv (cloudfe);
                reroutable = 0;
            }
            else
            if (frontends [0].revents & ZMQ_POLLIN) {
                msg = zmsg_recv (localfe);
                reroutable = 1;
            }
            else
```

```
                    break;      //  No work, go back to backends

            //  If reroutable, send to cloud 20% of the time
            //  Here we'd normally use cloud status information
            //
            if (reroutable && argc > 2 && randof (5) == 0) {
                //  Route to random broker peer
                int peer = randof (argc - 2) + 2;
                zmsg_pushmem (msg, argv [peer], strlen (argv [peer]));
                zmsg_send (&msg, cloudbe);
            }
            else {
                zframe_t *frame = (zframe_t *) zlist_pop (workers);
                zmsg_wrap (msg, frame);
                zmsg_send (&msg, localbe);
                capacity--;
            }
        }
    }
    //  When we're done, clean up properly
    while (zlist_size (workers)) {
        zframe_t *frame = (zframe_t *) zlist_pop (workers);
        zframe_destroy (&frame);
    }
    zlist_destroy (&workers);
    zctx_destroy (&ctx);
    return EXIT_SUCCESS;
}
```

Run this by, for instance, starting two instances of the broker in two windows:

```
peering2 me you
peering2 you me
```

Some comments on this code:

- In the C code at least, using the zmsg class makes life much easier, and our code much shorter. It's obviously an abstraction that works. If you build ØMQ applications in C, you should use CZMQ.

- Because we're not getting any state information from peers, we naively assume they are running. The code prompts you to confirm when you've started all the brokers. In the real case, we'd not send anything to brokers who had not told us they exist.

You can satisfy yourself that the code works by watching it run forever. If there were any misrouted messages, clients would end up blocking, and the brokers would stop printing trace information. You can prove that by killing either of the brokers. The other broker tries to send requests to the cloud, and one-by-one its clients block, waiting for an answer.

Putting it All Together

Let's put this together into a single package. As before, we'll run an entire cluster as one process. We're going to take the two previous examples and merge them into one properly working design that lets you simulate any number of clusters.

This code is the size of both previous prototypes together, at 270 LoC. That's pretty good for a simulation of a cluster that includes clients and workers and cloud workload distribution. Here is the code:

Example 36. Full cluster simulation (peering3.c)

```
//  Broker peering simulation (part 3)
//  Prototypes the full flow of status and tasks

#include "czmq.h"
#define NBR_CLIENTS 10
#define NBR_WORKERS 5
#define WORKER_READY   "\001"      //  Signals worker is ready

//  Our own name; in practice, this would be configured per node
static char *self;
```

This is the client task. It issues a burst of requests and then sleeps for a few seconds. This simulates sporadic activity; when a number of clients are active at once, the local workers should be overloaded. The client uses a REQ socket for requests and also pushes statistics to the monitor socket:

Example 36-1. Full cluster simulation (peering3.c) - client task

```
static void *
client_task (void *args)
{
    zctx_t *ctx = zctx_new ();
    void *client = zsocket_new (ctx, ZMQ_REQ);
    zsocket_connect (client, "ipc://%s-localfe.ipc", self);
    void *monitor = zsocket_new (ctx, ZMQ_PUSH);
    zsocket_connect (monitor, "ipc://%s-monitor.ipc", self);

    while (true) {
        sleep (randof (5));
        int burst = randof (15);
        while (burst--) {
            char task_id [5];
            sprintf (task_id, "%04X", randof (0x10000));

            //  Send request with random hex ID
            zstr_send (client, task_id);

            //  Wait max ten seconds for a reply, then complain
            zmq_pollitem_t pollset [1] = { { client, 0, ZMQ_POLLIN, 0 } };
```

```
                    int rc = zmq_poll (pollset, 1, 10 * 1000 * ZMQ_POLL_MSEC);
                    if (rc == -1)
                        break;              //  Interrupted

                    if (pollset [0].revents & ZMQ_POLLIN) {
                        char *reply = zstr_recv (client);
                        if (!reply)
                            break;              //  Interrupted
                        //  Worker is supposed to answer us with our task id
                        assert (streq (reply, task_id));
                        zstr_send (monitor, "%s", reply);
                        free (reply);
                    }
                    else {
                        zstr_send (monitor,
                            "E: CLIENT EXIT - lost task %s", task_id);
                        return NULL;
                    }
                }
            }
            zctx_destroy (&ctx);
            return NULL;
        }
```

This is the worker task, which uses a REQ socket to plug into the load-balancer. It's the same stub worker task that you've seen in other examples:

Example 36-2. Full cluster simulation (peering3.c) - worker task

```
static void *
worker_task (void *args)
{
    zctx_t *ctx = zctx_new ();
    void *worker = zsocket_new (ctx, ZMQ_REQ);
    zsocket_connect (worker, "ipc://%s-localbe.ipc", self);

    //  Tell broker we're ready for work
    zframe_t *frame = zframe_new (WORKER_READY, 1);
    zframe_send (&frame, worker, 0);

    //  Process messages as they arrive
    while (true) {
        zmsg_t *msg = zmsg_recv (worker);
        if (!msg)
            break;              //  Interrupted

        //  Workers are busy for 0/1 seconds
        sleep (randof (2));
        zmsg_send (&msg, worker);
    }
    zctx_destroy (&ctx);
```

```
        return NULL;
}
```

The main task begins by setting up all its sockets. The local frontend talks to clients, and our local backend talks to workers. The cloud frontend talks to peer brokers as if they were clients, and the cloud backend talks to peer brokers as if they were workers. The state backend publishes regular state messages, and the state frontend subscribes to all state backends to collect these messages. Finally, we use a PULL monitor socket to collect printable messages from tasks:

Example 36-3. Full cluster simulation (peering3.c) - main task

```
int main (int argc, char *argv [])
{
    //  First argument is this broker's name
    //  Other arguments are our peers' names
    if (argc < 2) {
        printf ("syntax: peering3 me {you}...\n");
        return 0;
    }
    self = argv [1];
    printf ("I: preparing broker at %s...\n", self);
    srandom ((unsigned) time (NULL));

    //  Prepare local frontend and backend
    zctx_t *ctx = zctx_new ();
    void *localfe = zsocket_new (ctx, ZMQ_ROUTER);
    zsocket_bind (localfe, "ipc://%s-localfe.ipc", self);

    void *localbe = zsocket_new (ctx, ZMQ_ROUTER);
    zsocket_bind (localbe, "ipc://%s-localbe.ipc", self);

    //  Bind cloud frontend to endpoint
    void *cloudfe = zsocket_new (ctx, ZMQ_ROUTER);
    zsockopt_set_identity (cloudfe, self);
    zsocket_bind (cloudfe, "ipc://%s-cloud.ipc", self);

    //  Connect cloud backend to all peers
    void *cloudbe = zsocket_new (ctx, ZMQ_ROUTER);
    zsockopt_set_identity (cloudbe, self);
    int argn;
    for (argn = 2; argn < argc; argn++) {
        char *peer = argv [argn];
        printf ("I: connecting to cloud frontend at '%s'\n", peer);
        zsocket_connect (cloudbe, "ipc://%s-cloud.ipc", peer);
    }
    //  Bind state backend to endpoint
    void *statebe = zsocket_new (ctx, ZMQ_PUB);
    zsocket_bind (statebe, "ipc://%s-state.ipc", self);
```

```
        //  Connect state frontend to all peers
        void *statefe = zsocket_new (ctx, ZMQ_SUB);
        zsockopt_set_subscribe (statefe, "");
        for (argn = 2; argn < argc; argn++) {
            char *peer = argv [argn];
            printf ("I: connecting to state backend at '%s'\n", peer);
            zsocket_connect (statefe, "ipc://%s-state.ipc", peer);
        }
        //  Prepare monitor socket
        void *monitor = zsocket_new (ctx, ZMQ_PULL);
        zsocket_bind (monitor, "ipc://%s-monitor.ipc", self);
```

After binding and connecting all our sockets, we start our child tasks - workers and clients:

Example 36-4. Full cluster simulation (peering3.c) - start child tasks

```
        int worker_nbr;
        for (worker_nbr = 0; worker_nbr < NBR_WORKERS; worker_nbr++)
            zthread_new (worker_task, NULL);

        //  Start local clients
        int client_nbr;
        for (client_nbr = 0; client_nbr < NBR_CLIENTS; client_nbr++)
            zthread_new (client_task, NULL);

        //  Queue of available workers
        int local_capacity = 0;
        int cloud_capacity = 0;
        zlist_t *workers = zlist_new ();
```

The main loop has two parts. First, we poll workers and our two service sockets (statefe and monitor), in any case. If we have no ready workers, then there's no point in looking at incoming requests. These can remain on their internal ØMQ queues:

Example 36-5. Full cluster simulation (peering3.c) - main loop

```
        while (true) {
            zmq_pollitem_t primary [] = {
                { localbe, 0, ZMQ_POLLIN, 0 },
                { cloudbe, 0, ZMQ_POLLIN, 0 },
                { statefe, 0, ZMQ_POLLIN, 0 },
                { monitor, 0, ZMQ_POLLIN, 0 }
            };
            //  If we have no workers ready, wait indefinitely
            int rc = zmq_poll (primary, 4,
                local_capacity? 1000 * ZMQ_POLL_MSEC: -1);
            if (rc == -1)
                break;              //  Interrupted

            //  Track if capacity changes during this iteration
```

```c
        int previous = local_capacity;
        zmsg_t *msg = NULL;         //  Reply from local worker

        if (primary [0].revents & ZMQ_POLLIN) {
            msg = zmsg_recv (localbe);
            if (!msg)
                break;              //  Interrupted
            zframe_t *identity = zmsg_unwrap (msg);
            zlist_append (workers, identity);
            local_capacity++;

            //  If it's READY, don't route the message any further
            zframe_t *frame = zmsg_first (msg);
            if (memcmp (zframe_data (frame), WORKER_READY, 1) == 0)
                zmsg_destroy (&msg);
        }
        //  Or handle reply from peer broker
        else
        if (primary [1].revents & ZMQ_POLLIN) {
            msg = zmsg_recv (cloudbe);
            if (!msg)
                break;              //  Interrupted
            //  We don't use peer broker identity for anything
            zframe_t *identity = zmsg_unwrap (msg);
            zframe_destroy (&identity);
        }
        //  Route reply to cloud if it's addressed to a broker
        for (argn = 2; msg && argn < argc; argn++) {
            char *data = (char *) zframe_data (zmsg_first (msg));
            size_t size = zframe_size (zmsg_first (msg));
            if (size == strlen (argv [argn])
            &&  memcmp (data, argv [argn], size) == 0)
                zmsg_send (&msg, cloudfe);
        }
        //  Route reply to client if we still need to
        if (msg)
            zmsg_send (&msg, localfe);
```

If we have input messages on our statefe or monitor sockets, we can process these immediately:

Example 36-6. Full cluster simulation (peering3.c) - handle state messages

```c
        if (primary [2].revents & ZMQ_POLLIN) {
            char *peer = zstr_recv (statefe);
            char *status = zstr_recv (statefe);
            cloud_capacity = atoi (status);
            free (peer);
            free (status);
        }
        if (primary [3].revents & ZMQ_POLLIN) {
```

```
            char *status = zstr_recv (monitor);
            printf ("%s\n", status);
            free (status);
        }
```

Now route as many clients requests as we can handle. If we have local capacity, we poll both localfe and cloudfe. If we have cloud capacity only, we poll just localfe. We route any request locally if we can, else we route to the cloud.

Example 36-7. Full cluster simulation (peering3.c) - route client requests

```
        while (local_capacity + cloud_capacity) {
            zmq_pollitem_t secondary [] = {
                { localfe, 0, ZMQ_POLLIN, 0 },
                { cloudfe, 0, ZMQ_POLLIN, 0 }
            };
            if (local_capacity)
                rc = zmq_poll (secondary, 2, 0);
            else
                rc = zmq_poll (secondary, 1, 0);
            assert (rc >= 0);

            if (secondary [0].revents & ZMQ_POLLIN)
                msg = zmsg_recv (localfe);
            else
            if (secondary [1].revents & ZMQ_POLLIN)
                msg = zmsg_recv (cloudfe);
            else
                break;      //  No work, go back to primary

            if (local_capacity) {
                zframe_t *frame = (zframe_t *) zlist_pop (workers);
                zmsg_wrap (msg, frame);
                zmsg_send (&msg, localbe);
                local_capacity--;
            }
            else {
                //  Route to random broker peer
                int peer = randof (argc - 2) + 2;
                zmsg_pushmem (msg, argv [peer], strlen (argv [peer]));
                zmsg_send (&msg, cloudbe);
            }
        }
```

We broadcast capacity messages to other peers; to reduce chatter, we do this only if our capacity changed.

Example 36-8. Full cluster simulation (peering3.c) - broadcast capacity

```
        if (local_capacity != previous) {
            //  We stick our own identity onto the envelope
```

```
                zstr_sendm (statebe, self);
                //  Broadcast new capacity
                zstr_send (statebe, "%d", local_capacity);
            }
        }
        //  When we're done, clean up properly
        while (zlist_size (workers)) {
            zframe_t *frame = (zframe_t *) zlist_pop (workers);
            zframe_destroy (&frame);
        }
        zlist_destroy (&workers);
        zctx_destroy (&ctx);
        return EXIT_SUCCESS;
    }
```

It's a nontrivial program and took about a day to get working. These are the highlights:

- The client threads detect and report a failed request. They do this by polling for a response and if none arrives after a while (10 seconds), printing an error message.

- Client threads don't print directly, but instead send a message to a monitor socket (PUSH) that the main loop collects (PULL) and prints off. This is the first case we've seen of using ØMQ sockets for monitoring and logging; this is a big use case that we'll come back to later.

- Clients simulate varying loads to get the cluster 100% at random moments, so that tasks are shifted over to the cloud. The number of clients and workers, and delays in the client and worker threads control this. Feel free to play with them to see if you can make a more realistic simulation.

- The main loop uses two pollsets. It could in fact use three: information, backends, and frontends. As in the earlier prototype, there is no point in taking a frontend message if there is no backend capacity.

These are some of the problems that arose during development of this program:

- Clients would freeze, due to requests or replies getting lost somewhere. Recall that the ROUTER socket drops messages it can't route. The first tactic here was to modify the client thread to detect and report such problems. Secondly, I put zmsg_dump() calls after every receive and before every send in the main loop, until the origin of the problems was clear.

- The main loop was mistakenly reading from more than one ready socket. This caused the first message to be lost. I fixed that by reading only from the first ready socket.

- The zmsg class was not properly encoding UUIDs as C strings. This caused UUIDs that contain 0 bytes to be corrupted. I fixed that by modifying zmsg to encode UUIDs as printable hex strings.

This simulation does not detect disappearance of a cloud peer. If you start several peers and stop one, and it was broadcasting capacity to the others, they will continue to send it work even if it's gone. You can try this, and you will get clients that complain of lost requests. The solution is twofold: first, only keep the capacity information for a short time so that if a peer does disappear, its capacity is quickly set to zero. Second, add reliability to the request-reply chain. We'll look at reliability in the next chapter.

Chapter 4. Reliable Request-Reply Patterns

"Advanced Request-Reply Patterns" covered advanced uses of ØMQ's request-reply pattern with working examples. This chapter looks at the general question of reliability and builds a set of reliable messaging patterns on top of ØMQ's core request-reply pattern.

In this chapter, we focus heavily on user-space request-reply *patterns*, reusable models that help you design your own ØMQ architectures:

- The *Lazy Pirate* pattern: reliable request-reply from the client side
- The *Simple Pirate* pattern: reliable request-reply using load balancing
- The *Paranoid Pirate* pattern: reliable request-reply with heartbeating
- The *Majordomo* pattern: service-oriented reliable queuing
- The *Titanic* pattern: disk-based/disconnected reliable queuing
- The *Binary Star* pattern: primary-backup server failover
- The *Freelance* pattern: brokerless reliable request-reply

What is "Reliability"?

Most people who speak of "reliability" don't really know what they mean. We can only define reliability in terms of failure. That is, if we can handle a certain set of well-defined and understood failures, then we are reliable with respect to those failures. No more, no less. So let's look at the possible causes of failure in a distributed ØMQ application, in roughly descending order of probability:

- Application code is the worst offender. It can crash and exit, freeze and stop responding to input, run too slowly for its input, exhaust all memory, and so on.
- System code—such as brokers we write using ØMQ—can die for the same reasons as application code. System code *should* be more reliable than application code, but it can still crash and burn, and especially run out of memory if it tries to queue messages for slow clients.
- Message queues can overflow, typically in system code that has learned to deal brutally with slow clients. When a queue overflows, it starts to discard messages. So we get "lost" messages.

- Networks can fail (e.g., WiFi gets switched off or goes out of range). ØMQ will automatically reconnect in such cases, but in the meantime, messages may get lost.
- Hardware can fail and take with it all the processes running on that box.
- Networks can fail in exotic ways, e.g., some ports on a switch may die and those parts of the network become inaccessible.
- Entire data centers can be struck by lightning, earthquakes, fire, or more mundane power or cooling failures.

To make a software system fully reliable against *all* of these possible failures is an enormously difficult and expensive job and goes beyond the scope of this modest guide.

Because the first five cases in the above list cover 99.9% of real world requirements outside large companies (according to a highly scientific study I just ran, which also told me that 78% of statistics are made up on the spot, and moreover never to trust a statistic that we didn't falsify ourselves), that's what we'll examine. If you're a large company with money to spend on the last two cases, contact my company immediately! There's a large hole behind my beach house waiting to be converted into an executive swimming pool.

Designing Reliability

So to make things brutally simple, reliability is "keeping things working properly when code freezes or crashes", a situation we'll shorten to "dies". However, the things we want to keep working properly are more complex than just messages. We need to take each core ØMQ messaging pattern and see how to make it work (if we can) even when code dies.

Let's take them one-by-one:
- Request-reply: if the server dies (while processing a request), the client can figure that out because it won't get an answer back. Then it can give up in a huff, wait and try again later, find another server, and so on. As for the client dying, we can brush that off as "someone else's problem" for now.
- Pub-sub: if the client dies (having gotten some data), the server doesn't know about it. Pub-sub doesn't send any information back from client to server. But the client can contact the server out-of-band, e.g., via request-reply, and ask, "please resend everything I missed". As for the server dying, that's out of scope for here. Subscribers can also self-verify that they're not running too slowly, and take action (e.g., warn the operator and die) if they are.
- Pipeline: if a worker dies (while working), the ventilator doesn't know about it. Pipelines, like the grinding gears of time, only work in one direction. But the downstream collector can detect that one task didn't get done, and send a message back to the ventilator saying, "hey, resend task 324!" If the ventilator or collector dies, whatever upstream client originally sent the work batch can

get tired of waiting and resend the whole lot. It's not elegant, but system code should really not die often enough to matter.

In this chapter we'll focus on just on request-reply, which is the low-hanging fruit of reliable messaging.

The basic request-reply pattern (a REQ client socket doing a blocking send/receive to a REP server socket) scores low on handling the most common types of failure. If the server crashes while processing the request, the client just hangs forever. If the network loses the request or the reply, the client hangs forever.

Request-reply is still much better than TCP, thanks to ØMQ's ability to reconnect peers silently, to load balance messages, and so on. But it's still not good enough for real work. The only case where you can really trust the basic request-reply pattern is between two threads in the same process where there's no network or separate server process to die.

However, with a little extra work, this humble pattern becomes a good basis for real work across a distributed network, and we get a set of reliable request-reply (RRR) patterns that I like to call the *Pirate* patterns (you'll eventually get the joke, I hope).

There are, in my experience, roughly three ways to connect clients to servers. Each needs a specific approach to reliability:

- Multiple clients talking directly to a single server. Use case: a single well-known server to which clients need to talk. Types of failure we aim to handle: server crashes and restarts, and network disconnects.

- Multiple clients talking to a broker proxy that distributes work to multiple workers. Use case: service-oriented transaction processing. Types of failure we aim to handle: worker crashes and restarts, worker busy looping, worker overload, queue crashes and restarts, and network disconnects.

- Multiple clients talking to multiple servers with no intermediary proxies. Use case: distributed services such as name resolution. Types of failure we aim to handle: service crashes and restarts, service busy looping, service overload, and network disconnects.

Each of these approaches has its trade-offs and often you'll mix them. We'll look at all three in detail.

Client-Side Reliability (Lazy Pirate Pattern)

We can get very simple reliable request-reply with some changes to the client. We call this the Lazy Pirate pattern (see figure 47). Rather than doing a blocking receive, we:

- Poll the REQ socket and receive from it only when it's sure a reply has arrived.
- Resend a request, if no reply has arrived within a timeout period.
- Abandon the transaction if there is still no reply after several requests.

If you try to use a REQ socket in anything other than a strict send/receive fashion, you'll get an error (technically, the REQ socket implements a small finite-state machine to enforce the send/receive ping-pong, and so the error code is called "EFSM"). This is slightly annoying when we want to use REQ in a pirate pattern, because we may send several requests before getting a reply.

The pretty good brute force solution is to close and reopen the REQ socket after an error:

Example 37. Lazy Pirate client (lpclient.c)

```
//  Lazy Pirate client
//  Use zmq_poll to do a safe request-reply
//  To run, start lpserver and then randomly kill/restart it

#include "czmq.h"
#define REQUEST_TIMEOUT     2500    //  msecs, (> 1000!)
#define REQUEST_RETRIES     3       //  Before we abandon
#define SERVER_ENDPOINT     "tcp://localhost:5555"

int main (void)
{
    zctx_t *ctx = zctx_new ();
    printf ("I: connecting to server...\n");
    void *client = zsocket_new (ctx, ZMQ_REQ);
    assert (client);
    zsocket_connect (client, SERVER_ENDPOINT);

    int sequence = 0;
    int retries_left = REQUEST_RETRIES;
    while (retries_left && !zctx_interrupted) {
        //  We send a request, then we work to get a reply
        char request [10];
        sprintf (request, "%d", ++sequence);
        zstr_send (client, request);

        int expect_reply = 1;
        while (expect_reply) {
            //  Poll socket for a reply, with timeout
            zmq_pollitem_t items [] = { { client, 0, ZMQ_POLLIN, 0 } };
            int rc = zmq_poll (items, 1, REQUEST_TIMEOUT * ZMQ_POLL_MSEC);
            if (rc == -1)
                break;          //  Interrupted
```

Here we process a server reply and exit our loop if the reply is valid. If we didn't a reply we close the client socket and resend the request. We try a number of times before finally abandoning:

Example 37-1. Lazy Pirate client (lpclient.c) - process server reply

```
            if (items [0].revents & ZMQ_POLLIN) {
                //  We got a reply from the server, must match sequence
                char *reply = zstr_recv (client);
```

```
                    if (!reply)
                        break;      // Interrupted
                    if (atoi (reply) == sequence) {
                        printf ("I: server replied OK (%s)\n", reply);
                        retries_left = REQUEST_RETRIES;
                        expect_reply = 0;
                    }
                    else
                        printf ("E: malformed reply from server: %s\n",
                            reply);

                    free (reply);
                }
                else
                if (--retries_left == 0) {
                    printf ("E: server seems to be offline, abandoning\n");
                    break;
                }
                else {
                    printf ("W: no response from server, retrying...\n");
                    //  Old socket is confused; close it and open a new one
                    zsocket_destroy (ctx, client);
                    printf ("I: reconnecting to server...\n");
                    client = zsocket_new (ctx, ZMQ_REQ);
                    zsocket_connect (client, SERVER_ENDPOINT);
                    //  Send request again, on new socket
                    zstr_send (client, request);
                }
            }
        }
    }
    zctx_destroy (&ctx);
    return 0;
}
```

Run this together with the matching server:

Example 38. Lazy Pirate server (lpserver.c)

```
//  Lazy Pirate server
//  Binds REQ socket to tcp://*:5555
//  Like hwserver except:
//   - echoes request as-is
//   - randomly runs slowly, or exits to simulate a crash.

#include "zhelpers.h"

int main (void)
{
    srandom ((unsigned) time (NULL));

    void *context = zmq_ctx_new ();
```

```
    void *server = zmq_socket (context, ZMQ_REP);
    zmq_bind (server, "tcp://*:5555");

    int cycles = 0;
    while (1) {
        char *request = s_recv (server);
        cycles++;

        //  Simulate various problems, after a few cycles
        if (cycles > 3 && randof (3) == 0) {
            printf ("I: simulating a crash\n");
            break;
        }
        else
        if (cycles > 3 && randof (3) == 0) {
            printf ("I: simulating CPU overload\n");
            sleep (2);
        }
        printf ("I: normal request (%s)\n", request);
        sleep (1);              //  Do some heavy work
        s_send (server, request);
        free (request);
    }
    zmq_close (server);
    zmq_ctx_destroy (context);
    return 0;
}
```

To run this test case, start the client and the server in two console windows. The server will randomly misbehave after a few messages. You can check the client's response. Here is typical output from the server:

```
I: normal request (1)
I: normal request (2)
I: normal request (3)
I: simulating CPU
overload
I: normal request (4)
I: simulating a crash
```

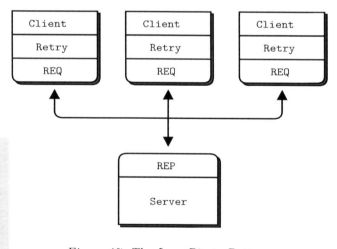

Figure 47. The Lazy Pirate Pattern

And here is the client's response:

```
I: connecting to server...
I: server replied OK (1)
I: server replied OK (2)
```

```
I: server replied OK (3)
W: no response from server, retrying...
I: connecting to server...
W: no response from server, retrying...
I: connecting to server...
E: server seems to be offline, abandoning
```

The client sequences each message and checks that replies come back exactly in order: that no requests or replies are lost, and no replies come back more than once, or out of order. Run the test a few times until you're convinced that this mechanism actually works. You don't need sequence numbers in a production application; they just help us trust our design.

The client uses a REQ socket, and does the brute force close/reopen because REQ sockets impose that strict send/receive cycle. You might be tempted to use a DEALER instead, but it would not be a good decision. First, it would mean emulating the secret sauce that REQ does with envelopes (if you've forgotten what that is, it's a good sign you don't want to have to do it). Second, it would mean potentially getting back replies that you didn't expect.

Handling failures only at the client works when we have a set of clients talking to a single server. It can handle a server crash, but only if recovery means restarting that same server. If there's a permanent error, such as a dead power supply on the server hardware, this approach won't work. Because the application code in servers is usually the biggest source of failures in any architecture, depending on a single server is not a great idea.

So, pros and cons:

- Pro: simple to understand and implement.
- Pro: works easily with existing client and server application code.
- Pro: ØMQ automatically retries the actual reconnection until it works.
- Con: doesn't failover to backup or alternate servers.

Basic Reliable Queuing (Simple Pirate Pattern)

Our second approach extends the Lazy Pirate pattern with a queue proxy that lets us talk, transparently, to multiple servers, which we can more accurately call "workers". We'll develop this in stages, starting with a minimal working model, the Simple Pirate pattern.

In all these Pirate patterns, workers are stateless. If the application requires some shared state, such as a shared database, we don't know about it as we design our messaging framework. Having a queue proxy means workers can come and go without clients knowing anything about it. If one worker dies, another takes over. This is a nice, simple topology with only one real weakness, namely the central queue itself, which can become a problem to manage, and a single point of failure.

The basis for the queue proxy is the load balancing broker from "Advanced Request-Reply Patterns". What is the very *minimum* we need to do to handle dead or blocked workers? Turns out, it's surprisingly little. We already have a retry mechanism in the client. So using the load balancing pattern will work pretty well. This fits with ØMQ's philosophy that we can extend a peer-to-peer pattern like request-reply by plugging naive proxies in the middle (see figure 48).

We don't need a special client; we're still using the Lazy Pirate client. Here is the queue, which is identical to the main task of the load balancing broker:

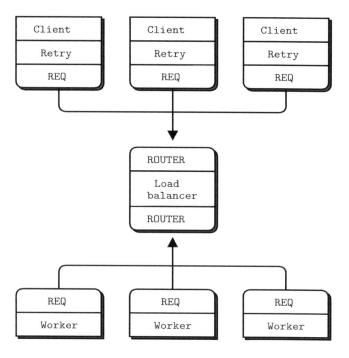

Figure 48. The Simple Pirate Pattern

Example 39. Simple Pirate queue (spqueue.c)

```
// Simple Pirate broker
// This is identical to load-balancing pattern, with no reliability
// mechanisms. It depends on the client for recovery. Runs forever.

#include "czmq.h"
#define WORKER_READY   "\001"      // Signals worker is ready

int main (void)
{
    zctx_t *ctx = zctx_new ();
    void *frontend = zsocket_new (ctx, ZMQ_ROUTER);
    void *backend = zsocket_new (ctx, ZMQ_ROUTER);
    zsocket_bind (frontend, "tcp://*:5555");    // For clients
    zsocket_bind (backend,  "tcp://*:5556");    // For workers

    // Queue of available workers
    zlist_t *workers = zlist_new ();

    // The body of this example is exactly the same as lbbroker2.
    ...
}
```

Here is the worker, which takes the Lazy Pirate server and adapts it for the load balancing pattern (using the REQ "ready" signaling):

Example 40. Simple Pirate worker (spworker.c)

```c
//  Simple Pirate worker
//  Connects REQ socket to tcp://*:5556
//  Implements worker part of load-balancing

#include "czmq.h"
#define WORKER_READY   "\001"      //  Signals worker is ready

int main (void)
{
    zctx_t *ctx = zctx_new ();
    void *worker = zsocket_new (ctx, ZMQ_REQ);

    //  Set random identity to make tracing easier
    srandom ((unsigned) time (NULL));
    char identity [10];
    sprintf (identity, "%04X-%04X", randof (0x10000), randof (0x10000));
    zmq_setsockopt (worker, ZMQ_IDENTITY, identity, strlen (identity));
    zsocket_connect (worker, "tcp://localhost:5556");

    //  Tell broker we're ready for work
    printf ("I: (%s) worker ready\n", identity);
    zframe_t *frame = zframe_new (WORKER_READY, 1);
    zframe_send (&frame, worker, 0);

    int cycles = 0;
    while (true) {
        zmsg_t *msg = zmsg_recv (worker);
        if (!msg)
            break;              //  Interrupted

        //  Simulate various problems, after a few cycles
        cycles++;
        if (cycles > 3 && randof (5) == 0) {
            printf ("I: (%s) simulating a crash\n", identity);
            zmsg_destroy (&msg);
            break;
        }
        else
        if (cycles > 3 && randof (5) == 0) {
            printf ("I: (%s) simulating CPU overload\n", identity);
            sleep (3);
            if (zctx_interrupted)
                break;
        }
        printf ("I: (%s) normal reply\n", identity);
        sleep (1);              //  Do some heavy work
```

```
        zmsg_send (&msg, worker);
    }
    zctx_destroy (&ctx);
    return 0;
}
```

To test this, start a handful of workers, a Lazy Pirate client, and the queue, in any order. You'll see that the workers eventually all crash and burn, and the client retries and then gives up. The queue never stops, and you can restart workers and clients ad nauseam. This model works with any number of clients and workers.

Robust Reliable Queuing (Paranoid Pirate Pattern)

The Simple Pirate Queue pattern works pretty well, especially because it's just a combination of two existing patterns. Still, it does have some weaknesses:

- It's not robust in the face of a queue crash and restart. The client will recover, but the workers won't. While ØMQ will reconnect workers' sockets automatically, as far as the newly started queue is concerned, the workers haven't signaled ready, so don't exist. To fix this, we have to do heartbeating from queue to worker so that the worker can detect when the queue has gone away.

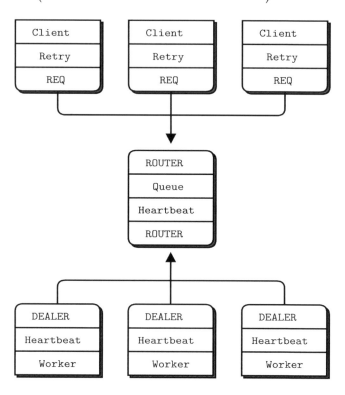

Figure 49. The Paranoid Pirate Pattern

- The queue does not detect worker failure, so if a worker dies while idle, the queue can't remove it from its worker queue until the queue sends it a request. The client waits and retries for nothing. It's not a critical problem, but it's not nice. To make this work properly, we do heartbeating from worker to queue, so that the queue can detect a lost worker at any stage.

We'll fix these in a properly pedantic Paranoid Pirate Pattern.

We previously used a REQ socket for the worker. For the Paranoid Pirate worker, we'll switch to a DEALER socket (see figure 49). This has the advantage of letting us send and receive messages at any time, rather than the lock-step send/receive that REQ imposes. The downside of DEALER is that we have to do our own envelope management (re-read "Advanced Request-Reply Patterns" for background on this concept).

We're still using the Lazy Pirate client. Here is the Paranoid Pirate queue proxy:

Example 41. Paranoid Pirate queue (ppqueue.c)

```
//  Paranoid Pirate queue

#include "czmq.h"
#define HEARTBEAT_LIVENESS  3       //  3-5 is reasonable
#define HEARTBEAT_INTERVAL  1000    //  msecs

//  Paranoid Pirate Protocol constants
#define PPP_READY       "\001"      //  Signals worker is ready
#define PPP_HEARTBEAT   "\002"      //  Signals worker heartbeat
```

Here we define the worker class; a structure and a set of functions that act as constructor, destructor, and methods on worker objects:

Example 41-1. Paranoid Pirate queue (ppqueue.c) - worker class structure

```
typedef struct {
    zframe_t *identity;         //  Identity of worker
    char *id_string;            //  Printable identity
    int64_t expiry;             //  Expires at this time
} worker_t;

//  Construct new worker
static worker_t *
s_worker_new (zframe_t *identity)
{
    worker_t *self = (worker_t *) zmalloc (sizeof (worker_t));
    self->identity = identity;
    self->id_string = zframe_strdup (identity);
    self->expiry = zclock_time ()
                 + HEARTBEAT_INTERVAL * HEARTBEAT_LIVENESS;
    return self;
}

//  Destroy specified worker object, including identity frame.
static void
s_worker_destroy (worker_t **self_p)
{
    assert (self_p);
    if (*self_p) {
        worker_t *self = *self_p;
```

```
            zframe_destroy (&self->identity);
            free (self->id_string);
            free (self);
            *self_p = NULL;
        }
    }
```

The ready method puts a worker to the end of the ready list:

Example 41-2. Paranoid Pirate queue (ppqueue.c) - worker ready method

```
static void
s_worker_ready (worker_t *self, zlist_t *workers)
{
    worker_t *worker = (worker_t *) zlist_first (workers);
    while (worker) {
        if (streq (self->id_string, worker->id_string)) {
            zlist_remove (workers, worker);
            s_worker_destroy (&worker);
            break;
        }
        worker = (worker_t *) zlist_next (workers);
    }
    zlist_append (workers, self);
}
```

The next method returns the next available worker identity:

Example 41-3. Paranoid Pirate queue (ppqueue.c) - get next available worker

```
static zframe_t *
s_workers_next (zlist_t *workers)
{
    worker_t *worker = zlist_pop (workers);
    assert (worker);
    zframe_t *frame = worker->identity;
    worker->identity = NULL;
    s_worker_destroy (&worker);
    return frame;
}
```

The purge method looks for and kills expired workers. We hold workers from oldest to most recent, so we stop at the first alive worker:

Example 41-4. Paranoid Pirate queue (ppqueue.c) - purge expired workers

```
static void
s_workers_purge (zlist_t *workers)
{
    worker_t *worker = (worker_t *) zlist_first (workers);
    while (worker) {
        if (zclock_time () < worker->expiry)
```

Code Connected Volume 1 - Chapter 4. Reliable Request-Reply Patterns   147

```
                break;              //  Worker is alive, we're done here

            zlist_remove (workers, worker);
            s_worker_destroy (&worker);
            worker = (worker_t *) zlist_first (workers);
        }
    }
```

The main task is a load-balancer with heartbeating on workers so we can detect crashed or blocked worker tasks:

Example 41-5. Paranoid Pirate queue (ppqueue.c) - main task

```
int main (void)
{
    zctx_t *ctx = zctx_new ();
    void *frontend = zsocket_new (ctx, ZMQ_ROUTER);
    void *backend = zsocket_new (ctx, ZMQ_ROUTER);
    zsocket_bind (frontend, "tcp://*:5555");    //  For clients
    zsocket_bind (backend,  "tcp://*:5556");    //  For workers

    //  List of available workers
    zlist_t *workers = zlist_new ();

    //  Send out heartbeats at regular intervals
    uint64_t heartbeat_at = zclock_time () + HEARTBEAT_INTERVAL;

    while (true) {
        zmq_pollitem_t items [] = {
            { backend,  0, ZMQ_POLLIN, 0 },
            { frontend, 0, ZMQ_POLLIN, 0 }
        };
        //  Poll frontend only if we have available workers
        int rc = zmq_poll (items, zlist_size (workers)? 2: 1,
            HEARTBEAT_INTERVAL * ZMQ_POLL_MSEC);
        if (rc == -1)
            break;              //  Interrupted

        //  Handle worker activity on backend
        if (items [0].revents & ZMQ_POLLIN) {
            //  Use worker identity for load-balancing
            zmsg_t *msg = zmsg_recv (backend);
            if (!msg)
                break;          //  Interrupted

            //  Any sign of life from worker means it's ready
            zframe_t *identity = zmsg_unwrap (msg);
            worker_t *worker = s_worker_new (identity);
            s_worker_ready (worker, workers);

            //  Validate control message, or return reply to client
```

```
                if (zmsg_size (msg) == 1) {
                    zframe_t *frame = zmsg_first (msg);
                    if (memcmp (zframe_data (frame), PPP_READY, 1)
                    &&  memcmp (zframe_data (frame), PPP_HEARTBEAT, 1)) {
                        printf ("E: invalid message from worker");
                        zmsg_dump (msg);
                    }
                    zmsg_destroy (&msg);
                }
                else
                    zmsg_send (&msg, frontend);
            }
            if (items [1].revents & ZMQ_POLLIN) {
                //  Now get next client request, route to next worker
                zmsg_t *msg = zmsg_recv (frontend);
                if (!msg)
                    break;          //  Interrupted
                zmsg_push (msg, s_workers_next (workers));
                zmsg_send (&msg, backend);
            }
```

We handle heartbeating after any socket activity. First, we send heartbeats to any idle workers if it's time. Then, we purge any dead workers:

Example 41-6. Paranoid Pirate queue (ppqueue.c) - handle heartbeating

```
            worker_t *worker = (worker_t *) zlist_first (workers);
            while (worker) {
                zframe_send (&worker->identity, backend,
                             ZFRAME_REUSE + ZFRAME_MORE);
                zframe_t *frame = zframe_new (PPP_HEARTBEAT, 1);
                zframe_send (&frame, backend, 0);
                worker = (worker_t *) zlist_next (workers);
            }
            heartbeat_at = zclock_time () + HEARTBEAT_INTERVAL;
        }
        s_workers_purge (workers);
    }
    //  When we're done, clean up properly
    while (zlist_size (workers)) {
        worker_t *worker = (worker_t *) zlist_pop (workers);
        s_worker_destroy (&worker);
    }
    zlist_destroy (&workers);
    zctx_destroy (&ctx);
    return 0;
}
```

The queue extends the load balancing pattern with heartbeating of workers. Heartbeating is one of those "simple" things that can be difficult to get right. I'll explain more about that in a second.

Here is the Paranoid Pirate worker:

Example 42. Paranoid Pirate worker (ppworker.c)

```
//  Paranoid Pirate worker

#include "czmq.h"
#define HEARTBEAT_LIVENESS  3       //  3-5 is reasonable
#define HEARTBEAT_INTERVAL  1000    //  msecs
#define INTERVAL_INIT       1000    //  Initial reconnect
#define INTERVAL_MAX        32000   //  After exponential backoff

//  Paranoid Pirate Protocol constants
#define PPP_READY       "\001"      //  Signals worker is ready
#define PPP_HEARTBEAT   "\002"      //  Signals worker heartbeat

//  Helper function that returns a new configured socket
//  connected to the Paranoid Pirate queue

static void *
s_worker_socket (zctx_t *ctx) {
    void *worker = zsocket_new (ctx, ZMQ_DEALER);
    zsocket_connect (worker, "tcp://localhost:5556");

    //  Tell queue we're ready for work
    printf ("I: worker ready\n");
    zframe_t *frame = zframe_new (PPP_READY, 1);
    zframe_send (&frame, worker, 0);

    return worker;
}
```

We have a single task that implements the worker side of the Paranoid Pirate Protocol (PPP). The interesting parts here are the heartbeating, which lets the worker detect if the queue has died, and vice versa:

Example 42-1. Paranoid Pirate worker (ppworker.c) - main task

```
int main (void)
{
    zctx_t *ctx = zctx_new ();
    void *worker = s_worker_socket (ctx);

    //  If liveness hits zero, queue is considered disconnected
    size_t liveness = HEARTBEAT_LIVENESS;
    size_t interval = INTERVAL_INIT;

    //  Send out heartbeats at regular intervals
    uint64_t heartbeat_at = zclock_time () + HEARTBEAT_INTERVAL;

    srandom ((unsigned) time (NULL));
```

```
        int cycles = 0;
        while (true) {
            zmq_pollitem_t items [] = { { worker,  0, ZMQ_POLLIN, 0 } };
            int rc = zmq_poll (items, 1, HEARTBEAT_INTERVAL * ZMQ_POLL_MSEC);
            if (rc == -1)
                break;              //  Interrupted

            if (items [0].revents & ZMQ_POLLIN) {
                //  Get message
                //   - 3-part envelope + content -> request
                //   - 1-part HEARTBEAT -> heartbeat
                zmsg_t *msg = zmsg_recv (worker);
                if (!msg)
                    break;          //  Interrupted
```

To test the robustness of the queue implementation we simulate various typical problems, such as the worker crashing or running very slowly. We do this after a few cycles so that the architecture can get up and running first:

Example 42-2. Paranoid Pirate worker (ppworker.c) - simulating problems

```
                cycles++;
                if (cycles > 3 && randof (5) == 0) {
                    printf ("I: simulating a crash\n");
                    zmsg_destroy (&msg);
                    break;
                }
                else
                if (cycles > 3 && randof (5) == 0) {
                    printf ("I: simulating CPU overload\n");
                    sleep (3);
                    if (zctx_interrupted)
                        break;
                }
                printf ("I: normal reply\n");
                zmsg_send (&msg, worker);
                liveness = HEARTBEAT_LIVENESS;
                sleep (1);          //  Do some heavy work
                if (zctx_interrupted)
                    break;
            }
            else
```

When we get a heartbeat message from the queue, it means the queue was (recently) alive, so we must reset our liveness indicator:

Example 42-3. Paranoid Pirate worker (ppworker.c) - handle heartbeats

```
                zframe_t *frame = zmsg_first (msg);
                if (memcmp (zframe_data (frame), PPP_HEARTBEAT, 1) == 0)
                    liveness = HEARTBEAT_LIVENESS;
```

```
                    else {
                        printf ("E: invalid message\n");
                        zmsg_dump (msg);
                    }
                    zmsg_destroy (&msg);
                }
                else {
                    printf ("E: invalid message\n");
                    zmsg_dump (msg);
                }
                interval = INTERVAL_INIT;
            }
            else
```

If the queue hasn't sent us heartbeats in a while, destroy the socket and reconnect. This is the simplest most brutal way of discarding any messages we might have sent in the meantime:

Example 42-4. Paranoid Pirate worker (ppworker.c) - detecting a dead queue

```
                printf ("W: heartbeat failure, can't reach queue\n");
                printf ("W: reconnecting in %zd msec...\n", interval);
                zclock_sleep (interval);

                if (interval < INTERVAL_MAX)
                    interval *= 2;
                zsocket_destroy (ctx, worker);
                worker = s_worker_socket (ctx);
                liveness = HEARTBEAT_LIVENESS;
            }
            //  Send heartbeat to queue if it's time
            if (zclock_time () > heartbeat_at) {
                heartbeat_at = zclock_time () + HEARTBEAT_INTERVAL;
                printf ("I: worker heartbeat\n");
                zframe_t *frame = zframe_new (PPP_HEARTBEAT, 1);
                zframe_send (&frame, worker, 0);
            }
        }
        zctx_destroy (&ctx);
        return 0;
    }
```

Some comments about this example:

- The code includes simulation of failures, as before. This makes it (a) very hard to debug, and (b) dangerous to reuse. When you want to debug this, disable the failure simulation.
- The worker uses a reconnect strategy similar to the one we designed for the Lazy Pirate client, with two major differences: (a) it does an exponential back-

off, and (b) it retries indefinitely (whereas the client retries a few times before reporting a failure).

Try the client, queue, and workers, such as by using a script like this:

```
ppqueue &
for i in 1 2 3 4; do
    ppworker &
    sleep 1
done
lpclient &
```

You should see the workers die one-by-one as they simulate a crash, and the client eventually give up. You can stop and restart the queue and both client and workers will reconnect and carry on. And no matter what you do to queues and workers, the client will never get an out-of-order reply: the whole chain either works, or the client abandons.

Heartbeating

Heartbeating solves the problem of knowing whether a peer is alive or dead. This is not an issue specific to ØMQ. TCP has a long timeout (30 minutes or so), that means that it can be impossible to know whether a peer has died, been disconnected, or gone on a weekend to Prague with a case of vodka, a redhead, and a large expense account.

It's is not easy to get heartbeating right. When writing the Paranoid Pirate examples, it took about five hours to get the heartbeating working properly. The rest of the request-reply chain took perhaps ten minutes. It is especially easy to create "false failures", i.e., when peers decide that they are disconnected because the heartbeats aren't sent properly.

We'll look at the three main answers people use for heartbeating with ØMQ.

Shrugging It Off

The most common approach is to do no heartbeating at all and hope for the best. Many if not most ØMQ applications do this. ØMQ encourages this by hiding peers in many cases. What problems does this approach cause?

- When we use a ROUTER socket in an application that tracks peers, as peers disconnect and reconnect, the application will leak memory (resources that the application holds for each peer) and get slower and slower.
- When we use SUB- or DEALER-based data recipients, we can't tell the difference between good silence (there's no data) and bad silence (the other end died). When a recipient knows the other side died, it can for example switch over to a backup route.
- If we use a TCP connection that stays silent for a long while, it will, in some networks, just die. Sending something (technically, a "keep-alive" more than a heartbeat), will keep the network alive.

One-Way Heartbeats

A second option is to send a heartbeat message from each node to its peers every second or so. When one node hears nothing from another within some timeout (several seconds, typically), it will treat that peer as dead. Sounds good, right? Sadly, no. This works in some cases but has nasty edge cases in others.

For pub-sub, this does work, and it's the only model you can use. SUB sockets cannot talk back to PUB sockets, but PUB sockets can happily send "I'm alive" messages to their subscribers.

As an optimization, you can send heartbeats only when there is no real data to send. Furthermore, you can send heartbeats progressively slower and slower, if network activity is an issue (e.g., on mobile networks where activity drains the battery). As long as the recipient can detect a failure (sharp stop in activity), that's fine.

Here are the typical problems with this design:

- It can be inaccurate when we send large amounts of data, as heartbeats will be delayed behind that data. If heartbeats are delayed, you can get false timeouts and disconnections due to network congestion. Thus, always treat *any* incoming data as a heartbeat, whether or not the sender optimizes out heartbeats.

- While the pub-sub pattern will drop messages for disappeared recipients, PUSH and DEALER sockets will queue them. So if you send heartbeats to a dead peer and it comes back, it will get all the heartbeats you sent, which can be thousands. Whoa, whoa!

- This design assumes that heartbeat timeouts are the same across the whole network. But that won't be accurate. Some peers will want very aggressive heartbeating in order to detect faults rapidly. And some will want very relaxed heartbeating, in order to let sleeping networks lie and save power.

Ping-Pong Heartbeats

The third option is to use a ping-pong dialog. One peer sends a ping command to the other, which replies with a pong command. Neither command has any payload. Pings and pongs are not correlated. Because the roles of "client" and "server" are arbitrary in some networks, we usually specify that either peer can in fact send a ping and expect a pong in response. However, because the timeouts depend on network topologies known best to dynamic clients, it is usually the client that pings the server.

This works for all ROUTER-based brokers. The same optimizations we used in the second model make this work even better: treat any incoming data as a pong, and only send a ping when not otherwise sending data.

Heartbeating for Paranoid Pirate

For Paranoid Pirate, we chose the second approach. It might not have been the simplest option: if designing this today, I'd probably try a ping-pong approach instead.

However the principles are similar. The heartbeat messages flow asynchronously in both directions, and either peer can decide the other is "dead" and stop talking to it.

In the worker, this is how we handle heartbeats from the queue:

- We calculate a *liveness*, which is how many heartbeats we can still miss before deciding the queue is dead. It starts at three and we decrement it each time we miss a heartbeat.
- We wait, in the `zmq_poll` loop, for one second each time, which is our heartbeat interval.
- If there's any message from the queue during that time, we reset our liveness to three.
- If there's no message during that time, we count down our liveness.
- If the liveness reaches zero, we consider the queue dead.
- If the queue is dead, we destroy our socket, create a new one, and reconnect.
- To avoid opening and closing too many sockets, we wait for a certain interval before reconnecting, and we double the interval each time until it reaches 32 seconds.

And this is how we handle heartbeats *to* the queue:

- We calculate when to send the next heartbeat; this is a single variable because we're talking to one peer, the queue.
- In the `zmq_poll` loop, whenever we pass this time, we send a heartbeat to the queue.

Here's the essential heartbeating code for the worker:

```
#define HEARTBEAT_LIVENESS   3       //  3-5 is reasonable
#define HEARTBEAT_INTERVAL   1000    //  msecs
#define INTERVAL_INIT        1000    //  Initial reconnect
#define INTERVAL_MAX         32000   //  After exponential backoff

...
//  If liveness hits zero, queue is considered disconnected
size_t liveness = HEARTBEAT_LIVENESS;
size_t interval = INTERVAL_INIT;

//  Send out heartbeats at regular intervals
uint64_t heartbeat_at = zclock_time () + HEARTBEAT_INTERVAL;

while (true) {
    zmq_pollitem_t items [] = { { worker,  0, ZMQ_POLLIN, 0 } };
    int rc = zmq_poll (items, 1, HEARTBEAT_INTERVAL * ZMQ_POLL_MSEC);

    if (items [0].revents & ZMQ_POLLIN) {
        //  Receive any message from queue
        liveness = HEARTBEAT_LIVENESS;
        interval = INTERVAL_INIT;
```

```
        }
        else
        if (--liveness == 0) {
            zclock_sleep (interval);
            if (interval < INTERVAL_MAX)
                interval *= 2;
            zsocket_destroy (ctx, worker);
            ...
            liveness = HEARTBEAT_LIVENESS;
        }
        //  Send heartbeat to queue if it's time
        if (zclock_time () > heartbeat_at) {
            heartbeat_at = zclock_time () + HEARTBEAT_INTERVAL;
            //  Send heartbeat message to queue
        }
    }
```

The queue does the same, but manages an expiration time for each worker.

Here are some tips for your own heartbeating implementation:

- Use `zmq_poll` or a reactor as the core of your application's main task.
- Start by building the heartbeating between peers, test it by simulating failures, and *then* build the rest of the message flow. Adding heartbeating afterwards is much trickier.
- Use simple tracing, i.e., print to console, to get this working. To help you trace the flow of messages between peers, use a dump method such as zmsg offers, and number your messages incrementally so you can see if there are gaps.
- In a real application, heartbeating must be configurable and usually negotiated with the peer. Some peers will want aggressive heartbeating, as low as 10 msecs. Other peers will be far away and want heartbeating as high as 30 seconds.
- If you have different heartbeat intervals for different peers, your poll timeout should be the lowest (shortest time) of these. Do not use an infinite timeout.
- Do heartbeating on the same socket you use for messages, so your heartbeats also act as a *keep-alive* to stop the network connection from going stale (some firewalls can be unkind to silent connections).

Contracts and Protocols

If you're paying attention, you'll realize that Paranoid Pirate is not interoperable with Simple Pirate, because of the heartbeats. But how do we define "interoperable"? To guarantee interoperability, we need a kind of contract, an agreement that lets different teams in different times and places write code that is guaranteed to work together. We call this a "protocol".

It's fun to experiment without specifications, but that's not a sensible basis for real applications. What happens if we want to write a worker in another language? Do we have to read code to see how things work? What if we want to change the protocol for some reason? Even a simple protocol will, if it's successful, evolve and become more complex.

Lack of contracts is a sure sign of a disposable application. So let's write a contract for this protocol. How do we do that?

There's a wiki at rfc.zeromq.org[14] that we made especially as a home for public ØMQ contracts.

To create a new specification, register on the wiki if needed, and follow the instructions. It's fairly straightforward, though writing technical texts is not everyone's cup of tea.

It took me about fifteen minutes to draft the new Pirate Pattern Protocol[15]. It's not a big specification, but it does capture enough to act as the basis for arguments ("your queue isn't PPP compatible; please fix it!").

Turning PPP into a real protocol would take more work:

- There should be a protocol version number in the READY command so that it's possible to distinguish between different versions of PPP.
- Right now, READY and HEARTBEAT are not entirely distinct from requests and replies. To make them distinct, we would need a message structure that includes a "message type" part.

Service-Oriented Reliable Queuing (Majordomo Pattern)

The nice thing about progress is how fast it happens when lawyers and committees aren't involved. The one-page MDP specification[16] turns PPP into something more solid (see figure 50). This is how we should design complex architectures: start by writing down the contracts, and only *then* write software to implement them.

The Majordomo Protocol (MDP) extends and improves on PPP in one interesting way: it adds a "service name" to

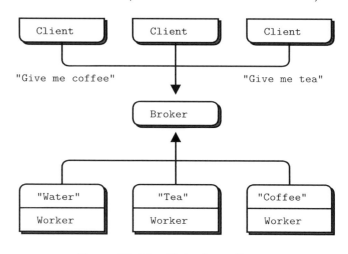

Figure 50. The Majordomo Pattern

requests that the client sends, and asks workers to register for specific services. Adding service names turns our Paranoid Pirate queue into a service-oriented broker. The nice thing about MDP is that it came out of working code, a simpler ancestor protocol

---

14   http://rfc.zeromq.org
15   http://rfc.zeromq.org/spec:6
16   http://rfc.zeromq.org/spec:7

(PPP), and a precise set of improvements that each solved a clear problem. This made it easy to draft.

To implement Majordomo, we need to write a framework for clients and workers. It's really not sane to ask every application developer to read the spec and make it work, when they could be using a simpler API that does the work for them.

So while our first contract (MDP itself) defines how the pieces of our distributed architecture talk to each other, our second contract defines how user applications talk to the technical framework we're going to design.

Majordomo has two halves, a client side and a worker side. Because we'll write both client and worker applications, we will need two APIs. Here is a sketch for the client API, using a simple object-oriented approach:

```
mdcli_t *mdcli_new     (char *broker);
void     mdcli_destroy (mdcli_t **self_p);
zmsg_t  *mdcli_send    (mdcli_t *self, char *service, zmsg_t **request_p);
```

That's it. We open a session to the broker, send a request message, get a reply message back, and eventually close the connection. Here's a sketch for the worker API:

```
mdwrk_t *mdwrk_new     (char *broker,char *service);
void     mdwrk_destroy (mdwrk_t **self_p);
zmsg_t  *mdwrk_recv    (mdwrk_t *self, zmsg_t *reply);
```

It's more or less symmetrical, but the worker dialog is a little different. The first time a worker does a recv(), it passes a null reply. Thereafter, it passes the current reply, and gets a new request.

The client and worker APIs were fairly simple to construct because they're heavily based on the Paranoid Pirate code we already developed. Here is the client API:

Example 43. Majordomo client API (mdcliapi.c)

```
//  mdcliapi class - Majordomo Protocol Client API
//  Implements the MDP/Worker spec at http://rfc.zeromq.org/spec:7.

#include "mdcliapi.h"

//  Structure of our class
//  We access these properties only via class methods

struct _mdcli_t {
    zctx_t *ctx;                //  Our context
    char *broker;
    void *client;               //  Socket to broker
    int verbose;                //  Print activity to stdout
    int timeout;                //  Request timeout
    int retries;                //  Request retries
};

//  Connect or reconnect to broker
```

```
void s_mdcli_connect_to_broker (mdcli_t *self)
{
    if (self->client)
        zsocket_destroy (self->ctx, self->client);
    self->client = zsocket_new (self->ctx, ZMQ_REQ);
    zmq_connect (self->client, self->broker);
    if (self->verbose)
        zclock_log ("I: connecting to broker at %s...", self->broker);
}
```

Here we have the constructor and destructor for our class:

Example 43-1. Majordomo client API (mdcliapi.c) - constructor and destructor

```
//  Constructor

mdcli_t *
mdcli_new (char *broker, int verbose)
{
    assert (broker);

    mdcli_t *self = (mdcli_t *) zmalloc (sizeof (mdcli_t));
    self->ctx = zctx_new ();
    self->broker = strdup (broker);
    self->verbose = verbose;
    self->timeout = 2500;           //  msecs
    self->retries = 3;              //  Before we abandon

    s_mdcli_connect_to_broker (self);
    return self;
}

//  Destructor

void
mdcli_destroy (mdcli_t **self_p)
{
    assert (self_p);
    if (*self_p) {
        mdcli_t *self = *self_p;
        zctx_destroy (&self->ctx);
        free (self->broker);
        free (self);
        *self_p = NULL;
    }
}
```

These are the class methods. We can set the request timeout and number of retry attempts before sending requests:

Example 43-2. Majordomo client API (mdcliapi.c) - configure retry behavior

```
//  Set request timeout

void
mdcli_set_timeout (mdcli_t *self, int timeout)
{
    assert (self);
    self->timeout = timeout;
}

//  Set request retries

void
mdcli_set_retries (mdcli_t *self, int retries)
{
    assert (self);
    self->retries = retries;
}
```

Here is the `send` method. It sends a request to the broker and gets a reply even if it has to retry several times. It takes ownership of the request message, and destroys it when sent. It returns the reply message, or NULL if there was no reply after multiple attempts:

Example 43-3. Majordomo client API (mdcliapi.c) - send request and wait for reply

```
zmsg_t *
mdcli_send (mdcli_t *self, char *service, zmsg_t **request_p)
{
    assert (self);
    assert (request_p);
    zmsg_t *request = *request_p;

    //  Prefix request with protocol frames
    //  Frame 1: "MDPCxy" (six bytes, MDP/Client x.y)
    //  Frame 2: Service name (printable string)
    zmsg_pushstr (request, service);
    zmsg_pushstr (request, MDPC_CLIENT);
    if (self->verbose) {
        zclock_log ("I: send request to '%s' service:", service);
        zmsg_dump (request);
    }
    int retries_left = self->retries;
    while (retries_left && !zctx_interrupted) {
        zmsg_t *msg = zmsg_dup (request);
        zmsg_send (&msg, self->client);
```

```
            zmq_pollitem_t items [] = {
                { self->client, 0, ZMQ_POLLIN, 0 }
            };
```

On any blocking call, libzmq will return -1 if there was an error; we could in theory check for different error codes, but in practice it's OK to assume it was EINTR (Ctrl-C):

Example 43-4. Majordomo client API (mdcliapi.c) - body of send

```
            int rc = zmq_poll (items, 1, self->timeout * ZMQ_POLL_MSEC);
            if (rc == -1)
                break;          //  Interrupted

            //  If we got a reply, process it
            if (items [0].revents & ZMQ_POLLIN) {
                zmsg_t *msg = zmsg_recv (self->client);
                if (self->verbose) {
                    zclock_log ("I: received reply:");
                    zmsg_dump (msg);
                }
                //  We would handle malformed replies better in real code
                assert (zmsg_size (msg) >= 3);

                zframe_t *header = zmsg_pop (msg);
                assert (zframe_streq (header, MDPC_CLIENT));
                zframe_destroy (&header);

                zframe_t *reply_service = zmsg_pop (msg);
                assert (zframe_streq (reply_service, service));
                zframe_destroy (&reply_service);

                zmsg_destroy (&request);
                return msg;     //  Success
            }
            else
            if (--retries_left) {
                if (self->verbose)
                    zclock_log ("W: no reply, reconnecting...");
                s_mdcli_connect_to_broker (self);
            }
            else {
                if (self->verbose)
                    zclock_log ("W: permanent error, abandoning");
                break;          //  Give up
            }
        }
        if (zctx_interrupted)
            printf ("W: interrupt received, killing client...\n");
        zmsg_destroy (&request);
```

```
        return NULL;
}
```

Let's see how the client API looks in action, with an example test program that does 100K request-reply cycles:

Example 44. Majordomo client application (mdclient.c)

```
//  Majordomo Protocol client example
//  Uses the mdcli API to hide all MDP aspects

//  Lets us build this source without creating a library
#include "mdcliapi.c"

int main (int argc, char *argv [])
{
    int verbose = (argc > 1 && streq (argv [1], "-v"));
    mdcli_t *session = mdcli_new ("tcp://localhost:5555", verbose);

    int count;
    for (count = 0; count < 100000; count++) {
        zmsg_t *request = zmsg_new ();
        zmsg_pushstr (request, "Hello world");
        zmsg_t *reply = mdcli_send (session, "echo", &request);
        if (reply)
            zmsg_destroy (&reply);
        else
            break;              //  Interrupt or failure
    }
    printf ("%d requests/replies processed\n", count);
    mdcli_destroy (&session);
    return 0;
}
```

And here is the worker API:

Example 45. Majordomo worker API (mdwrkapi.c)

```
//  mdwrkapi class - Majordomo Protocol Worker API
//  Implements the MDP/Worker spec at http://rfc.zeromq.org/spec:7.

#include "mdwrkapi.h"

//  Reliability parameters
#define HEARTBEAT_LIVENESS  3       //  3-5 is reasonable
```

This is the structure of a worker API instance. We use a pseudo-OO approach in a lot of the C examples, as well as the CZMQ binding:

Example 45-1. Majordomo worker API (mdwrkapi.c) - worker class structure

```
//  Structure of our class
//  We access these properties only via class methods

struct _mdwrk_t {
    zctx_t *ctx;                // Our context
    char *broker;
    char *service;
    void *worker;               // Socket to broker
    int verbose;                // Print activity to stdout

    //  Heartbeat management
    uint64_t heartbeat_at;      // When to send HEARTBEAT
    size_t liveness;            // How many attempts left
    int heartbeat;              // Heartbeat delay, msecs
    int reconnect;              // Reconnect delay, msecs

    int expect_reply;           // Zero only at start
    zframe_t *reply_to;         // Return identity, if any
};
```

We have two utility functions; to send a message to the broker and to (re)connect to the broker:

Example 45-2. Majordomo worker API (mdwrkapi.c) - utility functions

```
//  Send message to broker
//  If no msg is provided, creates one internally

static void
s_mdwrk_send_to_broker (mdwrk_t *self, char *command, char *option,
                        zmsg_t *msg)
{
    msg = msg? zmsg_dup (msg): zmsg_new ();

    //  Stack protocol envelope to start of message
    if (option)
        zmsg_pushstr (msg, option);
    zmsg_pushstr (msg, command);
    zmsg_pushstr (msg, MDPW_WORKER);
    zmsg_pushstr (msg, "");

    if (self->verbose) {
        zclock_log ("I: sending %s to broker",
            mdps_commands [(int) *command]);
        zmsg_dump (msg);
    }
```

```
        zmsg_send (&msg, self->worker);
    }

    //  Connect or reconnect to broker

    void s_mdwrk_connect_to_broker (mdwrk_t *self)
    {
        if (self->worker)
            zsocket_destroy (self->ctx, self->worker);
        self->worker = zsocket_new (self->ctx, ZMQ_DEALER);
        zmq_connect (self->worker, self->broker);
        if (self->verbose)
            zclock_log ("I: connecting to broker at %s...", self->broker);

        //  Register service with broker
        s_mdwrk_send_to_broker (self, MDPW_READY, self->service, NULL);

        //  If liveness hits zero, queue is considered disconnected
        self->liveness = HEARTBEAT_LIVENESS;
        self->heartbeat_at = zclock_time () + self->heartbeat;
    }
```

Here we have the constructor and destructor for our mdwrk class:

Example 45-3. Majordomo worker API (mdwrkapi.c) - constructor and destructor

```
    //  Constructor

    mdwrk_t *
    mdwrk_new (char *broker,char *service, int verbose)
    {
        assert (broker);
        assert (service);

        mdwrk_t *self = (mdwrk_t *) zmalloc (sizeof (mdwrk_t));
        self->ctx = zctx_new ();
        self->broker = strdup (broker);
        self->service = strdup (service);
        self->verbose = verbose;
        self->heartbeat = 2500;     //  msecs
        self->reconnect = 2500;     //  msecs

        s_mdwrk_connect_to_broker (self);
        return self;
    }

    //  Destructor

    void
    mdwrk_destroy (mdwrk_t **self_p)
    {
```

```
        assert (self_p);
        if (*self_p) {
            mdwrk_t *self = *self_p;
            zctx_destroy (&self->ctx);
            free (self->broker);
            free (self->service);
            free (self);
            *self_p = NULL;
        }
    }
```

We provide two methods to configure the worker API. You can set the heartbeat interval and retries to match the expected network performance.

Example 45-4. Majordomo worker API (mdwrkapi.c) - configure worker

```
//  Set heartbeat delay

void
mdwrk_set_heartbeat (mdwrk_t *self, int heartbeat)
{
    self->heartbeat = heartbeat;
}

//  Set reconnect delay

void
mdwrk_set_reconnect (mdwrk_t *self, int reconnect)
{
    self->reconnect = reconnect;
}
```

This is the `recv` method; it's a little misnamed since it first sends any reply and then waits for a new request. If you have a better name for this, let me know.

Example 45-5. Majordomo worker API (mdwrkapi.c) - recv method

```
//  Send reply, if any, to broker and wait for next request.

zmsg_t *
mdwrk_recv (mdwrk_t *self, zmsg_t **reply_p)
{
    //  Format and send the reply if we were provided one
    assert (reply_p);
    zmsg_t *reply = *reply_p;
    assert (reply || !self->expect_reply);
    if (reply) {
        assert (self->reply_to);
        zmsg_wrap (reply, self->reply_to);
        s_mdwrk_send_to_broker (self, MDPW_REPLY, NULL, reply);
        zmsg_destroy (reply_p);
```

```
        }
        self->expect_reply = 1;
        
        while (true) {
            zmq_pollitem_t items [] = {
                { self->worker, 0, ZMQ_POLLIN, 0 } };
            int rc = zmq_poll (items, 1, self->heartbeat * ZMQ_POLL_MSEC);
            if (rc == -1)
                break;              //  Interrupted
            
            if (items [0].revents & ZMQ_POLLIN) {
                zmsg_t *msg = zmsg_recv (self->worker);
                if (!msg)
                    break;          //  Interrupted
                if (self->verbose) {
                    zclock_log ("I: received message from broker:");
                    zmsg_dump (msg);
                }
                self->liveness = HEARTBEAT_LIVENESS;
                
                //  Don't try to handle errors, just assert noisily
                assert (zmsg_size (msg) >= 3);
                
                zframe_t *empty = zmsg_pop (msg);
                assert (zframe_streq (empty, ""));
                zframe_destroy (&empty);
                
                zframe_t *header = zmsg_pop (msg);
                assert (zframe_streq (header, MDPW_WORKER));
                zframe_destroy (&header);
                
                zframe_t *command = zmsg_pop (msg);
                if (zframe_streq (command, MDPW_REQUEST)) {
                    //  We should pop and save as many addresses as there are
                    //  up to a null part, but for now, just save one...
                    self->reply_to = zmsg_unwrap (msg);
                    zframe_destroy (&command);
```

Here is where we actually have a message to process; we return it to the caller application:

Example 45-6. Majordomo worker API (mdwrkapi.c) - process message

```
                    return msg;     //  We have a request to process
                }
                else
                if (zframe_streq (command, MDPW_HEARTBEAT))
                    ;               //  Do nothing for heartbeats
                else
                if (zframe_streq (command, MDPW_DISCONNECT))
                    s_mdwrk_connect_to_broker (self);
```

```
                else {
                    zclock_log ("E: invalid input message");
                    zmsg_dump (msg);
                }
                zframe_destroy (&command);
                zmsg_destroy (&msg);
            }
            else
            if (--self->liveness == 0) {
                if (self->verbose)
                    zclock_log ("W: disconnected from broker - retrying...");
                zclock_sleep (self->reconnect);
                s_mdwrk_connect_to_broker (self);
            }
            // Send HEARTBEAT if it's time
            if (zclock_time () > self->heartbeat_at) {
                s_mdwrk_send_to_broker (self, MDPW_HEARTBEAT, NULL, NULL);
                self->heartbeat_at = zclock_time () + self->heartbeat;
            }
        }
    }
    if (zctx_interrupted)
        printf ("W: interrupt received, killing worker...\n");
    return NULL;
}
```

Let's see how the worker API looks in action, with an example test program that implements an echo service:

Example 46. Majordomo worker application (mdworker.c)

```
//  Majordomo Protocol worker example
//  Uses the mdwrk API to hide all MDP aspects

//  Lets us build this source without creating a library
#include "mdwrkapi.c"

int main (int argc, char *argv [])
{
    int verbose = (argc > 1 && streq (argv [1], "-v"));
    mdwrk_t *session = mdwrk_new (
        "tcp://localhost:5555", "echo", verbose);

    zmsg_t *reply = NULL;
    while (true) {
        zmsg_t *request = mdwrk_recv (session, &reply);
        if (request == NULL)
            break;              //  Worker was interrupted
        reply = request;        //  Echo is complex... :-)
    }
    mdwrk_destroy (&session);
```

```
        return 0;
}
```

Here are some things to note about the worker API code:

- The APIs are single-threaded. This means, for example, that the worker won't send heartbeats in the background. Happily, this is exactly what we want: if the worker application gets stuck, heartbeats will stop and the broker will stop sending requests to the worker.

- The worker API doesn't do an exponential back-off; it's not worth the extra complexity.

- The APIs don't do any error reporting. If something isn't as expected, they raise an assertion (or exception depending on the language). This is ideal for a reference implementation, so any protocol errors show immediately. For real applications, the API should be robust against invalid messages.

You might wonder why the worker API is manually closing its socket and opening a new one, when ØMQ will automatically reconnect a socket if the peer disappears and comes back. Look back at the Simple Pirate and Paranoid Pirate workers to understand. Although ØMQ will automatically reconnect workers if the broker dies and comes back up, this isn't sufficient to re-register the workers with the broker. I know of at least two solutions. The simplest, which we use here, is for the worker to monitor the connection using heartbeats, and if it decides the broker is dead, to close its socket and start afresh with a new socket. The alternative is for the broker to challenge unknown workers when it gets a heartbeat from the worker and ask them to re-register. That would require protocol support.

Now let's design the Majordomo broker. Its core structure is a set of queues, one per service. We will create these queues as workers appear (we could delete them as workers disappear, but forget that for now because it gets complex). Additionally, we keep a queue of workers per service.

And here is the broker:

Example 47. Majordomo broker (mdbroker.c)

```
//  Majordomo Protocol broker
//  A minimal C implementation of the Majordomo Protocol as defined in
//  http://rfc.zeromq.org/spec:7 and http://rfc.zeromq.org/spec:8.

#include "czmq.h"
#include "mdp.h"

//  We'd normally pull these from config data

#define HEARTBEAT_LIVENESS  3       //  3-5 is reasonable
#define HEARTBEAT_INTERVAL  2500    //  msecs
#define HEARTBEAT_EXPIRY    HEARTBEAT_INTERVAL * HEARTBEAT_LIVENESS
```

The broker class defines a single broker instance:

Example 47-1. Majordomo broker (mdbroker.c) - broker class structure

```
typedef struct {
    zctx_t *ctx;                //  Our context
    void *socket;               //  Socket for clients & workers
    int verbose;                //  Print activity to stdout
    char *endpoint;             //  Broker binds to this endpoint
    zhash_t *services;          //  Hash of known services
    zhash_t *workers;           //  Hash of known workers
    zlist_t *waiting;           //  List of waiting workers
    uint64_t heartbeat_at;      //  When to send HEARTBEAT
} broker_t;

static broker_t *
    s_broker_new (int verbose);
static void
    s_broker_destroy (broker_t **self_p);
static void
    s_broker_bind (broker_t *self, char *endpoint);
static void
    s_broker_worker_msg (broker_t *self, zframe_t *sender, zmsg_t *msg);
static void
    s_broker_client_msg (broker_t *self, zframe_t *sender, zmsg_t *msg);
static void
    s_broker_purge (broker_t *self);
```

The service class defines a single service instance:

Example 47-2. Majordomo broker (mdbroker.c) - service class structure

```
typedef struct {
    broker_t *broker;           //  Broker instance
    char *name;                 //  Service name
    zlist_t *requests;          //  List of client requests
    zlist_t *waiting;           //  List of waiting workers
    size_t workers;             //  How many workers we have
} service_t;

static service_t *
    s_service_require (broker_t *self, zframe_t *service_frame);
static void
    s_service_destroy (void *argument);
static void
    s_service_dispatch (service_t *service, zmsg_t *msg);
```

The worker class defines a single worker, idle or active:

Example 47-3. Majordomo broker (mdbroker.c) - worker class structure

```
typedef struct {
    broker_t *broker;           //  Broker instance
    char *id_string;            //  Identity of worker as string
    zframe_t *identity;         //  Identity frame for routing
    service_t *service;         //  Owning service, if known
    int64_t expiry;             //  When worker expires, if no heartbeat
} worker_t;

static worker_t *
    s_worker_require (broker_t *self, zframe_t *identity);
static void
    s_worker_delete (worker_t *self, int disconnect);
static void
    s_worker_destroy (void *argument);
static void
    s_worker_send (worker_t *self, char *command, char *option,
                   zmsg_t *msg);
static void
    s_worker_waiting (worker_t *self);
```

Here are the constructor and destructor for the broker:

Example 47-4. Majordomo broker (mdbroker.c) - broker constructor and destructor

```
static broker_t *
s_broker_new (int verbose)
{
    broker_t *self = (broker_t *) zmalloc (sizeof (broker_t));

    //  Initialize broker state
    self->ctx = zctx_new ();
    self->socket = zsocket_new (self->ctx, ZMQ_ROUTER);
    self->verbose = verbose;
    self->services = zhash_new ();
    self->workers = zhash_new ();
    self->waiting = zlist_new ();
    self->heartbeat_at = zclock_time () + HEARTBEAT_INTERVAL;
    return self;
}

static void
s_broker_destroy (broker_t **self_p)
{
    assert (self_p);
    if (*self_p) {
        broker_t *self = *self_p;
        zctx_destroy (&self->ctx);
```

```
            zhash_destroy (&self->services);
            zhash_destroy (&self->workers);
            zlist_destroy (&self->waiting);
            free (self);
            *self_p = NULL;
        }
    }
```

This method binds the broker instance to an endpoint. We can call this multiple times. Note that MDP uses a single socket for both clients and workers:

Example 47-5. Majordomo broker (mdbroker.c) - broker bind method

```
void
s_broker_bind (broker_t *self, char *endpoint)
{
    zsocket_bind (self->socket, endpoint);
    zclock_log ("I: MDP broker/0.2.0 is active at %s", endpoint);
}
```

This method processes one READY, REPLY, HEARTBEAT, or DISCONNECT message sent to the broker by a worker:

Example 47-6. Majordomo broker (mdbroker.c) - broker worker_msg method

```
static void
s_broker_worker_msg (broker_t *self, zframe_t *sender, zmsg_t *msg)
{
    assert (zmsg_size (msg) >= 1);     //  At least, command

    zframe_t *command = zmsg_pop (msg);
    char *id_string = zframe_strhex (sender);
    int worker_ready = (zhash_lookup (self->workers, id_string) != NULL);
    free (id_string);
    worker_t *worker = s_worker_require (self, sender);

    if (zframe_streq (command, MDPW_READY)) {
        if (worker_ready)              //  Not first command in session
            s_worker_delete (worker, 1);
        else
        if (zframe_size (sender) >= 4  //  Reserved service name
        &&  memcmp (zframe_data (sender), "mmi.", 4) == 0)
            s_worker_delete (worker, 1);
        else {
            //  Attach worker to service and mark as idle
            zframe_t *service_frame = zmsg_pop (msg);
            worker->service = s_service_require (self, service_frame);
            worker->service->workers++;
            s_worker_waiting (worker);
            zframe_destroy (&service_frame);
        }
```

```
        }
        else
        if (zframe_streq (command, MDPW_REPLY)) {
            if (worker_ready) {
                //  Remove and save client return envelope and insert the
                //   protocol header and service name, then rewrap envelope.
                zframe_t *client = zmsg_unwrap (msg);
                zmsg_pushstr (msg, worker->service->name);
                zmsg_pushstr (msg, MDPC_CLIENT);
                zmsg_wrap (msg, client);
                zmsg_send (&msg, self->socket);
                s_worker_waiting (worker);
            }
            else
                s_worker_delete (worker, 1);
        }
        else
        if (zframe_streq (command, MDPW_HEARTBEAT)) {
            if (worker_ready)
                worker->expiry = zclock_time () + HEARTBEAT_EXPIRY;
            else
                s_worker_delete (worker, 1);
        }
        else
        if (zframe_streq (command, MDPW_DISCONNECT))
            s_worker_delete (worker, 0);
        else {
            zclock_log ("E: invalid input message");
            zmsg_dump (msg);
        }
        free (command);
        zmsg_destroy (&msg);
}
```

Process a request coming from a client. We implement MMI requests directly here (at present, we implement only the mmi.service request):

Example 47-7. Majordomo broker (mdbroker.c) - broker client_msg method

```
static void
s_broker_client_msg (broker_t *self, zframe_t *sender, zmsg_t *msg)
{
    assert (zmsg_size (msg) >= 2);      //  Service name + body

    zframe_t *service_frame = zmsg_pop (msg);
    service_t *service = s_service_require (self, service_frame);

    //  Set reply return identity to client sender
    zmsg_wrap (msg, zframe_dup (sender));

    //  If we got a MMI service request, process that internally
```

```
            if (zframe_size (service_frame) >= 4
            &&  memcmp (zframe_data (service_frame), "mmi.", 4) == 0) {
                char *return_code;
                if (zframe_streq (service_frame, "mmi.service")) {
                    char *name = zframe_strdup (zmsg_last (msg));
                    service_t *service =
                        (service_t *) zhash_lookup (self->services, name);
                    return_code = service && service->workers? "200": "404";
                    free (name);
                }
                else
                    return_code = "501";

                zframe_reset (zmsg_last (msg), return_code, strlen (return_code));

                //  Remove & save client return envelope and insert the
                //  protocol header and service name, then rewrap envelope.
                zframe_t *client = zmsg_unwrap (msg);
                zmsg_push (msg, zframe_dup (service_frame));
                zmsg_pushstr (msg, MDPC_CLIENT);
                zmsg_wrap (msg, client);
                zmsg_send (&msg, self->socket);
            }
            else
                //  Else dispatch the message to the requested service
                s_service_dispatch (service, msg);
        zframe_destroy (&service_frame);
}
```

This method deletes any idle workers that haven't pinged us in a while. We hold workers from oldest to most recent so we can stop scanning whenever we find a live worker. This means we'll mainly stop at the first worker, which is essential when we have large numbers of workers (we call this method in our critical path):

Example 47-8. Majordomo broker (mdbroker.c) - broker purge method

```
static void
s_broker_purge (broker_t *self)
{
    worker_t *worker = (worker_t *) zlist_first (self->waiting);
    while (worker) {
        if (zclock_time () < worker->expiry)
            break;                  //  Worker is alive, we're done here
        if (self->verbose)
            zclock_log ("I: deleting expired worker: %s",
                        worker->id_string);

        s_worker_delete (worker, 0);
        worker = (worker_t *) zlist_first (self->waiting);
    }
}
```

Here is the implementation of the methods that work on a service:

Example 47-9. Majordomo broker (mdbroker.c) - service methods

```c
//  Lazy constructor that locates a service by name or creates a new
//  service if there is no service already with that name.

static service_t *
s_service_require (broker_t *self, zframe_t *service_frame)
{
    assert (service_frame);
    char *name = zframe_strdup (service_frame);

    service_t *service =
        (service_t *) zhash_lookup (self->services, name);
    if (service == NULL) {
        service = (service_t *) zmalloc (sizeof (service_t));
        service->broker = self;
        service->name = name;
        service->requests = zlist_new ();
        service->waiting = zlist_new ();
        zhash_insert (self->services, name, service);
        zhash_freefn (self->services, name, s_service_destroy);
        if (self->verbose)
            zclock_log ("I: added service: %s", name);
    }
    else
        free (name);

    return service;
}

//  Service destructor is called automatically whenever the service is
//  removed from broker->services.

static void
s_service_destroy (void *argument)
{
    service_t *service = (service_t *) argument;
    while (zlist_size (service->requests)) {
        zmsg_t *msg = zlist_pop (service->requests);
        zmsg_destroy (&msg);
    }
    zlist_destroy (&service->requests);
    zlist_destroy (&service->waiting);
    free (service->name);
    free (service);
}
```

This method sends requests to waiting workers:

Example 47-10. Majordomo broker (mdbroker.c) - service dispatch method

```
static void
s_service_dispatch (service_t *self, zmsg_t *msg)
{
    assert (self);
    if (msg)                      //  Queue message if any
        zlist_append (self->requests, msg);

    s_broker_purge (self->broker);
    while (zlist_size (self->waiting) && zlist_size (self->requests)) {
        worker_t *worker = zlist_pop (self->waiting);
        zlist_remove (self->broker->waiting, worker);
        zmsg_t *msg = zlist_pop (self->requests);
        s_worker_send (worker, MDPW_REQUEST, NULL, msg);
        zmsg_destroy (&msg);
    }
}
```

Here is the implementation of the methods that work on a worker:

Example 47-11. Majordomo broker (mdbroker.c) - worker methods

```
//  Lazy constructor that locates a worker by identity, or creates a new
//  worker if there is no worker already with that identity.

static worker_t *
s_worker_require (broker_t *self, zframe_t *identity)
{
    assert (identity);

    //  self->workers is keyed off worker identity
    char *id_string = zframe_strhex (identity);
    worker_t *worker =
        (worker_t *) zhash_lookup (self->workers, id_string);

    if (worker == NULL) {
        worker = (worker_t *) zmalloc (sizeof (worker_t));
        worker->broker = self;
        worker->id_string = id_string;
        worker->identity = zframe_dup (identity);
        zhash_insert (self->workers, id_string, worker);
        zhash_freefn (self->workers, id_string, s_worker_destroy);
        if (self->verbose)
            zclock_log ("I: registering new worker: %s", id_string);
    }
    else
        free (id_string);
    return worker;
```

```
}

// This method deletes the current worker.

static void
s_worker_delete (worker_t *self, int disconnect)
{
    assert (self);
    if (disconnect)
        s_worker_send (self, MDPW_DISCONNECT, NULL, NULL);

    if (self->service) {
        zlist_remove (self->service->waiting, self);
        self->service->workers--;
    }
    zlist_remove (self->broker->waiting, self);
    //  This implicitly calls s_worker_destroy
    zhash_delete (self->broker->workers, self->id_string);
}

// Worker destructor is called automatically whenever the worker is
// removed from broker->workers.

static void
s_worker_destroy (void *argument)
{
    worker_t *self = (worker_t *) argument;
    zframe_destroy (&self->identity);
    free (self->id_string);
    free (self);
}
```

This method formats and sends a command to a worker. The caller may also provide a command option, and a message payload:

Example 47-12. Majordomo broker (mdbroker.c) - worker send method

```
static void
s_worker_send (worker_t *self, char *command, char *option, zmsg_t *msg)
{
    msg = msg? zmsg_dup (msg): zmsg_new ();

    //  Stack protocol envelope to start of message
    if (option)
        zmsg_pushstr (msg, option);
    zmsg_pushstr (msg, command);
    zmsg_pushstr (msg, MDPW_WORKER);

    //  Stack routing envelope to start of message
    zmsg_wrap (msg, zframe_dup (self->identity));
```

```
        if (self->broker->verbose) {
            zclock_log ("I: sending %s to worker",
                mdps_commands [(int) *command]);
            zmsg_dump (msg);
        }
        zmsg_send (&msg, self->broker->socket);
    }

    //  This worker is now waiting for work

    static void
    s_worker_waiting (worker_t *self)
    {
        //  Queue to broker and service waiting lists
        assert (self->broker);
        zlist_append (self->broker->waiting, self);
        zlist_append (self->service->waiting, self);
        self->expiry = zclock_time () + HEARTBEAT_EXPIRY;
        s_service_dispatch (self->service, NULL);
    }
```

Finally, here is the main task. We create a new broker instance and then process messages on the broker socket:

Example 47-13. Majordomo broker (mdbroker.c) - main task

```
    int main (int argc, char *argv [])
    {
        int verbose = (argc > 1 && streq (argv [1], "-v"));

        broker_t *self = s_broker_new (verbose);
        s_broker_bind (self, "tcp://*:5555");

        //  Get and process messages forever or until interrupted
        while (true) {
            zmq_pollitem_t items [] = {
                { self->socket,  0, ZMQ_POLLIN, 0 } };
            int rc = zmq_poll (items, 1, HEARTBEAT_INTERVAL * ZMQ_POLL_MSEC);
            if (rc == -1)
                break;              //  Interrupted

            //  Process next input message, if any
            if (items [0].revents & ZMQ_POLLIN) {
                zmsg_t *msg = zmsg_recv (self->socket);
                if (!msg)
                    break;          //  Interrupted
                if (self->verbose) {
                    zclock_log ("I: received message:");
                    zmsg_dump (msg);
                }
                zframe_t *sender = zmsg_pop (msg);
```

```
                    zframe_t *empty  = zmsg_pop (msg);
                    zframe_t *header = zmsg_pop (msg);

                    if (zframe_streq (header, MDPC_CLIENT))
                        s_broker_client_msg (self, sender, msg);
                    else
                    if (zframe_streq (header, MDPW_WORKER))
                        s_broker_worker_msg (self, sender, msg);
                    else {
                        zclock_log ("E: invalid message:");
                        zmsg_dump (msg);
                        zmsg_destroy (&msg);
                    }
                    zframe_destroy (&sender);
                    zframe_destroy (&empty);
                    zframe_destroy (&header);
                }
                //  Disconnect and delete any expired workers
                //  Send heartbeats to idle workers if needed
                if (zclock_time () > self->heartbeat_at) {
                    s_broker_purge (self);
                    worker_t *worker = (worker_t *) zlist_first (self->waiting);
                    while (worker) {
                        s_worker_send (worker, MDPW_HEARTBEAT, NULL, NULL);
                        worker = (worker_t *) zlist_next (self->waiting);
                    }
                    self->heartbeat_at = zclock_time () + HEARTBEAT_INTERVAL;
                }
            }
            if (zctx_interrupted)
                printf ("W: interrupt received, shutting down...\n");

            s_broker_destroy (&self);
            return 0;
        }
```

This is by far the most complex example we've seen. It's almost 500 lines of code. To write this and make it somewhat robust took two days. However, this is still a short piece of code for a full service-oriented broker.

Here are some things to note about the broker code:

- The Majordomo Protocol lets us handle both clients and workers on a single socket. This is nicer for those deploying and managing the broker: it just sits on one ØMQ endpoint rather than the two that most proxies need.

- The broker implements all of MDP/0.1 properly (as far as I know), including disconnection if the broker sends invalid commands, heartbeating, and the rest.

- It can be extended to run multiple threads, each managing one socket and one set of clients and workers. This could be interesting for segmenting large architectures. The C code is already organized around a broker class to make this trivial.

- A primary/failover or live/live broker reliability model is easy, as the broker essentially has no state except service presence. It's up to clients and workers to choose another broker if their first choice isn't up and running.

- The examples use five-second heartbeats, mainly to reduce the amount of output when you enable tracing. Realistic values would be lower for most LAN applications. However, any retry has to be slow enough to allow for a service to restart, say 10 seconds at least.

We later improved and extended the protocol and the Majordomo implementation, which now sits in its own Github project. If you want a properly usable Majordomo stack, use the GitHub project.

Asynchronous Majordomo Pattern

The Majordomo implementation in the previous section is simple and stupid. The client is just the original Simple Pirate, wrapped up in a sexy API. When I fire up a client, broker, and worker on a test box, it can process 100,000 requests in about 14 seconds. That is partially due to the code, which cheerfully copies message frames around as if CPU cycles were free. But the real problem is that we're doing network round-trips. ØMQ disables Nagle's algorithm[17], but round-tripping is still slow.

Theory is great in theory, but in practice, practice is better. Let's measure the actual cost of round-tripping with a simple test program. This sends a bunch of messages, first waiting for a reply to each message, and second as a batch, reading all the replies back as a batch. Both approaches do the same work, but they give very different results. We mock up a client, broker, and worker:

Example 48. Round-trip demonstrator (tripping.c)

```
//  Round-trip demonstrator
//  While this example runs in a single process, that is just to make
//  it easier to start and stop the example. The client task signals to
//  main when it's ready.

#include "czmq.h"

static void
client_task (void *args, zctx_t *ctx, void *pipe)
{
    void *client = zsocket_new (ctx, ZMQ_DEALER);
    zsocket_connect (client, "tcp://localhost:5555");
    printf ("Setting up test...\n");
    zclock_sleep (100);

    int requests;
```

---

17 http://en.wikipedia.org/wiki/Nagles_algorithm

```c
        int64_t start;

        printf ("Synchronous round-trip test...\n");
        start = zclock_time ();
        for (requests = 0; requests < 10000; requests++) {
            zstr_send (client, "hello");
            char *reply = zstr_recv (client);
            free (reply);
        }
        printf (" %d calls/second\n",
            (1000 * 10000) / (int) (zclock_time () - start));

        printf ("Asynchronous round-trip test...\n");
        start = zclock_time ();
        for (requests = 0; requests < 100000; requests++)
            zstr_send (client, "hello");
        for (requests = 0; requests < 100000; requests++) {
            char *reply = zstr_recv (client);
            free (reply);
        }
        printf (" %d calls/second\n",
            (1000 * 100000) / (int) (zclock_time () - start));
        zstr_send (pipe, "done");
}
```

Here is the worker task. All it does is receive a message, and bounce it back the way it came:

Example 48-1. Round-trip demonstrator (tripping.c) - worker task

```c
static void *
worker_task (void *args)
{
    zctx_t *ctx = zctx_new ();
    void *worker = zsocket_new (ctx, ZMQ_DEALER);
    zsocket_connect (worker, "tcp://localhost:5556");

    while (true) {
        zmsg_t *msg = zmsg_recv (worker);
        zmsg_send (&msg, worker);
    }
    zctx_destroy (&ctx);
    return NULL;
}
```

Here is the broker task. It uses the `zmq_proxy` function to switch messages between frontend and backend:

Example 48-2. Round-trip demonstrator (tripping.c) - broker task

```
static void *
broker_task (void *args)
{
    //  Prepare our context and sockets
    zctx_t *ctx = zctx_new ();
    void *frontend = zsocket_new (ctx, ZMQ_DEALER);
    zsocket_bind (frontend, "tcp://*:5555");
    void *backend = zsocket_new (ctx, ZMQ_DEALER);
    zsocket_bind (backend, "tcp://*:5556");
    zmq_proxy (frontend, backend, NULL);
    zctx_destroy (&ctx);
    return NULL;
}
```

Finally, here's the main task, which starts the client, worker, and broker, and then runs until the client signals it to stop:

Example 48-3. Round-trip demonstrator (tripping.c) - main task

```
int main (void)
{
    //  Create threads
    zctx_t *ctx = zctx_new ();
    void *client = zthread_fork (ctx, client_task, NULL);
    zthread_new (worker_task, NULL);
    zthread_new (broker_task, NULL);

    //  Wait for signal on client pipe
    char *signal = zstr_recv (client);
    free (signal);

    zctx_destroy (&ctx);
    return 0;
}
```

On my development box, this program says:

```
Setting up test...
Synchronous round-trip test...
 9057 calls/second
Asynchronous round-trip test...
 173010 calls/second
```

Note that the client thread does a small pause before starting. This is to get around one of the "features" of the router socket: if you send a message with the address of a peer that's not yet connected, the message gets discarded. In this example we don't use the load balancing mechanism, so without the sleep, if the worker thread is too slow to connect, it will lose messages, making a mess of our test.

As we see, round-tripping in the simplest case is 20 times slower than the asynchronous, "shove it down the pipe as fast as it'll go" approach. Let's see if we can apply this to Majordomo to make it faster.

First, we modify the client API to send and receive in two separate methods:

```
mdcli_t *mdcli_new     (char *broker);
void     mdcli_destroy (mdcli_t **self_p);
int      mdcli_send    (mdcli_t *self, char *service, zmsg_t **request_p);
zmsg_t  *mdcli_recv    (mdcli_t *self);
```

It's literally a few minutes' work to refactor the synchronous client API to become asynchronous:

Example 49. Majordomo asynchronous client API (mdcliapi2.c)

```
//  mdcliapi2 class - Majordomo Protocol Client API
//  Implements the MDP/Worker spec at http://rfc.zeromq.org/spec:7.

#include "mdcliapi2.h"

//  Structure of our class
//  We access these properties only via class methods

struct _mdcli_t {
    zctx_t *ctx;                //  Our context
    char *broker;
    void *client;               //  Socket to broker
    int verbose;                //  Print activity to stdout
    int timeout;                //  Request timeout
};

//  Connect or reconnect to broker. In this asynchronous class we use a
//  DEALER socket instead of a REQ socket; this lets us send any number
//  of requests without waiting for a reply.

void s_mdcli_connect_to_broker (mdcli_t *self)
{
    if (self->client)
        zsocket_destroy (self->ctx, self->client);
    self->client = zsocket_new (self->ctx, ZMQ_DEALER);
    zmq_connect (self->client, self->broker);
    if (self->verbose)
        zclock_log ("I: connecting to broker at %s...", self->broker);
}

//  The constructor and destructor are the same as in mdcliapi, except
//  we don't do retries, so there's no retries property.
```

...
...

The differences are:

- We use a DEALER socket instead of REQ, so we emulate REQ with an empty delimiter frame before each request and each response.
- We don't retry requests; if the application needs to retry, it can do this itself.
- We break the synchronous send method into separate send and recv methods.
- The send method is asynchronous and returns immediately after sending. The caller can thus send a number of messages before getting a response.
- The recv method waits for (with a timeout) one response and returns that to the caller.

And here's the corresponding client test program, which sends 100,000 messages and then receives 100,00 back:

Example 50. Majordomo client application (mdclient2.c)

```
//  Majordomo Protocol client example - asynchronous
//  Uses the mdcli API to hide all MDP aspects

//  Lets us build this source without creating a library
#include "mdcliapi2.c"

int main (int argc, char *argv [])
{
    int verbose = (argc > 1 && streq (argv [1], "-v"));
    mdcli_t *session = mdcli_new ("tcp://localhost:5555", verbose);

    int count;
    for (count = 0; count < 100000; count++) {
        zmsg_t *request = zmsg_new ();
        zmsg_pushstr (request, "Hello world");
        mdcli_send (session, "echo", &request);
    }
    for (count = 0; count < 100000; count++) {
        zmsg_t *reply = mdcli_recv (session);
        if (reply)
            zmsg_destroy (&reply);
        else
            break;              //  Interrupted by Ctrl-C
    }
    printf ("%d replies received\n", count);
    mdcli_destroy (&session);
    return 0;
}
```

The broker and worker are unchanged because we've not modified the protocol at all. We see an immediate improvement in performance. Here's the synchronous client chugging through 100K request-reply cycles:

```
$ time mdclient
100000 requests/replies processed

real    0m14.088s
user    0m1.310s
sys     0m2.670s
```

And here's the asynchronous client, with a single worker:

```
$ time mdclient2
100000 replies received

real    0m8.730s
user    0m0.920s
sys     0m1.550s
```

Twice as fast. Not bad, but let's fire up 10 workers and see how it handles the traffic

```
$ time mdclient2
100000 replies received

real    0m3.863s
user    0m0.730s
sys     0m0.470s
```

It isn't fully asynchronous because workers get their messages on a strict last-used basis. But it will scale better with more workers. On my PC, after eight or so workers, it doesn't get any faster. Four cores only stretches so far. But we got a 4x improvement in throughput with just a few minutes' work. The broker is still unoptimized. It spends most of its time copying message frames around, instead of doing zero-copy, which it could. But we're getting 25K reliable request/reply calls a second, with pretty low effort.

However, the asynchronous Majordomo pattern isn't all roses. It has a fundamental weakness, namely that it cannot survive a broker crash without more work. If you look at the `mdcliapi2` code you'll see it does not attempt to reconnect after a failure. A proper reconnect would require the following:

- A number on every request and a matching number on every reply, which would ideally require a change to the protocol to enforce.
- Tracking and holding onto all outstanding requests in the client API, i.e., those for which no reply has yet been received.
- In case of failover, for the client API to *resend* all outstanding requests to the broker.

It's not a deal breaker, but it does show that performance often means complexity. Is this worth doing for Majordomo? It depends on your use case. For a name lookup service you call once per session, no. For a web frontend serving thousands of clients, probably yes.

Service Discovery

So, we have a nice service-oriented broker, but we have no way of knowing whether a particular service is available or not. We know whether a request failed, but we don't know why. It is useful to be able to ask the broker, "is the echo service running?" The most obvious way would be to modify our MDP/Client protocol to add commands to ask this. But MDP/Client has the great charm of being simple. Adding service discovery to it would make it as complex as the MDP/Worker protocol.

Another option is to do what email does, and ask that undeliverable requests be returned. This can work well in an asynchronous world, but it also adds complexity. We need ways to distinguish returned requests from replies and to handle these properly.

Let's try to use what we've already built, building on top of MDP instead of modifying it. Service discovery is, itself, a service. It might indeed be one of several management services, such as "disable service X", "provide statistics", and so on. What we want is a general, extensible solution that doesn't affect the protocol or existing applications.

So here's a small RFC that layers this on top of MDP: the Majordomo Management Interface (MMI)[18]. We already implemented it in the broker, though unless you read the whole thing you probably missed that. I'll explain how it works in the broker:

- When a client requests a service that starts with `mmi.`, instead of routing this to a worker, we handle it internally.
- We handle just one service in this broker, which is `mmi.service`, the service discovery service.
- The payload for the request is the name of an external service (a real one, provided by a worker).
- The broker returns "200" (OK) or "404" (Not found), depending on whether there are workers registered for that service or not.

Here's how we use the service discovery in an application:

Example 51. Service discovery over Majordomo (mmiecho.c)

```
//  MMI echo query example

//  Lets us build this source without creating a library
#include "mdcliapi.c"

int main (int argc, char *argv [])
{
```

---

18 http://rfc.zeromq.org/spec:8

```
        int verbose = (argc > 1 && streq (argv [1], "-v"));
        mdcli_t *session = mdcli_new ("tcp://localhost:5555", verbose);

        //  This is the service we want to look up
        zmsg_t *request = zmsg_new ();
        zmsg_addstr (request, "echo");

        //  This is the service we send our request to
        zmsg_t *reply = mdcli_send (session, "mmi.service", &request);

        if (reply) {
            char *reply_code = zframe_strdup (zmsg_first (reply));
            printf ("Lookup echo service: %s\n", reply_code);
            free (reply_code);
            zmsg_destroy (&reply);
        }
        else
            printf ("E: no response from broker, make sure it's running\n");

        mdcli_destroy (&session);
        return 0;
    }
```

Try this with and without a worker running, and you should see the little program report "200" or "404" accordingly. The implementation of MMI in our example broker is flimsy. For example, if a worker disappears, services remain "present". In practice, a broker should remove services that have no workers after some configurable timeout.

Idempotent Services

Idempotency is not something you take a pill for. What it means is that it's safe to repeat an operation. Checking the clock is idempotent. Lending ones credit card to ones children is not. While many client-to-server use cases are idempotent, some are not. Examples of idempotent use cases include:

- Stateless task distribution, i.e., a pipeline where the servers are stateless workers that compute a reply based purely on the state provided by a request. In such a case, it's safe (though inefficient) to execute the same request many times.
- A name service that translates logical addresses into endpoints to bind or connect to. In such a case, it's safe to make the same lookup request many times.

And here are examples of a non-idempotent use cases:

- A logging service. One does not want the same log information recorded more than once.
- Any service that has impact on downstream nodes, e.g., sends on information to other nodes. If that service gets the same request more than once, downstream nodes will get duplicate information.

- Any service that modifies shared data in some non-idempotent way; e.g., a service that debits a bank account is not idempotent without extra work.

When our server applications are not idempotent, we have to think more carefully about when exactly they might crash. If an application dies when it's idle, or while it's processing a request, that's usually fine. We can use database transactions to make sure a debit and a credit are always done together, if at all. If the server dies while sending its reply, that's a problem, because as far as it's concerned, it has done its work.

If the network dies just as the reply is making its way back to the client, the same problem arises. The client will think the server died and will resend the request, and the server will do the same work twice, which is not what we want.

To handle non-idempotent operations, use the fairly standard solution of detecting and rejecting duplicate requests. This means:

- The client must stamp every request with a unique client identifier and a unique message number.
- The server, before sending back a reply, stores it using the combination of client ID and message number as a key.
- The server, when getting a request from a given client, first checks whether it has a reply for that client ID and message number. If so, it does not process the request, but just resends the reply.

Disconnected Reliability (Titanic Pattern)

Once you realize that Majordomo is a "reliable" message broker, you might be tempted to add some spinning rust (that is, ferrous-based hard disk platters). After all, this works for all the enterprise messaging systems. It's such a tempting idea that it's a little sad to have to be negative toward it. But brutal cynicism is one of my specialties. So, some reasons you don't want rust-based brokers sitting in the center of your architecture are:

- As you've seen, the Lazy Pirate client performs surprisingly well. It works across a whole range of architectures, from direct client-to-server to distributed queue proxies. It does tend to assume that workers are stateless and idempotent. But we can work around that limitation without resorting to rust.
- Rust brings a whole set of problems, from slow performance to additional pieces that you have to manage, repair, and handle 6 a.m. panics from, as they inevitably break at the start of daily operations. The beauty of the Pirate patterns in general is their simplicity. They won't crash. And if you're still worried about the hardware, you can move to a peer-to-peer pattern that has no broker at all. I'll explain later in this chapter.

Having said this, however, there is one sane use case for rust-based reliability, which is an asynchronous disconnected network. It solves a major problem with Pirate, namely that a client has to wait for an answer in real time. If clients and workers are only sporadically connected (think of email as an analogy), we can't use a stateless network between clients and workers. We have to put state in the middle.

So, here's the Titanic pattern (see figure 51), in which we write messages to disk to ensure they never get lost, no matter how sporadically clients and workers are connected. As we did for service discovery, we're going to layer Titanic on top of MDP rather than extend it. It's wonderfully lazy because it means we can implement our fire-and-forget reliability in a specialized worker, rather than in the broker. This is excellent for several reasons:

- It is *much* easier because we divide and conquer: the broker handles message routing and the worker handles reliability.
- It lets us mix brokers written in one language with workers written in another.
- It lets us evolve the fire-and-forget technology independently.

The only downside is that there's an extra network hop between broker and hard disk. The benefits are easily worth it.

There are many ways to make a persistent request-reply architecture. We'll aim for one that is simple and painless. The simplest design I could come up with, after playing with this for a few hours, is a "proxy service". That is, Titanic doesn't affect workers at all. If a client wants a reply immediately, it talks directly to a service and hopes the service is available. If a client is happy to wait a while, it talks to Titanic instead and asks, "hey, buddy, would you take care of this for me while I go buy my groceries?"

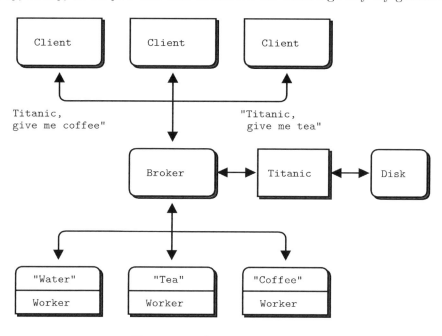

Figure 51. The Titanic Pattern

Titanic is thus both a worker and a client. The dialog between client and Titanic goes along these lines:

- Client: Please accept this request for me. Titanic: OK, done.

- Client: Do you have a reply for me? Titanic: Yes, here it is. Or, no, not yet.
- Client: OK, you can wipe that request now, I'm happy. Titanic: OK, done.

Whereas the dialog between Titanic and broker and worker goes like this:
- Titanic: Hey, Broker, is there an coffee service? Broker: Uhm, Yeah, seems like.
- Titanic: Hey, coffee service, please handle this for me.
- Coffee: Sure, here you are.
- Titanic: Sweeeeet!

You can work through this and the possible failure scenarios. If a worker crashes while processing a request, Titanic retries indefinitely. If a reply gets lost somewhere, Titanic will retry. If the request gets processed but the client doesn't get the reply, it will ask again. If Titanic crashes while processing a request or a reply, the client will try again. As long as requests are fully committed to safe storage, work can't get lost.

The handshaking is pedantic, but can be pipelined, i.e., clients can use the asynchronous Majordomo pattern to do a lot of work and then get the responses later.

We need some way for a client to request *its* replies. We'll have many clients asking for the same services, and clients disappear and reappear with different identities. Here is a simple, reasonably secure solution:

- Every request generates a universally unique ID (UUID), which Titanic returns to the client after it has queued the request.
- When a client asks for a reply, it must specify the UUID for the original request.

In a realistic case, the client would want to store its request UUIDs safely, e.g., in a local database.

Before we jump off and write yet another formal specification (fun, fun!), let's consider how the client talks to Titanic. One way is to use a single service and send it three different request types. Another way, which seems simpler, is to use three services:

- `titanic.request`: store a request message, and return a UUID for the request.
- `titanic.reply`: fetch a reply, if available, for a given request UUID.
- `titanic.close`: confirm that a reply has been stored and processed.

We'll just make a multithreaded worker, which as we've seen from our multithreading experience with ØMQ, is trivial. However, let's first sketch what Titanic would look like in terms of ØMQ messages and frames. This gives us the Titanic Service Protocol (TSP)[19].

Using TSP is clearly more work for client applications than accessing a service directly via MDP. Here's the shortest robust "echo" client example:

Example 52. Titanic client example (ticlient.c)

```
//  Titanic client example
//  Implements client side of http://rfc.zeromq.org/spec:9
```

---

19 http://rfc.zeromq.org/spec:9

```c
// Lets build this source without creating a library
#include "mdcliapi.c"

// Calls a TSP service
// Returns response if successful (status code 200 OK), else NULL
//
static zmsg_t *
s_service_call (mdcli_t *session, char *service, zmsg_t **request_p)
{
    zmsg_t *reply = mdcli_send (session, service, request_p);
    if (reply) {
        zframe_t *status = zmsg_pop (reply);
        if (zframe_streq (status, "200")) {
            zframe_destroy (&status);
            return reply;
        }
        else
        if (zframe_streq (status, "400")) {
            printf ("E: client fatal error, aborting\n");
            exit (EXIT_FAILURE);
        }
        else
        if (zframe_streq (status, "500")) {
            printf ("E: server fatal error, aborting\n");
            exit (EXIT_FAILURE);
        }
    }
    else
        exit (EXIT_SUCCESS);    //  Interrupted or failed

    zmsg_destroy (&reply);
    return NULL;            //  Didn't succeed; don't care why not
}
```

The main task tests our service call by sending an echo request:

Example 52-1. Titanic client example (ticlient.c) - main task

```c
int main (int argc, char *argv [])
{
    int verbose = (argc > 1 && streq (argv [1], "-v"));
    mdcli_t *session = mdcli_new ("tcp://localhost:5555", verbose);

    //  1. Send 'echo' request to Titanic
    zmsg_t *request = zmsg_new ();
    zmsg_addstr (request, "echo");
    zmsg_addstr (request, "Hello world");
    zmsg_t *reply = s_service_call (
        session, "titanic.request", &request);
```

```
            zframe_t *uuid = NULL;
        if (reply) {
            uuid = zmsg_pop (reply);
            zmsg_destroy (&reply);
            zframe_print (uuid, "I: request UUID ");
        }
        //  2. Wait until we get a reply
        while (!zctx_interrupted) {
            zclock_sleep (100);
            request = zmsg_new ();
            zmsg_add (request, zframe_dup (uuid));
            zmsg_t *reply = s_service_call (
                session, "titanic.reply", &request);

            if (reply) {
                char *reply_string = zframe_strdup (zmsg_last (reply));
                printf ("Reply: %s\n", reply_string);
                free (reply_string);
                zmsg_destroy (&reply);

                //  3. Close request
                request = zmsg_new ();
                zmsg_add (request, zframe_dup (uuid));
                reply = s_service_call (session, "titanic.close", &request);
                zmsg_destroy (&reply);
                break;
            }
            else {
                printf ("I: no reply yet, trying again...\n");
                zclock_sleep (5000);     //  Try again in 5 seconds
            }
        }
        zframe_destroy (&uuid);
        mdcli_destroy (&session);
        return 0;
    }
```

Of course this can be, and should be, wrapped up in some kind of framework or API. It's not healthy to ask average application developers to learn the full details of messaging: it hurts their brains, costs time, and offers too many ways to make buggy complexity. Additionally, it makes it hard to add intelligence.

For example, this client blocks on each request whereas in a real application, we'd want to be doing useful work while tasks are executed. This requires some nontrivial plumbing to build a background thread and talk to that cleanly. It's the kind of thing you want to wrap in a nice simple API that the average developer cannot misuse. It's the same approach that we used for Majordomo.

Here's the Titanic implementation. This server handles the three services using three threads, as proposed. It does full persistence to disk using the most brutal approach possible: one file per message. It's so simple, it's scary. The only complex part is that it keeps a separate queue of all requests, to avoid reading the directory over and over:

Example 53. Titanic broker example (titanic.c)

```c
//  Titanic service
//  Implements server side of http://rfc.zeromq.org/spec:9

//  Lets us build this source without creating a library
#include "mdwrkapi.c"
#include "mdcliapi.c"

#include "zfile.h"
#include <uuid/uuid.h>

//  Return a new UUID as a printable character string
//  Caller must free returned string when finished with it

static char *
s_generate_uuid (void)
{
    char hex_char [] = "0123456789ABCDEF";
    char *uuidstr = zmalloc (sizeof (uuid_t) * 2 + 1);
    uuid_t uuid;
    uuid_generate (uuid);
    int byte_nbr;
    for (byte_nbr = 0; byte_nbr < sizeof (uuid_t); byte_nbr++) {
        uuidstr [byte_nbr * 2 + 0] = hex_char [uuid [byte_nbr] >> 4];
        uuidstr [byte_nbr * 2 + 1] = hex_char [uuid [byte_nbr] & 15];
    }
    return uuidstr;
}

//  Returns freshly allocated request filename for given UUID

#define TITANIC_DIR ".titanic"

static char *
s_request_filename (char *uuid) {
    char *filename = malloc (256);
    snprintf (filename, 256, TITANIC_DIR "/%s.req", uuid);
    return filename;
}

//  Returns freshly allocated reply filename for given UUID

static char *
s_reply_filename (char *uuid) {
```

```
    char *filename = malloc (256);
    snprintf (filename, 256, TITANIC_DIR "/%s.rep", uuid);
    return filename;
}
```

The titanic.request task waits for requests to this service. It writes each request to disk and returns a UUID to the client. The client picks up the reply asynchronously using the titanic.reply service:

Example 53-1. Titanic broker example (titanic.c) - Titanic request service

```
static void
titanic_request (void *args, zctx_t *ctx, void *pipe)
{
    mdwrk_t *worker = mdwrk_new (
        "tcp://localhost:5555", "titanic.request", 0);
    zmsg_t *reply = NULL;

    while (true) {
        //  Send reply if it's not null
        //  And then get next request from broker
        zmsg_t *request = mdwrk_recv (worker, &reply);
        if (!request)
            break;      //  Interrupted, exit

        //  Ensure message directory exists
        zfile_mkdir (TITANIC_DIR);

        //  Generate UUID and save message to disk
        char *uuid = s_generate_uuid ();
        char *filename = s_request_filename (uuid);
        FILE *file = fopen (filename, "w");
        assert (file);
        zmsg_save (request, file);
        fclose (file);
        free (filename);
        zmsg_destroy (&request);

        //  Send UUID through to message queue
        reply = zmsg_new ();
        zmsg_addstr (reply, uuid);
        zmsg_send (&reply, pipe);

        //  Now send UUID back to client
        //  Done by the mdwrk_recv() at the top of the loop
        reply = zmsg_new ();
        zmsg_addstr (reply, "200");
        zmsg_addstr (reply, uuid);
        free (uuid);
    }
```

```
        mdwrk_destroy (&worker);
}
```

The `titanic.reply` task checks if there's a reply for the specified request (by UUID), and returns a 200 (OK), 300 (Pending), or 400 (Unknown) accordingly:

Example 53-2. Titanic broker example (titanic.c) - Titanic reply service

```
static void *
titanic_reply (void *context)
{
    mdwrk_t *worker = mdwrk_new (
        "tcp://localhost:5555", "titanic.reply", 0);
    zmsg_t *reply = NULL;

    while (true) {
        zmsg_t *request = mdwrk_recv (worker, &reply);
        if (!request)
            break;      //  Interrupted, exit

        char *uuid = zmsg_popstr (request);
        char *req_filename = s_request_filename (uuid);
        char *rep_filename = s_reply_filename (uuid);
        if (zfile_exists (rep_filename)) {
            FILE *file = fopen (rep_filename, "r");
            assert (file);
            reply = zmsg_load (NULL, file);
            zmsg_pushstr (reply, "200");
            fclose (file);
        }
        else {
            reply = zmsg_new ();
            if (zfile_exists (req_filename))
                zmsg_pushstr (reply, "300"); //Pending
            else
                zmsg_pushstr (reply, "400"); //Unknown
        }
        zmsg_destroy (&request);
        free (uuid);
        free (req_filename);
        free (rep_filename);
    }
    mdwrk_destroy (&worker);
    return 0;
}
```

The `titanic.close` task removes any waiting replies for the request (specified by UUID). It's idempotent, so it is safe to call more than once in a row:

Example 53-3. Titanic broker example (titanic.c) - Titanic close task

```c
static void *
titanic_close (void *context)
{
    mdwrk_t *worker = mdwrk_new (
        "tcp://localhost:5555", "titanic.close", 0);
    zmsg_t *reply = NULL;

    while (true) {
        zmsg_t *request = mdwrk_recv (worker, &reply);
        if (!request)
            break;      //  Interrupted, exit

        char *uuid = zmsg_popstr (request);
        char *req_filename = s_request_filename (uuid);
        char *rep_filename = s_reply_filename (uuid);
        zfile_delete (req_filename);
        zfile_delete (rep_filename);
        free (uuid);
        free (req_filename);
        free (rep_filename);

        zmsg_destroy (&request);
        reply = zmsg_new ();
        zmsg_addstr (reply, "200");
    }
    mdwrk_destroy (&worker);
    return 0;
}
```

This is the main thread for the Titanic worker. It starts three child threads; for the request, reply, and close services. It then dispatches requests to workers using a simple brute force disk queue. It receives request UUIDs from the `titanic.request` service, saves these to a disk file, and then throws each request at MDP workers until it gets a response.

Example 53-4. Titanic broker example (titanic.c) - worker task

```c
static int s_service_success (char *uuid);

int main (int argc, char *argv [])
{
    int verbose = (argc > 1 && streq (argv [1], "-v"));
    zctx_t *ctx = zctx_new ();

    void *request_pipe = zthread_fork (ctx, titanic_request, NULL);
    zthread_new (titanic_reply, NULL);
```

```
        zthread_new (titanic_close, NULL);

    //  Main dispatcher loop
    while (true) {
        //  We'll dispatch once per second, if there's no activity
        zmq_pollitem_t items [] = { { request_pipe, 0, ZMQ_POLLIN, 0 } };
        int rc = zmq_poll (items, 1, 1000 * ZMQ_POLL_MSEC);
        if (rc == -1)
            break;              //  Interrupted
        if (items [0].revents & ZMQ_POLLIN) {
            //  Ensure message directory exists
            zfile_mkdir (TITANIC_DIR);

            //  Append UUID to queue, prefixed with '-' for pending
            zmsg_t *msg = zmsg_recv (request_pipe);
            if (!msg)
                break;          //  Interrupted
            FILE *file = fopen (TITANIC_DIR "/queue", "a");
            char *uuid = zmsg_popstr (msg);
            fprintf (file, "-%s\n", uuid);
            fclose (file);
            free (uuid);
            zmsg_destroy (&msg);
        }
        //  Brute force dispatcher
        char entry [] = "?.......:.......:.......:.......:";
        FILE *file = fopen (TITANIC_DIR "/queue", "r+");
        while (file && fread (entry, 33, 1, file) == 1) {
            //  UUID is prefixed with '-' if still waiting
            if (entry [0] == '-') {
                if (verbose)
                    printf ("I: processing request %s\n", entry + 1);
                if (s_service_success (entry + 1)) {
                    //  Mark queue entry as processed
                    fseek (file, -33, SEEK_CUR);
                    fwrite ("+", 1, 1, file);
                    fseek (file, 32, SEEK_CUR);
                }
            }
            //  Skip end of line, LF or CRLF
            if (fgetc (file) == '\r')
                fgetc (file);
            if (zctx_interrupted)
                break;
        }
        if (file)
            fclose (file);
    }
    return 0;
}
```

Here, we first check if the requested MDP service is defined or not, using a MMI lookup to the Majordomo broker. If the service exists, we send a request and wait for a reply using the conventional MDP client API. This is not meant to be fast, just very simple:

Example 53-5. Titanic broker example (titanic.c) - try to call a service

```
static int
s_service_success (char *uuid)
{
    // Load request message, service will be first frame
    char *filename = s_request_filename (uuid);
    FILE *file = fopen (filename, "r");
    free (filename);

    // If the client already closed request, treat as successful
    if (!file)
        return 1;

    zmsg_t *request = zmsg_load (NULL, file);
    fclose (file);
    zframe_t *service = zmsg_pop (request);
    char *service_name = zframe_strdup (service);

    // Create MDP client session with short timeout
    mdcli_t *client = mdcli_new ("tcp://localhost:5555", FALSE);
    mdcli_set_timeout (client, 1000);   //  1 sec
    mdcli_set_retries (client, 1);      //  only 1 retry

    // Use MMI protocol to check if service is available
    zmsg_t *mmi_request = zmsg_new ();
    zmsg_add (mmi_request, service);
    zmsg_t *mmi_reply = mdcli_send (client, "mmi.service", &mmi_request);
    int service_ok = (mmi_reply
        && zframe_streq (zmsg_first (mmi_reply), "200"));
    zmsg_destroy (&mmi_reply);

    int result = 0;
    if (service_ok) {
        zmsg_t *reply = mdcli_send (client, service_name, &request);
        if (reply) {
            filename = s_reply_filename (uuid);
            FILE *file = fopen (filename, "w");
            assert (file);
            zmsg_save (reply, file);
            fclose (file);
            free (filename);
            result = 1;
        }
        zmsg_destroy (&reply);
```

```
    }
    else
        zmsg_destroy (&request);

    mdcli_destroy (&client);
    free (service_name);
    return result;
}
```

To test this, start `mdbroker` and `titanic`, and then run `ticlient`. Now start `mdworker` arbitrarily, and you should see the client getting a response and exiting happily.

Some notes about this code:

- Note that some loops start by sending, others by receiving messages. This is because Titanic acts both as a client and a worker in different roles.

- We send requests only to services that appear to be running, using MMI. This works as well as the MMI implementation in the broker.

- We use an inproc connection to send new request data from the `titanic.request` service through to the main dispatcher. This saves the dispatcher from having to scan the disk directory, load all request files, and sort them by date/time.

The important thing about this example is not performance (which, although I haven't tested it, is surely terrible), but how well it implements the reliability contract. To try it, start the mdbroker and titanic programs. Then start the ticlient, and then start the mdworker echo service. You can run all four of these using the -v option to do verbose activity tracing. You can stop and restart any piece *except the client* and nothing will get lost.

If you want to use Titanic in real cases, you'll rapidly be asking "how do we make this faster?"

Here's what I'd do, starting with the example implementation:

- Use a single disk file for all data, rather than multiple files. Operating systems are usually better at handling a few large files than many smaller ones.

- Organize that disk file as a circular buffer so that new requests can be written contiguously (with very occasional wraparound). One thread, writing full speed to a disk file, can work rapidly.

- Keep the index in memory and rebuild the index at startup time, from the disk buffer. This saves the extra disk head flutter needed to keep the index fully safe on disk. You would want an fsync after every message, or every N milliseconds if you were prepared to lose the last M messages in case of a system failure.

- Use a solid-state drive rather than spinning iron oxide platters.

- Pre-allocate the entire file, or allocate it in large chunks, which allows the circular buffer to grow and shrink as needed. This avoids fragmentation and ensures that most reads and writes are contiguous.

And so on. What I'd not recommend is storing messages in a database, not even a "fast" key/value store, unless you really like a specific database and don't have performance worries. You will pay a steep price for the abstraction, ten to a thousand times over a raw disk file.

If you want to make Titanic *even more reliable*, duplicate the requests to a second server, which you'd place in a second location just far away enough to survive a nuclear attack on your primary location, yet not so far that you get too much latency.

If you want to make Titanic *much faster and less reliable*, store requests and replies purely in memory. This will give you the functionality of a disconnected network, but requests won't survive a crash of the Titanic server itself.

High-Availability Pair (Binary Star Pattern)

The Binary Star pattern puts two servers in a primary-backup high-availability pair (see figure 52). At any given time, one of these (the active) accepts connections from client applications. The other (the passive) does nothing, but the two servers monitor each other. If the active disappears from the network, after a certain time the passive takes over as active.

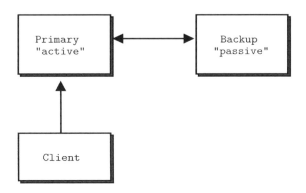

Figure 52. High-Availability Pair, Normal Operation

We developed the Binary Star pattern at iMatix for our OpenAMQ server[20]. We designed it:

- To provide a straightforward high-availability solution.
- To be simple enough to actually understand and use.
- To fail over reliably when needed, and only when needed.

Assuming we have a Binary Star pair running, here are the different scenarios that will result in a failover (see figure 53):

- The hardware running the primary server has a fatal problem (power supply explodes, machine catches fire, or someone simply unplugs it by mistake), and disappears. Applications see this, and reconnect to the backup server.
- The network segment on which the primary server sits crashes—perhaps a router gets hit by a power spike—and applications start to reconnect to the backup server.
- The primary server crashes or is killed by the operator and does not restart automatically.

---

20 http://www.openamq.org

Recovery from failover works as follows:

- The operators restart the primary server and fix whatever problems were causing it to disappear from the network.
- The operators stop the backup server at a moment when it will cause minimal disruption to applications.
- When applications have reconnected to the primary server, the operators restart the backup server.

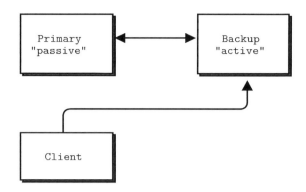

Figure 53. High-availability Pair During Failover

Recovery (to using the primary server as active) is a manual operation. Painful experience teaches us that automatic recovery is undesirable. There are several reasons:

- Failover creates an interruption of service to applications, possibly lasting 10-30 seconds. If there is a real emergency, this is much better than total outage. But if recovery creates a further 10-30 second outage, it is better that this happens off-peak, when users have gone off the network.
- When there is an emergency, the absolute first priority is certainty for those trying to fix things. Automatic recovery creates uncertainty for system administrators, who can no longer be sure which server is in charge without double-checking.
- Automatic recovery can create situations where networks fail over and then recover, placing operators in the difficult position of analyzing what happened. There was an interruption of service, but the cause isn't clear.

Having said this, the Binary Star pattern will fail back to the primary server if this is running (again) and the backup server fails. In fact, this is how we provoke recovery.

The shutdown process for a Binary Star pair is to either:

1. Stop the passive server and then stop the active server at any later time, or
2. Stop both servers in any order but within a few seconds of each other.

Stopping the active and then the passive server with any delay longer than the failover timeout will cause applications to disconnect, then reconnect, and then disconnect again, which may disturb users.

Detailed Requirements

Binary Star is as simple as it can be, while still working accurately. In fact, the current design is the third complete redesign. Each of the previous designs we found to be too complex, trying to do too much, and we stripped out functionality until we came to a design that was understandable, easy to use, and reliable enough to be worth using.

These are our requirements for a high-availability architecture:

- The failover is meant to provide insurance against catastrophic system failures, such as hardware breakdown, fire, accident, and so on. There are simpler ways to recover from ordinary server crashes and we already covered these.
- Failover time should be under 60 seconds and preferably under 10 seconds.
- Failover has to happen automatically, whereas recovery must happen manually. We want applications to switch over to the backup server automatically, but we do not want them to switch back to the primary server except when the operators have fixed whatever problem there was and decided that it is a good time to interrupt applications again.
- The semantics for client applications should be simple and easy for developers to understand. Ideally, they should be hidden in the client API.
- There should be clear instructions for network architects on how to avoid designs that could lead to *split brain syndrome*, in which both servers in a Binary Star pair think they are the active server.
- There should be no dependencies on the order in which the two servers are started.
- It must be possible to make planned stops and restarts of either server without stopping client applications (though they may be forced to reconnect).
- Operators must be able to monitor both servers at all times.
- It must be possible to connect the two servers using a high-speed dedicated network connection. That is, failover synchronization must be able to use a specific IP route.

We make the following assumptions:

- A single backup server provides enough insurance; we don't need multiple levels of backup.
- The primary and backup servers are equally capable of carrying the application load. We do not attempt to balance load across the servers.
- There is sufficient budget to cover a fully redundant backup server that does nothing almost all the time.

We don't attempt to cover the following:

- The use of an active backup server or load balancing. In a Binary Star pair, the backup server is inactive and does no useful work until the primary server goes offline.
- The handling of persistent messages or transactions in any way. We assume the existence of a network of unreliable (and probably untrusted) servers or Binary Star pairs.

- Any automatic exploration of the network. The Binary Star pair is manually and explicitly defined in the network and is known to applications (at least in their configuration data).
- Replication of state or messages between servers. All server-side state must be recreated by applications when they fail over.

Here is the key terminology that we use in Binary Star:

- *Primary*: the server that is normally or initially active.
- *Backup*: the server that is normally passive. It will become active if and when the primary server disappears from the network, and when client applications ask the backup server to connect.
- *Active*: the server that accepts client connections. There is at most one active server.
- *Passive*: the server that takes over if the active disappears. Note that when a Binary Star pair is running normally, the primary server is active, and the backup is passive. When a failover has happened, the roles are switched.

To configure a Binary Star pair, you need to:

1. Tell the primary server where the backup server is located.
2. Tell the backup server where the primary server is located.
3. Optionally, tune the failover response times, which must be the same for both servers.

The main tuning concern is how frequently you want the servers to check their peering status, and how quickly you want to activate failover. In our example, the failover timeout value defaults to 2,000 msec. If you reduce this, the backup server will take over as active more rapidly but may take over in cases where the primary server could recover. For example, you may have wrapped the primary server in a shell script that restarts it if it crashes. In that case, the timeout should be higher than the time needed to restart the primary server.

For client applications to work properly with a Binary Star pair, they must:

1. Know both server addresses.
2. Try to connect to the primary server, and if that fails, to the backup server.
3. Detect a failed connection, typically using heartbeating.
4. Try to reconnect to the primary, and then backup (in that order), with a delay between retries that is at least as high as the server failover timeout.
5. Recreate all of the state they require on a server.
6. Retransmit messages lost during a failover, if messages need to be reliable.

It's not trivial work, and we'd usually wrap this in an API that hides it from real end-user applications.

These are the main limitations of the Binary Star pattern:

- A server process cannot be part of more than one Binary Star pair.

- A primary server can have a single backup server, and no more.
- The passive server does no useful work, and is thus wasted.
- The backup server must be capable of handling full application loads.
- Failover configuration cannot be modified at runtime.
- Client applications must do some work to benefit from failover.

Preventing Split-Brain Syndrome

Split-brain syndrome occurs when different parts of a cluster think they are active at the same time. It causes applications to stop seeing each other. Binary Star has an algorithm for detecting and eliminating split brain, which is based on a three-way decision mechanism (a server will not decide to become active until it gets application connection requests and it cannot see its peer server).

However, it is still possible to (mis)design a network to fool this algorithm. A typical scenario would be a Binary Star pair, that is distributed between two buildings, where each building also had a set of applications and where there was a single network link between both buildings. Breaking this link would create two sets of client applications, each with half of the Binary Star pair, and each failover server would become active.

To prevent split-brain situations, we must connect a Binary Star pair using a dedicated network link, which can be as simple as plugging them both into the same switch or, better, using a crossover cable directly between two machines.

We must not split a Binary Star architecture into two islands, each with a set of applications. While this may be a common type of network architecture, you should use federation, not high-availability failover, in such cases.

A suitably paranoid network configuration would use two private cluster interconnects, rather than a single one. Further, the network cards used for the cluster would be different from those used for message traffic, and possibly even on different paths on the server hardware. The goal is to separate possible failures in the network from possible failures in the cluster. Network ports can have a relatively high failure rate.

Binary Star Implementation

Without further ado, here is a proof-of-concept implementation of the Binary Star server. The primary and backup servers run the same code, you choose their roles when you run the code:

Example 54. Binary Star server (bstarsrv.c)

```
//  Binary Star server proof-of-concept implementation. This server does no
//  real work; it just demonstrates the Binary Star failover model.

#include "czmq.h"

//  States we can be in at any point in time
```

```
typedef enum {
    STATE_PRIMARY = 1,          //  Primary, waiting for peer to connect
    STATE_BACKUP  = 2,          //  Backup, waiting for peer to connect
    STATE_ACTIVE  = 3,          //  Active - accepting connections
    STATE_PASSIVE = 4           //  Passive - not accepting connections
} state_t;

// Events, which start with the states our peer can be in
typedef enum {
    PEER_PRIMARY = 1,           //  HA peer is pending primary
    PEER_BACKUP  = 2,           //  HA peer is pending backup
    PEER_ACTIVE  = 3,           //  HA peer is active
    PEER_PASSIVE = 4,           //  HA peer is passive
    CLIENT_REQUEST = 5          //  Client makes request
} event_t;

// Our finite state machine
typedef struct {
    state_t state;              //  Current state
    event_t event;              //  Current event
    int64_t peer_expiry;        //  When peer is considered 'dead'
} bstar_t;

// We send state information this often
// If peer doesn't respond in two heartbeats, it is 'dead'
#define HEARTBEAT 1000          //  In msecs
```

The heart of the Binary Star design is its finite-state machine (FSM). The FSM runs one event at a time. We apply an event to the current state, which checks if the event is accepted, and if so, sets a new state:

Example 54-1. Binary Star server (bstarsrv.c) - Binary Star state machine

```
static Bool
s_state_machine (bstar_t *fsm)
{
    Bool exception = FALSE;

    //  These are the PRIMARY and BACKUP states; we're waiting to become
    //  ACTIVE or PASSIVE depending on events we get from our peer:
    if (fsm->state == STATE_PRIMARY) {
        if (fsm->event == PEER_BACKUP) {
            printf ("I: connected to backup (passive), ready active\n");
            fsm->state = STATE_ACTIVE;
        }
        else
        if (fsm->event == PEER_ACTIVE) {
            printf ("I: connected to backup (active), ready passive\n");
            fsm->state = STATE_PASSIVE;
        }
        //  Accept client connections
```

```
        }
        else
        if (fsm->state == STATE_BACKUP) {
            if (fsm->event == PEER_ACTIVE) {
                printf ("I: connected to primary (active), ready passive\n");
                fsm->state = STATE_PASSIVE;
            }
            else
            //  Reject client connections when acting as backup
            if (fsm->event == CLIENT_REQUEST)
                exception = TRUE;
        }
        else
```

These are the ACTIVE and PASSIVE states:

Example 54-2. Binary Star server (bstarsrv.c) - active and passive states

```
        if (fsm->state == STATE_ACTIVE) {
            if (fsm->event == PEER_ACTIVE) {
                //  Two actives would mean split-brain
                printf ("E: fatal error - dual actives, aborting\n");
                exception = TRUE;
            }
        }
        else
        //  Server is passive
        //  CLIENT_REQUEST events can trigger failover if peer looks dead
        if (fsm->state == STATE_PASSIVE) {
            if (fsm->event == PEER_PRIMARY) {
                //  Peer is restarting - become active, peer will go passive
                printf ("I: primary (passive) is restarting, ready active\n");
                fsm->state = STATE_ACTIVE;
            }
            else
            if (fsm->event == PEER_BACKUP) {
                //  Peer is restarting - become active, peer will go passive
                printf ("I: backup (passive) is restarting, ready active\n");
                fsm->state = STATE_ACTIVE;
            }
            else
            if (fsm->event == PEER_PASSIVE) {
                //  Two passives would mean cluster would be non-responsive
                printf ("E: fatal error - dual passives, aborting\n");
                exception = TRUE;
            }
            else
            if (fsm->event == CLIENT_REQUEST) {
                //  Peer becomes active if timeout has passed
                //  It's the client request that triggers the failover
                assert (fsm->peer_expiry > 0);
```

```
            if (zclock_time () >= fsm->peer_expiry) {
                //  If peer is dead, switch to the active state
                printf ("I: failover successful, ready active\n");
                fsm->state = STATE_ACTIVE;
            }
            else
                //  If peer is alive, reject connections
                exception = TRUE;
        }
    }
    return exception;
}
```

This is our main task. First we bind/connect our sockets with our peer and make sure we will get state messages correctly. We use three sockets; one to publish state, one to subscribe to state, and one for client requests/replies:

Example 54-3. Binary Star server (bstarsrv.c) - main task

```
int main (int argc, char *argv [])
{
    //  Arguments can be either of:
    //      -p  primary server, at tcp://localhost:5001
    //      -b  backup server, at tcp://localhost:5002
    zctx_t *ctx = zctx_new ();
    void *statepub = zsocket_new (ctx, ZMQ_PUB);
    void *statesub = zsocket_new (ctx, ZMQ_SUB);
    zsockopt_set_subscribe (statesub, "");
    void *frontend = zsocket_new (ctx, ZMQ_ROUTER);
    bstar_t fsm = { 0 };

    if (argc == 2 && streq (argv [1], "-p")) {
        printf ("I: Primary active, waiting for backup (passive)\n");
        zsocket_bind (frontend, "tcp://*:5001");
        zsocket_bind (statepub, "tcp://*:5003");
        zsocket_connect (statesub, "tcp://localhost:5004");
        fsm.state = STATE_PRIMARY;
    }
    else
    if (argc == 2 && streq (argv [1], "-b")) {
        printf ("I: Backup passive, waiting for primary (active)\n");
        zsocket_bind (frontend, "tcp://*:5002");
        zsocket_bind (statepub, "tcp://*:5004");
        zsocket_connect (statesub, "tcp://localhost:5003");
        fsm.state = STATE_BACKUP;
    }
    else {
        printf ("Usage: bstarsrv { -p | -b }\n");
        zctx_destroy (&ctx);
        exit (0);
    }
```

We now process events on our two input sockets, and process these events one at a time via our finite-state machine. Our "work" for a client request is simply to echo it back:

Example 54-4. Binary Star server (bstarsrv.c) - handling socket input

```
    //  Set timer for next outgoing state message
    int64_t send_state_at = zclock_time () + HEARTBEAT;
    while (!zctx_interrupted) {
        zmq_pollitem_t items [] = {
            { frontend, 0, ZMQ_POLLIN, 0 },
            { statesub, 0, ZMQ_POLLIN, 0 }
        };
        int time_left = (int) ((send_state_at - zclock_time ()));
        if (time_left < 0)
            time_left = 0;
        int rc = zmq_poll (items, 2, time_left * ZMQ_POLL_MSEC);
        if (rc == -1)
            break;              //  Context has been shut down

        if (items [0].revents & ZMQ_POLLIN) {
            //  Have a client request
            zmsg_t *msg = zmsg_recv (frontend);
            fsm.event = CLIENT_REQUEST;
            if (s_state_machine (&fsm) == FALSE)
                //  Answer client by echoing request back
                zmsg_send (&msg, frontend);
            else
                zmsg_destroy (&msg);
        }
        if (items [1].revents & ZMQ_POLLIN) {
            //  Have state from our peer, execute as event
            char *message = zstr_recv (statesub);
            fsm.event = atoi (message);
            free (message);
            if (s_state_machine (&fsm))
                break;          //  Error, so exit
            fsm.peer_expiry = zclock_time () + 2 * HEARTBEAT;
        }
        //  If we timed out, send state to peer
        if (zclock_time () >= send_state_at) {
            char message [2];
            sprintf (message, "%d", fsm.state);
            zstr_send (statepub, message);
            send_state_at = zclock_time () + HEARTBEAT;
        }
    }
    if (zctx_interrupted)
        printf ("W: interrupted\n");

    //  Shutdown sockets and context
```

```
        zctx_destroy (&ctx);
        return 0;
}
```

And here is the client:

Example 55. Binary Star client (bstarcli.c)

```
//  Binary Star client proof-of-concept implementation. This client does no
//  real work; it just demonstrates the Binary Star failover model.

#include "czmq.h"
#define REQUEST_TIMEOUT     1000    //  msecs
#define SETTLE_DELAY        2000    //  Before failing over

int main (void)
{
    zctx_t *ctx = zctx_new ();

    char *server [] = { "tcp://localhost:5001", "tcp://localhost:5002" };
    uint server_nbr = 0;

    printf ("I: connecting to server at %s...\n", server [server_nbr]);
    void *client = zsocket_new (ctx, ZMQ_REQ);
    zsocket_connect (client, server [server_nbr]);

    int sequence = 0;
    while (!zctx_interrupted) {
        //  We send a request, then we work to get a reply
        char request [10];
        sprintf (request, "%d", ++sequence);
        zstr_send (client, request);

        int expect_reply = 1;
        while (expect_reply) {
            //  Poll socket for a reply, with timeout
            zmq_pollitem_t items [] = { { client, 0, ZMQ_POLLIN, 0 } };
            int rc = zmq_poll (items, 1, REQUEST_TIMEOUT * ZMQ_POLL_MSEC);
            if (rc == -1)
                break;          //  Interrupted
```

We use a Lazy Pirate strategy in the client. If there's no reply within our timeout, we close the socket and try again. In Binary Star, it's the client vote that decides which server is primary; the client must therefore try to connect to each server in turn:

Example 55-1. Binary Star client (bstarcli.c) - main body of client

```
            if (items [0].revents & ZMQ_POLLIN) {
                //  We got a reply from the server, must match sequence
                char *reply = zstr_recv (client);
                if (atoi (reply) == sequence) {
```

```
                printf ("I: server replied OK (%s)\n", reply);
                expect_reply = 0;
                sleep (1);   //  One request per second
            }
            else
                printf ("E: bad reply from server: %s\n", reply);
            free (reply);
        }
        else {
            printf ("W: no response from server, failing over\n");

            //  Old socket is confused; close it and open a new one
            zsocket_destroy (ctx, client);
            server_nbr = (server_nbr + 1) % 2;
            zclock_sleep (SETTLE_DELAY);
            printf ("I: connecting to server at %s...\n",
                    server [server_nbr]);
            client = zsocket_new (ctx, ZMQ_REQ);
            zsocket_connect (client, server [server_nbr]);

            //  Send request again, on new socket
            zstr_send (client, request);
        }
    }
    }
    zctx_destroy (&ctx);
    return 0;
}
```

To test Binary Star, start the servers and client in any order:

```
bstarsrv -p      # Start primary
bstarsrv -b      # Start backup
bstarcli
```

You can then provoke failover by killing the primary server, and recovery by restarting the primary and killing the backup. Note how it's the client vote that triggers failover, and recovery.

Binary star is driven by a finite state machine (see figure 54). Events are the peer state, so "Peer Active" means the other server has told us it's active. "Client Request" means we've received a client request. "Client Vote" means we've received a client request AND our peer is inactive for two heartbeats.

Note that the servers use PUB-SUB sockets for state exchange. No other socket combination will work here. PUSH and DEALER block if there is no peer ready to receive a message. PAIR does not reconnect if the peer disappears and comes back. ROUTER needs the address of the peer before it can send it a message.

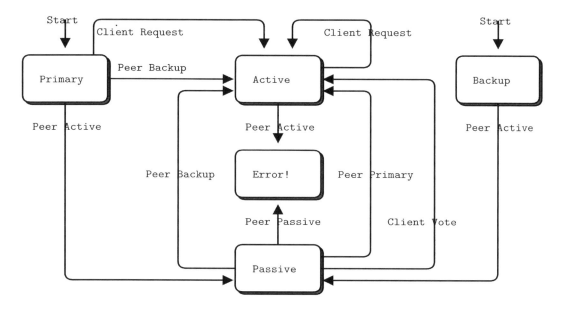

Figure 54. Binary Star Finite State Machine

Binary Star Reactor

Binary Star is useful and generic enough to package up as a reusable reactor class. The reactor then runs and calls our code whenever it has a message to process. This is much nicer than copying/pasting the Binary Star code into each server where we want that capability.

In C, we wrap the CZMQ `zloop` class that we saw before. `zloop` lets you register handlers to react on socket and timer events. In the Binary Star reactor, we provide handlers for voters and for state changes (active to passive, and vice versa). Here is the `bstar` API:

```
//  Create a new Binary Star instance, using local (bind) and
//  remote (connect) endpoints to set up the server peering.
bstar_t *bstar_new (int primary, char *local, char *remote);

//  Destroy a Binary Star instance
void bstar_destroy (bstar_t **self_p);

//  Return underlying zloop reactor, for timer and reader
//  registration and cancelation.
zloop_t *bstar_zloop (bstar_t *self);

//  Register voting reader
int bstar_voter (bstar_t *self, char *endpoint, int type,
                 zloop_fn handler, void *arg);

//  Register main state change handlers
void bstar_new_active (bstar_t *self, zloop_fn handler, void *arg);
void bstar_new_passive (bstar_t *self, zloop_fn handler, void *arg);
```

```
// Start the reactor, which ends if a callback function returns -1,
// or the process received SIGINT or SIGTERM.
int bstar_start (bstar_t *self);
```

And here is the class implementation:

Example 56. Binary Star core class (bstar.c)

```
//  bstar class - Binary Star reactor

#include "bstar.h"

//  States we can be in at any point in time
typedef enum {
    STATE_PRIMARY = 1,          //  Primary, waiting for peer to connect
    STATE_BACKUP = 2,           //  Backup, waiting for peer to connect
    STATE_ACTIVE = 3,           //  Active - accepting connections
    STATE_PASSIVE = 4           //  Passive - not accepting connections
} state_t;

//  Events, which start with the states our peer can be in
typedef enum {
    PEER_PRIMARY = 1,           //  HA peer is pending primary
    PEER_BACKUP = 2,            //  HA peer is pending backup
    PEER_ACTIVE = 3,            //  HA peer is active
    PEER_PASSIVE = 4,           //  HA peer is passive
    CLIENT_REQUEST = 5          //  Client makes request
} event_t;

//  Structure of our class

struct _bstar_t {
    zctx_t *ctx;                //  Our private context
    zloop_t *loop;              //  Reactor loop
    void *statepub;             //  State publisher
    void *statesub;             //  State subscriber
    state_t state;              //  Current state
    event_t event;              //  Current event
    int64_t peer_expiry;        //  When peer is considered 'dead'
    zloop_fn *voter_fn;         //  Voting socket handler
    void *voter_arg;            //  Arguments for voting handler
    zloop_fn *active_fn;        //  Call when become active
    void *active_arg;           //  Arguments for handler
    zloop_fn *passive_fn;       //  Call when become passive
    void *passive_arg;          //  Arguments for handler
};

//  The finite-state machine is the same as in the proof-of-concept server.
//  To understand this reactor in detail, first read the CZMQ zloop class.
...
```

This is the constructor for our bstar class. We have to tell it whether we're primary or backup server, as well as our local and remote endpoints to bind and connect to:

Example 56-1. Binary Star core class (bstar.c) - constructor

```
bstar_t *
bstar_new (int primary, char *local, char *remote)
{
    bstar_t
        *self;

    self = (bstar_t *) zmalloc (sizeof (bstar_t));

    //  Initialize the Binary Star
    self->ctx = zctx_new ();
    self->loop = zloop_new ();
    self->state = primary? STATE_PRIMARY: STATE_BACKUP;

    //  Create publisher for state going to peer
    self->statepub = zsocket_new (self->ctx, ZMQ_PUB);
    zsocket_bind (self->statepub, local);

    //  Create subscriber for state coming from peer
    self->statesub = zsocket_new (self->ctx, ZMQ_SUB);
    zsockopt_set_subscribe (self->statesub, "");
    zsocket_connect (self->statesub, remote);

    //  Set-up basic reactor events
    zloop_timer (self->loop, BSTAR_HEARTBEAT, 0, s_send_state, self);
    zmq_pollitem_t poller = { self->statesub, 0, ZMQ_POLLIN };
    zloop_poller (self->loop, &poller, s_recv_state, self);
    return self;
}
```

The destructor shuts down the bstar reactor:

Example 56-2. Binary Star core class (bstar.c) - destructor

```
void
bstar_destroy (bstar_t **self_p)
{
    assert (self_p);
    if (*self_p) {
        bstar_t *self = *self_p;
        zloop_destroy (&self->loop);
        zctx_destroy (&self->ctx);
        free (self);
        *self_p = NULL;
    }
}
```

This method returns the underlying zloop reactor, so we can add additional timers and readers:

Example 56-3. Binary Star core class (bstar.c) - zloop method

```
zloop_t *
bstar_zloop (bstar_t *self)
{
    return self->loop;
}
```

This method registers a client voter socket. Messages received on this socket provide the CLIENT_REQUEST events for the Binary Star FSM and are passed to the provided application handler. We require exactly one voter per bstar instance:

Example 56-4. Binary Star core class (bstar.c) - voter method

```
int
bstar_voter (bstar_t *self, char *endpoint, int type, zloop_fn handler,
             void *arg)
{
    // Hold actual handler+arg so we can call this later
    void *socket = zsocket_new (self->ctx, type);
    zsocket_bind (socket, endpoint);
    assert (!self->voter_fn);
    self->voter_fn = handler;
    self->voter_arg = arg;
    zmq_pollitem_t poller = { socket, 0, ZMQ_POLLIN };
    return zloop_poller (self->loop, &poller, s_voter_ready, self);
}
```

Register handlers to be called each time there's a state change:

Example 56-5. Binary Star core class (bstar.c) - register state-change handlers

```
void
bstar_new_active (bstar_t *self, zloop_fn handler, void *arg)
{
    assert (!self->active_fn);
    self->active_fn = handler;
    self->active_arg = arg;
}

void
bstar_new_passive (bstar_t *self, zloop_fn handler, void *arg)
{
    assert (!self->passive_fn);
    self->passive_fn = handler;
    self->passive_arg = arg;
}
```

Enable/disable verbose tracing, for debugging:

Example 56-6. Binary Star core class (bstar.c) - enable/disable tracing

```
void bstar_set_verbose (bstar_t *self, Bool verbose)
{
    zloop_set_verbose (self->loop, verbose);
}
```

Finally, start the configured reactor. It will end if any handler returns -1 to the reactor, or if the process receives SIGINT or SIGTERM:

Example 56-7. Binary Star core class (bstar.c) - start the reactor

```
int
bstar_start (bstar_t *self)
{
    assert (self->voter_fn);
    s_update_peer_expiry (self);
    return zloop_start (self->loop);
}
```

This gives us the following short main program for the server:

Example 57. Binary Star server, using core class (bstarsrv2.c)

```
//  Binary Star server, using bstar reactor

//  Lets us build this source without creating a library
#include "bstar.c"

//  Echo service
int s_echo (zloop_t *loop, zmq_pollitem_t *poller, void *arg)
{
    zmsg_t *msg = zmsg_recv (poller->socket);
    zmsg_send (&msg, poller->socket);
    return 0;
}

int main (int argc, char *argv [])
{
    //  Arguments can be either of:
    //      -p  primary server, at tcp://localhost:5001
    //      -b  backup server, at tcp://localhost:5002
    bstar_t *bstar;
    if (argc == 2 && streq (argv [1], "-p")) {
        printf ("I: Primary active, waiting for backup (passive)\n");
        bstar = bstar_new (BSTAR_PRIMARY,
            "tcp://*:5003", "tcp://localhost:5004");
        bstar_voter (bstar, "tcp://*:5001", ZMQ_ROUTER, s_echo, NULL);
    }
    else
```

```
        if (argc == 2 && streq (argv [1], "-b")) {
            printf ("I: Backup passive, waiting for primary (active)\n");
            bstar = bstar_new (BSTAR_BACKUP,
                "tcp://*:5004", "tcp://localhost:5003");
            bstar_voter (bstar, "tcp://*:5002", ZMQ_ROUTER, s_echo, NULL);
        }
        else {
            printf ("Usage: bstarsrvs { -p | -b }\n");
            exit (0);
        }
        bstar_start (bstar);
        bstar_destroy (&bstar);
        return 0;
    }
```

Brokerless Reliability (Freelance Pattern)

It might seem ironic to focus so much on broker-based reliability, when we often explain ØMQ as "brokerless messaging". However, in messaging, as in real life, the middleman is both a burden and a benefit. In practice, most messaging architectures benefit from a mix of distributed and brokered messaging. You get the best results when you can decide freely what trade-offs you want to make. This is why I can drive twenty minutes to a wholesaler to buy five cases of wine for a party, but I can also walk ten minutes to a corner store to buy one bottle for a dinner. Our highly context-sensitive relative valuations of time, energy, and cost are essential to the real world economy. And they are essential to an optimal message-based architecture.

This is why ØMQ does not *impose* a broker-centric architecture, though it does give you the tools to build brokers, aka *proxies*, and we've built a dozen or so different ones so far, just for practice.

So we'll end this chapter by deconstructing the broker-based reliability we've built so far, and turning it back into a distributed peer-to-peer architecture I call the Freelance pattern. Our use case will be a name resolution service. This is a common problem with ØMQ architectures: how do we know the endpoint to connect to? Hard-coding TCP/IP addresses in code is insanely fragile. Using configuration files creates an administration nightmare. Imagine if you had to hand-configure your web browser, on every PC or mobile phone you used, to realize that "google.com" was "74.125.230.82".

A ØMQ name service (and we'll make a simple implementation) must do the following:

- Resolve a logical name into at least a bind endpoint, and a connect endpoint. A realistic name service would provide multiple bind endpoints, and possibly multiple connect endpoints as well.

- Allow us to manage multiple parallel environments, e.g., "test" versus "production", without modifying code.

- Be reliable, because if it is unavailable, applications won't be able to connect to the network.

Putting a name service behind a service-oriented Majordomo broker is clever from some points of view. However, it's simpler and much less surprising to just expose the name service as a server to which clients can connect directly. If we do this right, the name service becomes the *only* global network endpoint we need to hard-code in our code or configuration files.

The types of failure we aim to handle are server crashes and restarts, server busy looping, server overload, and network issues. To get reliability, we'll create a pool of name servers so if one crashes or goes away, clients can connect to another, and so on. In practice, two would be enough. But for the example, we'll assume the pool can be any size (see figure 55).

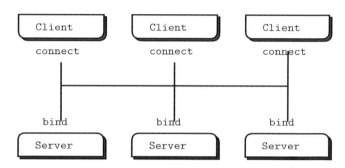

Figure 55. The Freelance Pattern

In this architecture, a large set of clients connect to a small set of servers directly. The servers bind to their respective addresses. It's fundamentally different from a broker-based approach like Majordomo, where workers connect to the broker. Clients have a couple of options:

- Use REQ sockets and the Lazy Pirate pattern. Easy, but would need some additional intelligence so clients don't stupidly try to reconnect to dead servers over and over.
- Use DEALER sockets and blast out requests (which will be load balanced to all connected servers) until they get a reply. Effective, but not elegant.
- Use ROUTER sockets so clients can address specific servers. But how does the client know the identity of the server sockets? Either the server has to ping the client first (complex), or the server has to use a hard-coded, fixed identity known to the client (nasty).

We'll develop each of these in the following subsections.

Model One: Simple Retry and Failover

So our menu appears to offer: simple, brutal, complex, or nasty. Let's start with simple and then work out the kinks. We take Lazy Pirate and rewrite it to work with multiple server endpoints.

Start one or several servers first, specifying a bind endpoint as the argument:

Example 58. Freelance server, Model One (flserver1.c)

```c
//  Freelance server - Model 1
//  Trivial echo service

#include "czmq.h"

int main (int argc, char *argv [])
{
    if (argc < 2) {
        printf ("I: syntax: %s <endpoint>\n", argv [0]);
        return 0;
    }
    zctx_t *ctx = zctx_new ();
    void *server = zsocket_new (ctx, ZMQ_REP);
    zsocket_bind (server, argv [1]);

    printf ("I: echo service is ready at %s\n", argv [1]);
    while (true) {
        zmsg_t *msg = zmsg_recv (server);
        if (!msg)
            break;              //  Interrupted
        zmsg_send (&msg, server);
    }
    if (zctx_interrupted)
        printf ("W: interrupted\n");

    zctx_destroy (&ctx);
    return 0;
}
```

Then start the client, specifying one or more connect endpoints as arguments:

Example 59. Freelance client, Model One (flclient1.c)

```c
//  Freelance client - Model 1
//  Uses REQ socket to query one or more services

#include "czmq.h"
#define REQUEST_TIMEOUT     1000
#define MAX_RETRIES         3       //  Before we abandon

static zmsg_t *
s_try_request (zctx_t *ctx, char *endpoint, zmsg_t *request)
{
    printf ("I: trying echo service at %s...\n", endpoint);
    void *client = zsocket_new (ctx, ZMQ_REQ);
    zsocket_connect (client, endpoint);
```

```
    //  Send request, wait safely for reply
    zmsg_t *msg = zmsg_dup (request);
    zmsg_send (&msg, client);
    zmq_pollitem_t items [] = { { client, 0, ZMQ_POLLIN, 0 } };
    zmq_poll (items, 1, REQUEST_TIMEOUT * ZMQ_POLL_MSEC);
    zmsg_t *reply = NULL;
    if (items [0].revents & ZMQ_POLLIN)
        reply = zmsg_recv (client);

    //  Close socket in any case, we're done with it now
    zsocket_destroy (ctx, client);
    return reply;
}
```

The client uses a Lazy Pirate strategy if it only has one server to talk to. If it has two or more servers to talk to, it will try each server just once:

Example 59-1. Freelance client, Model One (flclient1.c) - client task

```
int main (int argc, char *argv [])
{
    zctx_t *ctx = zctx_new ();
    zmsg_t *request = zmsg_new ();
    zmsg_addstr (request, "Hello world");
    zmsg_t *reply = NULL;

    int endpoints = argc - 1;
    if (endpoints == 0)
        printf ("I: syntax: %s <endpoint> ...\n", argv [0]);
    else
    if (endpoints == 1) {
        //  For one endpoint, we retry N times
        int retries;
        for (retries = 0; retries < MAX_RETRIES; retries++) {
            char *endpoint = argv [1];
            reply = s_try_request (ctx, endpoint, request);
            if (reply)
                break;          //  Successful
            printf ("W: no response from %s, retrying...\n", endpoint);
        }
    }
    else {
        //  For multiple endpoints, try each at most once
        int endpoint_nbr;
        for (endpoint_nbr = 0; endpoint_nbr < endpoints; endpoint_nbr++) {
            char *endpoint = argv [endpoint_nbr + 1];
            reply = s_try_request (ctx, endpoint, request);
            if (reply)
                break;          //  Successful
            printf ("W: no response from %s\n", endpoint);
        }
```

```
        }
        if (reply)
            printf ("Service is running OK\n");

        zmsg_destroy (&request);
        zmsg_destroy (&reply);
        zctx_destroy (&ctx);
        return 0;
    }
```

A sample run is:

```
flserver1 tcp://*:5555 &
flserver1 tcp://*:5556 &
flclient1 tcp://localhost:5555 tcp://localhost:5556
```

Although the basic approach is Lazy Pirate, the client aims to just get one successful reply. It has two techniques, depending on whether you are running a single server or multiple servers:

- With a single server, the client will retry several times, exactly as for Lazy Pirate.
- With multiple servers, the client will try each server at most once until it's received a reply or has tried all servers.

This solves the main weakness of Lazy Pirate, namely that it could not fail over to backup or alternate servers.

However, this design won't work well in a real application. If we're connecting many sockets and our primary name server is down, we're going to experience this painful timeout each time.

Model Two: Brutal Shotgun Massacre

Let's switch our client to using a DEALER socket. Our goal here is to make sure we get a reply back within the shortest possible time, no matter whether a particular server is up or down. Our client takes this approach:

- We set things up, connecting to all servers.
- When we have a request, we blast it out as many times as we have servers.
- We wait for the first reply, and take that.
- We ignore any other replies.

What will happen in practice is that when all servers are running, ØMQ will distribute the requests so that each server gets one request and sends one reply. When any server is offline and disconnected, ØMQ will distribute the requests to the remaining servers. So a server may in some cases get the same request more than once.

What's more annoying for the client is that we'll get multiple replies back, but there's no guarantee we'll get a precise number of replies. Requests and replies can get lost (e.g., if the server crashes while processing a request).

So we have to number requests and ignore any replies that don't match the request number. Our Model One server will work because it's an echo server, but coincidence is not a great basis for understanding. So we'll make a Model Two server that chews up the message and returns a correctly numbered reply with the content "OK". We'll use messages consisting of two parts: a sequence number and a body.

Start one or more servers, specifying a bind endpoint each time:

Example 60. Freelance server, Model Two (flserver2.c)

```c
//  Freelance server - Model 2
//  Does some work, replies OK, with message sequencing

#include "czmq.h"

int main (int argc, char *argv [])
{
    if (argc < 2) {
        printf ("I: syntax: %s <endpoint>\n", argv [0]);
        return 0;
    }
    zctx_t *ctx = zctx_new ();
    void *server = zsocket_new (ctx, ZMQ_REP);
    zsocket_bind (server, argv [1]);

    printf ("I: service is ready at %s\n", argv [1]);
    while (true) {
        zmsg_t *request = zmsg_recv (server);
        if (!request)
            break;          //  Interrupted
        //  Fail nastily if run against wrong client
        assert (zmsg_size (request) == 2);

        zframe_t *identity = zmsg_pop (request);
        zmsg_destroy (&request);

        zmsg_t *reply = zmsg_new ();
        zmsg_add (reply, identity);
        zmsg_addstr (reply, "OK");
        zmsg_send (&reply, server);
    }
    if (zctx_interrupted)
        printf ("W: interrupted\n");

    zctx_destroy (&ctx);
    return 0;
}
```

Then start the client, specifying the connect endpoints as arguments:

Example 61. Freelance client, Model Two (flclient2.c)

```
//  Freelance client - Model 2
//  Uses DEALER socket to blast one or more services

#include "czmq.h"

//  We design our client API as a class, using the CZMQ style
#ifdef __cplusplus
extern "C" {
#endif

typedef struct _flclient_t flclient_t;
flclient_t *flclient_new (void);
void        flclient_destroy (flclient_t **self_p);
void        flclient_connect (flclient_t *self, char *endpoint);
zmsg_t     *flclient_request (flclient_t *self, zmsg_t **request_p);

#ifdef __cplusplus
}
#endif

//  If not a single service replies within this time, give up
#define GLOBAL_TIMEOUT 2500

int main (int argc, char *argv [])
{
    if (argc == 1) {
        printf ("I: syntax: %s <endpoint> ...\n", argv [0]);
        return 0;
    }
    //  Create new freelance client object
    flclient_t *client = flclient_new ();

    //  Connect to each endpoint
    int argn;
    for (argn = 1; argn < argc; argn++)
        flclient_connect (client, argv [argn]);

    //  Send a bunch of name resolution 'requests', measure time
    int requests = 10000;
    uint64_t start = zclock_time ();
    while (requests--) {
        zmsg_t *request = zmsg_new ();
        zmsg_addstr (request, "random name");
        zmsg_t *reply = flclient_request (client, &request);
        if (!reply) {
            printf ("E: name service not available, aborting\n");
            break;
```

```
            }
            zmsg_destroy (&reply);
        }
        printf ("Average round trip cost: %d usec\n",
            (int) (zclock_time () - start) / 10);

        flclient_destroy (&client);
        return 0;
    }
```

Here is the `flclient` class implementation. Each instance has a context, a DEALER socket it uses to talk to the servers, a counter of how many servers it's connected to, and a request sequence number:

Example 61-1. Freelance client, Model Two (flclient2.c) - class implementation

```
    struct _flclient_t {
        zctx_t *ctx;        // Our context wrapper
        void *socket;       // DEALER socket talking to servers
        size_t servers;     // How many servers we have connected to
        uint sequence;      // Number of requests ever sent
    };

    // Constructor

    flclient_t *
    flclient_new (void)
    {
        flclient_t
            *self;

        self = (flclient_t *) zmalloc (sizeof (flclient_t));
        self->ctx = zctx_new ();
        self->socket = zsocket_new (self->ctx, ZMQ_DEALER);
        return self;
    }

    // Destructor

    void
    flclient_destroy (flclient_t **self_p)
    {
        assert (self_p);
        if (*self_p) {
            flclient_t *self = *self_p;
            zctx_destroy (&self->ctx);
            free (self);
            *self_p = NULL;
        }
    }
```

```
//  Connect to new server endpoint

void
flclient_connect (flclient_t *self, char *endpoint)
{
    assert (self);
    zsocket_connect (self->socket, endpoint);
    self->servers++;
}
```

This method does the hard work. It sends a request to all connected servers in parallel (for this to work, all connections must be successful and completed by this time). It then waits for a single successful reply, and returns that to the caller. Any other replies are just dropped:

Example 61-2. Freelance client, Model Two (flclient2.c) - request method

```
zmsg_t *
flclient_request (flclient_t *self, zmsg_t **request_p)
{
    assert (self);
    assert (*request_p);
    zmsg_t *request = *request_p;

    // Prefix request with sequence number and empty envelope
    char sequence_text [10];
    sprintf (sequence_text, "%u", ++self->sequence);
    zmsg_pushstr (request, sequence_text);
    zmsg_pushstr (request, "");

    // Blast the request to all connected servers
    int server;
    for (server = 0; server < self->servers; server++) {
        zmsg_t *msg = zmsg_dup (request);
        zmsg_send (&msg, self->socket);
    }
    // Wait for a matching reply to arrive from anywhere
    // Since we can poll several times, calculate each one
    zmsg_t *reply = NULL;
    uint64_t endtime = zclock_time () + GLOBAL_TIMEOUT;
    while (zclock_time () < endtime) {
        zmq_pollitem_t items [] = { { self->socket, 0, ZMQ_POLLIN, 0 } };
        zmq_poll (items, 1, (endtime - zclock_time ()) * ZMQ_POLL_MSEC);
        if (items [0].revents & ZMQ_POLLIN) {
            //  Reply is [empty][sequence][OK]
            reply = zmsg_recv (self->socket);
            assert (zmsg_size (reply) == 3);
            free (zmsg_popstr (reply));
            char *sequence = zmsg_popstr (reply);
            int sequence_nbr = atoi (sequence);
            free (sequence);
```

```
                if (sequence_nbr == self->sequence)
                    break;
                zmsg_destroy (&reply);
            }
        }
        zmsg_destroy (request_p);
        return reply;
    }
```

Here are some things to note about the client implementation:

- The client is structured as a nice little class-based API that hides the dirty work of creating ØMQ contexts and sockets and talking to the server. That is, if a shotgun blast to the midriff can be called "talking".
- The client will abandon the chase if it can't find *any* responsive server within a few seconds.
- The client has to create a valid REP envelope, i.e., add an empty message frame to the front of the message.

The client performs 10,000 name resolution requests (fake ones, as our server does essentially nothing) and measures the average cost. On my test box, talking to one server, this requires about 60 microseconds. Talking to three servers, it takes about 80 microseconds.

The pros and cons of our shotgun approach are:

- Pro: it is simple, easy to make and easy to understand.
- Pro: it does the job of failover, and works rapidly, so long as there is at least one server running.
- Con: it creates redundant network traffic.
- Con: we can't prioritize our servers, i.e., Primary, then Secondary.
- Con: the server can do at most one request at a time, period.

Model Three: Complex and Nasty

The shotgun approach seems too good to be true. Let's be scientific and work through all the alternatives. We're going to explore the complex/nasty option, even if it's only to finally realize that we preferred brutal. Ah, the story of my life.

We can solve the main problems of the client by switching to a ROUTER socket. That lets us send requests to specific servers, avoid servers we know are dead, and in general be as smart as we want to be. We can also solve the main problem of the server (single-threadedness) by switching to a ROUTER socket.

But doing ROUTER to ROUTER between two anonymous sockets (which haven't set an identity) is not possible. Both sides generate an identity (for the other peer) only when they receive a first message, and thus neither can talk to the other until it has first received a message. The only way out of this conundrum is to cheat, and use hard-coded identities in one direction. The proper way to cheat, in a client/server case, is to let the client "know" the identity of the server. Doing it the other way around would be insane, on top of complex and nasty, because any number of clients should be able to arise independently. Insane, complex, and nasty are great attributes for a genocidal dictator, but terrible ones for software.

Rather than invent yet another concept to manage, we'll use the connection endpoint as identity. This is a unique string on which both sides can agree without more prior knowledge than they already have for the shotgun model. It's a sneaky and effective way to connect two ROUTER sockets.

Remember how ØMQ identities work. The server ROUTER socket sets an identity before it binds its socket. When a client connects, they do a little handshake to exchange identities, before either side sends a real message. The client ROUTER socket, having not set an identity, sends a null identity to the server. The server generates a random UUID to designate the client for its own use. The server sends its identity (which we've agreed is going to be an endpoint string) to the client.

This means that our client can route a message to the server (i.e., send on its ROUTER socket, specifying the server endpoint as identity) as soon as the connection is established. That's not *immediately* after doing a zmq_connect(), but some random time thereafter. Herein lies one problem: we don't know when the server will actually be available and complete its connection handshake. If the server is online, it could be after a few milliseconds. If the server is down and the sysadmin is out to lunch, it could be an hour from now.

There's a small paradox here. We need to know when servers become connected and available for work. In the Freelance pattern, unlike the broker-based patterns we saw earlier in this chapter, servers are silent until spoken to. Thus we can't talk to a server until it's told us it's online, which it can't do until we've asked it.

My solution is to mix in a little of the shotgun approach from model 2, meaning we'll fire (harmless) shots at anything we can, and if anything moves, we know it's alive. We're not going to fire real requests, but rather a kind of ping-pong heartbeat.

This brings us to the realm of protocols again, so here's a short spec that defines how a Freelance client and server exchange ping-pong commands and request-reply commands[21].

It is short and sweet to implement as a server. Here's our echo server, Model Three, now speaking FLP:

Example 62. Freelance server, Model Three (flserver3.c)

```
// Freelance server - Model 3
// Uses an ROUTER/ROUTER socket but just one thread

#include "czmq.h"

int main (int argc, char *argv [])
{
```

---

21 http://rfc.zeromq.org/spec:10

```c
    int verbose = (argc > 1 && streq (argv [1], "-v"));

    zctx_t *ctx = zctx_new ();

    //  Prepare server socket with predictable identity
    char *bind_endpoint = "tcp://*:5555";
    char *connect_endpoint = "tcp://localhost:5555";
    void *server = zsocket_new (ctx, ZMQ_ROUTER);
    zmq_setsockopt (server,
        ZMQ_IDENTITY, connect_endpoint, strlen (connect_endpoint));
    zsocket_bind (server, bind_endpoint);
    printf ("I: service is ready at %s\n", bind_endpoint);

    while (!zctx_interrupted) {
        zmsg_t *request = zmsg_recv (server);
        if (verbose && request)
            zmsg_dump (request);
        if (!request)
            break;              //  Interrupted

        //  Frame 0: identity of client
        //  Frame 1: PING, or client control frame
        //  Frame 2: request body
        zframe_t *identity = zmsg_pop (request);
        zframe_t *control = zmsg_pop (request);
        zmsg_t *reply = zmsg_new ();
        if (zframe_streq (control, "PING"))
            zmsg_addstr (reply, "PONG");
        else {
            zmsg_add (reply, control);
            zmsg_addstr (reply, "OK");
        }
        zmsg_destroy (&request);
        zmsg_push (reply, identity);
        if (verbose && reply)
            zmsg_dump (reply);
        zmsg_send (&reply, server);
    }
    if (zctx_interrupted)
        printf ("W: interrupted\n");

    zctx_destroy (&ctx);
    return 0;
}
```

The Freelance client, however, has gotten large. For clarity, it's split into an example application and a class that does the hard work. Here's the top-level application:

Example 63. Freelance client, Model Three (flclient3.c)

```
//  Freelance client - Model 3
//  Uses flcliapi class to encapsulate Freelance pattern

//  Lets us build this source without creating a library
#include "flcliapi.c"

int main (void)
{
    //  Create new freelance client object
    flcliapi_t *client = flcliapi_new ();

    //  Connect to several endpoints
    flcliapi_connect (client, "tcp://localhost:5555");
    flcliapi_connect (client, "tcp://localhost:5556");
    flcliapi_connect (client, "tcp://localhost:5557");

    //  Send a bunch of name resolution 'requests', measure time
    int requests = 1000;
    uint64_t start = zclock_time ();
    while (requests--) {
        zmsg_t *request = zmsg_new ();
        zmsg_addstr (request, "random name");
        zmsg_t *reply = flcliapi_request (client, &request);
        if (!reply) {
            printf ("E: name service not available, aborting\n");
            break;
        }
        zmsg_destroy (&reply);
    }
    printf ("Average round trip cost: %d usec\n",
        (int) (zclock_time () - start) / 10);

    flcliapi_destroy (&client);
    return 0;
}
```

And here, almost as complex and large as the Majordomo broker, is the client API class:

Example 64. Freelance client API (flcliapi.c)

```
//  flcliapi class - Freelance Pattern agent class
//  Implements the Freelance Protocol at http://rfc.zeromq.org/spec:10

#include "flcliapi.h"
```

```
//  If no server replies within this time, abandon request
#define GLOBAL_TIMEOUT  3000    //  msecs
//  PING interval for servers we think are alive
#define PING_INTERVAL   2000    //  msecs
//  Server considered dead if silent for this long
#define SERVER_TTL      6000    //  msecs
```

This API works in two halves, a common pattern for APIs that need to run in the background. One half is an frontend object our application creates and works with; the other half is a backend "agent" that runs in a background thread. The frontend talks to the backend over an inproc pipe socket:

Example 64-1. Freelance client API (flcliapi.c) - API structure

```
//  Structure of our frontend class

struct _flcliapi_t {
    zctx_t *ctx;        //  Our context wrapper
    void *pipe;         //  Pipe through to flcliapi agent
};

//  This is the thread that handles our real flcliapi class
static void flcliapi_agent (void *args, zctx_t *ctx, void *pipe);

//  Constructor

flcliapi_t *
flcliapi_new (void)
{
    flcliapi_t
        *self;

    self = (flcliapi_t *) zmalloc (sizeof (flcliapi_t));
    self->ctx = zctx_new ();
    self->pipe = zthread_fork (self->ctx, flcliapi_agent, NULL);
    return self;
}

//  Destructor

void
flcliapi_destroy (flcliapi_t **self_p)
{
    assert (self_p);
    if (*self_p) {
        flcliapi_t *self = *self_p;
        zctx_destroy (&self->ctx);
        free (self);
        *self_p = NULL;
    }
}
```

To implement the connect method, the frontend object sends a multipart message to the backend agent. The first part is a string "CONNECT", and the second part is the endpoint. It waits 100msec for the connection to come up, which isn't pretty, but saves us from sending all requests to a single server, at startup time:

Example 64-2. Freelance client API (flcliapi.c) - connect method

```
void
flcliapi_connect (flcliapi_t *self, char *endpoint)
{
    assert (self);
    assert (endpoint);
    zmsg_t *msg = zmsg_new ();
    zmsg_addstr (msg, "CONNECT");
    zmsg_addstr (msg, endpoint);
    zmsg_send (&msg, self->pipe);
    zclock_sleep (100);     //  Allow connection to come up
}
```

To implement the request method, the frontend object sends a message to the backend, specifying a command "REQUEST" and the request message:

Example 64-3. Freelance client API (flcliapi.c) - request method

```
zmsg_t *
flcliapi_request (flcliapi_t *self, zmsg_t **request_p)
{
    assert (self);
    assert (*request_p);

    zmsg_pushstr (*request_p, "REQUEST");
    zmsg_send (request_p, self->pipe);
    zmsg_t *reply = zmsg_recv (self->pipe);
    if (reply) {
        char *status = zmsg_popstr (reply);
        if (streq (status, "FAILED"))
            zmsg_destroy (&reply);
        free (status);
    }
    return reply;
}
```

Here we see the backend agent. It runs as an attached thread, talking to its parent over a pipe socket. It is a fairly complex piece of work so we'll break it down into pieces. First, the agent manages a set of servers, using our familiar class approach:

Example 64-4. Freelance client API (flcliapi.c) - backend agent

```
//  Simple class for one server we talk to

typedef struct {
```

```
    char *endpoint;            //  Server identity/endpoint
    uint alive;                //  1 if known to be alive
    int64_t ping_at;           //  Next ping at this time
    int64_t expires;           //  Expires at this time
} server_t;

server_t *
server_new (char *endpoint)
{
    server_t *self = (server_t *) zmalloc (sizeof (server_t));
    self->endpoint = strdup (endpoint);
    self->alive = 0;
    self->ping_at = zclock_time () + PING_INTERVAL;
    self->expires = zclock_time () + SERVER_TTL;
    return self;
}

void
server_destroy (server_t **self_p)
{
    assert (self_p);
    if (*self_p) {
        server_t *self = *self_p;
        free (self->endpoint);
        free (self);
        *self_p = NULL;
    }
}

int
server_ping (const char *key, void *server, void *socket)
{
    server_t *self = (server_t *) server;
    if (zclock_time () >= self->ping_at) {
        zmsg_t *ping = zmsg_new ();
        zmsg_addstr (ping, self->endpoint);
        zmsg_addstr (ping, "PING");
        zmsg_send (&ping, socket);
        self->ping_at = zclock_time () + PING_INTERVAL;
    }
    return 0;
}

int
server_tickless (const char *key, void *server, void *arg)
{
    server_t *self = (server_t *) server;
    uint64_t *tickless = (uint64_t *) arg;
    if (*tickless > self->ping_at)
        *tickless = self->ping_at;
```

```
        return 0;
}
```

We build the agent as a class that's capable of processing messages coming in from its various sockets:

Example 64-5. Freelance client API (flcliapi.c) - backend agent class

```
//  Simple class for one background agent

typedef struct {
    zctx_t *ctx;                //  Own context
    void *pipe;                 //  Socket to talk back to application
    void *router;               //  Socket to talk to servers
    zhash_t *servers;           //  Servers we've connected to
    zlist_t *actives;           //  Servers we know are alive
    uint sequence;              //  Number of requests ever sent
    zmsg_t *request;            //  Current request if any
    zmsg_t *reply;              //  Current reply if any
    int64_t expires;            //  Timeout for request/reply
} agent_t;

agent_t *
agent_new (zctx_t *ctx, void *pipe)
{
    agent_t *self = (agent_t *) zmalloc (sizeof (agent_t));
    self->ctx = ctx;
    self->pipe = pipe;
    self->router = zsocket_new (self->ctx, ZMQ_ROUTER);
    self->servers = zhash_new ();
    self->actives = zlist_new ();
    return self;
}

void
agent_destroy (agent_t **self_p)
{
    assert (self_p);
    if (*self_p) {
        agent_t *self = *self_p;
        zhash_destroy (&self->servers);
        zlist_destroy (&self->actives);
        zmsg_destroy (&self->request);
        zmsg_destroy (&self->reply);
        free (self);
        *self_p = NULL;
    }
}
```

This method processes one message from our frontend class (it's going to be CONNECT or REQUEST):

Example 64-6. Freelance client API (flcliapi.c) - control messages

```c
//  Callback when we remove server from agent 'servers' hash table

static void
s_server_free (void *argument)
{
    server_t *server = (server_t *) argument;
    server_destroy (&server);
}

void
agent_control_message (agent_t *self)
{
    zmsg_t *msg = zmsg_recv (self->pipe);
    char *command = zmsg_popstr (msg);

    if (streq (command, "CONNECT")) {
        char *endpoint = zmsg_popstr (msg);
        printf ("I: connecting to %s...\n", endpoint);
        int rc = zmq_connect (self->router, endpoint);
        assert (rc == 0);
        server_t *server = server_new (endpoint);
        zhash_insert (self->servers, endpoint, server);
        zhash_freefn (self->servers, endpoint, s_server_free);
        zlist_append (self->actives, server);
        server->ping_at = zclock_time () + PING_INTERVAL;
        server->expires = zclock_time () + SERVER_TTL;
        free (endpoint);
    }
    else
    if (streq (command, "REQUEST")) {
        assert (!self->request);      //  Strict request-reply cycle
        //  Prefix request with sequence number and empty envelope
        char sequence_text [10];
        sprintf (sequence_text, "%u", ++self->sequence);
        zmsg_pushstr (msg, sequence_text);
        //  Take ownership of request message
        self->request = msg;
        msg = NULL;
        //  Request expires after global timeout
        self->expires = zclock_time () + GLOBAL_TIMEOUT;
    }
    free (command);
    zmsg_destroy (&msg);
}
```

This method processes one message from a connected server:

Example 64-7. Freelance client API (flcliapi.c) - router messages

```
void
agent_router_message (agent_t *self)
{
    zmsg_t *reply = zmsg_recv (self->router);

    //  Frame 0 is server that replied
    char *endpoint = zmsg_popstr (reply);
    server_t *server =
        (server_t *) zhash_lookup (self->servers, endpoint);
    assert (server);
    free (endpoint);
    if (!server->alive) {
        zlist_append (self->actives, server);
        server->alive = 1;
    }
    server->ping_at = zclock_time () + PING_INTERVAL;
    server->expires = zclock_time () + SERVER_TTL;

    //  Frame 1 may be sequence number for reply
    char *sequence = zmsg_popstr (reply);
    if (atoi (sequence) == self->sequence) {
        zmsg_pushstr (reply, "OK");
        zmsg_send (&reply, self->pipe);
        zmsg_destroy (&self->request);
    }
    else
        zmsg_destroy (&reply);
}
```

Finally, here's the agent task itself, which polls its two sockets and processes incoming messages:

Example 64-8. Freelance client API (flcliapi.c) - backend agent implementation

```
static void
flcliapi_agent (void *args, zctx_t *ctx, void *pipe)
{
    agent_t *self = agent_new (ctx, pipe);

    zmq_pollitem_t items [] = {
        { self->pipe, 0, ZMQ_POLLIN, 0 },
        { self->router, 0, ZMQ_POLLIN, 0 }
    };
    while (!zctx_interrupted) {
        //  Calculate tickless timer, up to 1 hour
        uint64_t tickless = zclock_time () + 1000 * 3600;
        if (self->request
```

```
                && tickless > self->expires)
                    tickless = self->expires;
            zhash_foreach (self->servers, server_tickless, &tickless);

            int rc = zmq_poll (items, 2,
                (tickless - zclock_time ()) * ZMQ_POLL_MSEC);
            if (rc == -1)
                break;              //  Context has been shut down

            if (items [0].revents & ZMQ_POLLIN)
                agent_control_message (self);

            if (items [1].revents & ZMQ_POLLIN)
                agent_router_message (self);

            //  If we're processing a request, dispatch to next server
            if (self->request) {
                if (zclock_time () >= self->expires) {
                    //  Request expired, kill it
                    zstr_send (self->pipe, "FAILED");
                    zmsg_destroy (&self->request);
                }
                else {
                    //  Find server to talk to, remove any expired ones
                    while (zlist_size (self->actives)) {
                        server_t *server =
                            (server_t *) zlist_first (self->actives);
                        if (zclock_time () >= server->expires) {
                            zlist_pop (self->actives);
                            server->alive = 0;
                        }
                        else {
                            zmsg_t *request = zmsg_dup (self->request);
                            zmsg_pushstr (request, server->endpoint);
                            zmsg_send (&request, self->router);
                            break;
                        }
                    }
                }
            }
            //  Disconnect and delete any expired servers
            //  Send heartbeats to idle servers if needed
            zhash_foreach (self->servers, server_ping, self->router);
        }
        agent_destroy (&self);
    }
```

This API implementation is fairly sophisticated and uses a couple of techniques that we've not seen before.

- **Multithreaded API**: the client API consists of two parts, a synchronous flcliapi class that runs in the application thread, and an asynchronous *agent* class that runs as a background thread. Remember how ØMQ makes it easy to create multithreaded apps. The flcliapi and agent classes talk to each other with messages over an inproc socket. All ØMQ aspects (such as creating and destroying a context) are hidden in the API. The agent in effect acts like a mini-broker, talking to servers in the background, so that when we make a request, it can make a best effort to reach a server it believes is available.

- **Tickless poll timer**: in previous poll loops we always used a fixed tick interval, e.g., 1 second, which is simple enough but not excellent on power-sensitive clients (such as notebooks or mobile phones), where waking the CPU costs power. For fun, and to help save the planet, the agent uses a *tickless timer*, which calculates the poll delay based on the next timeout we're expecting. A proper implementation would keep an ordered list of timeouts. We just check all timeouts and calculate the poll delay until the next one.

Conclusion

In this chapter, we've seen a variety of reliable request-reply mechanisms, each with certain costs and benefits. The example code is largely ready for real use, though it is not optimized. Of all the different patterns, the two that stand out for production use are the Majordomo pattern, for broker-based reliability, and the Freelance pattern, for brokerless reliability.

Chapter 5. Advanced Pub-Sub Patterns

In "Advanced Request-Reply Patterns" and "Reliable Request-Reply Patterns" we looked at advanced use of ØMQ's request-reply pattern. If you managed to digest all that, congratulations. In this chapter we'll focus on publish-subscribe and extend ØMQ's core pub-sub pattern with higher-level patterns for performance, reliability, state distribution, and monitoring.

We'll cover:

- When to use publish-subscribe.
- How to handle too-slow subscribers (the *Suicidal Snail* pattern).
- How to design high-speed subscribers (the *Black Box* pattern).
- How to monitor a pub-sub network (the *Espresso* pattern).
- How to build a shared key-value store (the *Clone* pattern).
- How to use reactors to simplify complex servers.
- How to use the Binary Star pattern to add failover to a server.

Pros and Cons of Pub-Sub

ØMQ's low-level patterns have their different characters. Pub-sub addresses an old messaging problem, which is *multicast* or *group messaging*. It has that unique mix of meticulous simplicity and brutal indifference that characterizes ØMQ. It's worth understanding the trade-offs that pub-sub makes, how these benefit us, and how we can work around them if needed.

First, PUB sends each message to "all of many", whereas PUSH and DEALER rotate messages to "one of many". You cannot simply replace PUSH with PUB or vice versa and hope that things will work. This bears repeating because people seem to quite often suggest doing this.

More profoundly, pub-sub is aimed at scalability. This means large volumes of data, sent rapidly to many recipients. If you need millions of messages per second sent to thousands of points, you'll appreciate pub-sub a lot more than if you need a few messages a second sent to a handful of recipients.

To get scalability, pub-sub uses the same trick as push-pull, which is to get rid of back-chatter. This means that recipients don't talk back to senders. There are some exceptions, e.g., SUB sockets will send subscriptions to PUB sockets, but it's anonymous and infrequent.

Killing back-chatter is essential to real scalability. With pub-sub, it's how the pattern can map cleanly to the PGM multicast protocol, which is handled by the network switch. In other words, subscribers don't connect to the publisher at all, they connect to a multicast *group* on the switch, to which the publisher sends its messages.

When we remove back-chatter, our overall message flow becomes *much* simpler, which lets us make simpler APIs, simpler protocols, and in general reach many more people. But we also remove any possibility to coordinate senders and receivers. What this means is:

- Publishers can't tell when subscribers are successfully connected, both on initial connections, and on reconnections after network failures.
- Subscribers can't tell publishers anything that would allow publishers to control the rate of messages they send. Publishers only have one setting, which is *full-speed*, and subscribers must either keep up or lose messages.
- Publishers can't tell when subscribers have disappeared due to processes crashing, networks breaking, and so on.

The downside is that we actually need all of these if we want to do reliable multicast. The ØMQ pub-sub pattern will lose messages arbitrarily when a subscriber is connecting, when a network failure occurs, or just if the subscriber or network can't keep up with the publisher.

The upside is that there are many use cases where *almost* reliable multicast is just fine. When we need this back-chatter, we can either switch to using ROUTER-DEALER (which I tend to do for most normal volume cases), or we can add a separate channel for synchronization (we'll see an example of this later in this chapter).

Pub-sub is like a radio broadcast; you miss everything before you join, and then how much information you get depends on the quality of your reception. Surprisingly, this model is useful and widespread because it maps perfectly to real world distribution of information. Think of Facebook and Twitter, the BBC World Service, and the sports results.

As we did for request-reply, let's define *reliability* in terms of what can go wrong. Here are the classic failure cases for pub-sub:

- Subscribers join late, so they miss messages the server already sent.
- Subscribers can fetch messages too slowly, so queues build up and then overflow.
- Subscribers can drop off and lose messages while they are away.
- Subscribers can crash and restart, and lose whatever data they already received.
- Networks can become overloaded and drop data (specifically, for PGM).
- Networks can become too slow, so publisher-side queues overflow and publishers crash.

A lot more can go wrong but these are the typical failures we see in a realistic system. Since v3.x, ØMQ forces default limits on its internal buffers (the so-called high-water mark or HWM), so publisher crashes are rarer unless you deliberately set the HWM to infinite.

All of these failure cases have answers, though not always simple ones. Reliability requires complexity that most of us don't need, most of the time, which is why ØMQ doesn't attempt to provide it out of the box (even if there was one global design for reliability, which there isn't).

Pub-Sub Tracing (Espresso Pattern)

Let's start this chapter by looking at a way to trace pub-sub networks. In "Sockets and Patterns" we saw a simple proxy that used these to do transport bridging. The zmq_proxy() method has three arguments: a *frontend* and *backend* socket that it bridges together, and a *capture* socket to which it will send all messages.

The code is deceptively simple:

Example 65. Espresso Pattern (espresso.c)

```
//  Espresso Pattern
//  This shows how to capture data using a pub-sub proxy

#include "czmq.h"

//  The subscriber thread requests messages starting with
//  A and B, then reads and counts incoming messages.

static void
subscriber_thread (void *args, zctx_t *ctx, void *pipe)
{
    //  Subscribe to "A" and "B"
    void *subscriber = zsocket_new (ctx, ZMQ_SUB);
    zsocket_connect (subscriber, "tcp://localhost:6001");
    zsockopt_set_subscribe (subscriber, "A");
    zsockopt_set_subscribe (subscriber, "B");

    int count = 0;
    while (count < 5) {
        char *string = zstr_recv (subscriber);
        if (!string)
            break;              //  Interrupted
        free (string);
        count++;
    }
    zsocket_destroy (ctx, subscriber);
}
```

The publisher sends random messages starting with A-J:

Example 65-1. Espresso Pattern (espresso.c) - publisher thread

```
static void
publisher_thread (void *args, zctx_t *ctx, void *pipe)
{
    void *publisher = zsocket_new (ctx, ZMQ_PUB);
    zsocket_bind (publisher, "tcp://*:6000");

    while (!zctx_interrupted) {
        char string [10];
        sprintf (string, "%c-%05d", randof (10) + 'A', randof (100000));
        if (zstr_send (publisher, string) == -1)
            break;              //  Interrupted
        zclock_sleep (100);     //  Wait for 1/10th second
    }
}
```

The listener receives all messages flowing through the proxy, on its pipe. In CZMQ, the pipe is a pair of ZMQ_PAIR sockets that connect attached child threads. In other languages your mileage may vary:

Example 65-2. Espresso Pattern (espresso.c) - listener thread

```
static void
listener_thread (void *args, zctx_t *ctx, void *pipe)
{
    //  Print everything that arrives on pipe
    while (true) {
        zframe_t *frame = zframe_recv (pipe);
        if (!frame)
            break;              //  Interrupted
        zframe_print (frame, NULL);
        zframe_destroy (&frame);
    }
}
```

The main task starts the subscriber and publisher, and then sets itself up as a listening proxy. The listener runs as a child thread:

Example 65-3. Espresso Pattern (espresso.c) - main thread

```
int main (void)
{
    //  Start child threads
    zctx_t *ctx = zctx_new ();
    zthread_fork (ctx, publisher_thread, NULL);
    zthread_fork (ctx, subscriber_thread, NULL);

    void *subscriber = zsocket_new (ctx, ZMQ_XSUB);
    zsocket_connect (subscriber, "tcp://localhost:6000");
```

```
        void *publisher = zsocket_new (ctx, ZMQ_XPUB);
        zsocket_bind (publisher, "tcp://*:6001");
        void *listener = zthread_fork (ctx, listener_thread, NULL);
        zmq_proxy (subscriber, publisher, listener);

        puts (" interrupted");
        //  Tell attached threads to exit
        zctx_destroy (&ctx);
        return 0;
}
```

Espresso works by creating a listener thread that reads a PAIR socket and prints anything it gets. That PAIR socket is one end of a pipe; the other end (another PAIR) is the socket we pass to `zmq_proxy()`. In practice, you'd filter interesting messages to get the essence of what you want to track (hence the name of the pattern).

The subscriber thread subscribes to "A" and "B", receives five messages, and then destroys its socket. When you run the example, the listener prints two subscription messages, five data messages, two unsubscribe messages, and then silence:

```
[002] 0141
[002] 0142
[007] B-91164
[007] B-12979
[007] A-52599
[007] A-06417
[007] A-45770
[002] 0041
[002] 0042
```

This shows neatly how the publisher socket stops sending data when there are no subscribers for it. The publisher thread is still sending messages. The socket just drops them silently.

Last Value Caching

If you've used commercial pub-sub systems, you may be used to some features that are missing in the fast and cheerful ØMQ pub-sub model. One of these is *last value caching* (LVC). This solves the problem of how a new subscriber catches up when it joins the network. The theory is that publishers get notified when a new subscriber joins and subscribes to some specific topics. The publisher can then rebroadcast the last message for those topics.

I've already explained why publishers don't get notified when there are new subscribers, because in large pub-sub systems, the volumes of data make it pretty much impossible. To make really large-scale pub-sub networks, you need a protocol like PGM that exploits an upscale Ethernet switch's ability to multicast data to thousands of subscribers. Trying to do a TCP unicast from the publisher to each of thousands of subscribers just doesn't scale. You get weird spikes, unfair distribution (some subscribers getting the message before others), network congestion, and general unhappiness.

PGM is a one-way protocol: the publisher sends a message to a multicast address at the switch, which then rebroadcasts that to all interested subscribers. The publisher never sees when subscribers join or leave: this all happens in the switch, which we don't really want to start reprogramming.

However, in a lower-volume network with a few dozen subscribers and a limited number of topics, we can use TCP and then the XSUB and XPUB sockets *do* talk to each other as we just saw in the Espresso pattern.

Can we make an LVC using ØMQ? The answer is yes, if we make a proxy that sits between the publisher and subscribers; an analog for the PGM switch, but one we can program ourselves.

I'll start by making a publisher and subscriber that highlight the worst case scenario. This publisher is pathological. It starts by immediately sending messages to each of a thousand topics, and then it sends one update a second to a random topic. A subscriber connects, and subscribes to a topic. Without LVC, a subscriber would have to wait an average of 500 seconds to get any data. To add some drama, let's pretend there's an escaped convict called Gregor threatening to rip the head off Roger the toy bunny if we can't fix that 8.3 minutes' delay.

Here's the publisher code. Note that it has the command line option to connect to some address, but otherwise binds to an endpoint. We'll use this later to connect to our last value cache:

Example 66. Pathologic Publisher (pathopub.c)

```
//  Pathological publisher
//  Sends out 1,000 topics and then one random update per second

#include "czmq.h"

int main (int argc, char *argv [])
{
    zctx_t *context = zctx_new ();
    void *publisher = zsocket_new (context, ZMQ_PUB);
    if (argc == 2)
        zsocket_connect (publisher, argv [1]);
    else
        zsocket_bind (publisher, "tcp://*:5556");

    //  Ensure subscriber connection has time to complete
    sleep (1);

    //  Send out all 1,000 topic messages
    int topic_nbr;
    for (topic_nbr = 0; topic_nbr < 1000; topic_nbr++) {
        zstr_sendm (publisher, "%03d", topic_nbr, ZMQ_SNDMORE);
        zstr_send (publisher, "Save Roger");
```

```
        }
        //  Send one random update per second
        srandom ((unsigned) time (NULL));
        while (!zctx_interrupted) {
            sleep (1);
            zstr_sendm (publisher, "%03d", randof (1000), ZMQ_SNDMORE);
            zstr_send (publisher, "Off with his head!");
        }
        zctx_destroy (&context);
        return 0;
    }
```

And here's the subscriber:

Example 67. Pathologic Subscriber (pathosub.c)

```
//  Pathological subscriber
//  Subscribes to one random topic and prints received messages

#include "czmq.h"

int main (int argc, char *argv [])
{
    zctx_t *context = zctx_new ();
    void *subscriber = zsocket_new (context, ZMQ_SUB);
    if (argc == 2)
        zsocket_connect (subscriber, argv [1]);
    else
        zsocket_connect (subscriber, "tcp://localhost:5556");

    srandom ((unsigned) time (NULL));
    char subscription [5];
    sprintf (subscription, "%03d", randof (1000));
    zsocket_set_subscribe (subscriber, subscription);

    while (true) {
        char *topic = zstr_recv (subscriber);
        if (!topic)
            break;
        char *data = zstr_recv (subscriber);
        assert (streq (topic, subscription));
        puts (data);
        free (topic);
        free (data);
    }
    zctx_destroy (&context);
    return 0;
}
```

Try building and running these: first the subscriber, then the publisher. You'll see the subscriber reports getting "Save Roger" as you'd expect:

```
./pathosub &
./pathopub
```

It's when you run a second subscriber that you understand Roger's predicament. You have to leave it an awful long time before it reports getting any data. So, here's our last value cache. As I promised, it's a proxy that binds to two sockets and then handles messages on both:

Example 68. Last Value Caching Proxy (lvcache.c)

```
//  Last value cache
//  Uses XPUB subscription messages to re-send data

#include "czmq.h"

int main (void)
{
    zctx_t *context = zctx_new ();
    void *frontend = zsocket_new (context, ZMQ_SUB);
    zsocket_bind (frontend, "tcp://*:5557");
    void *backend = zsocket_new (context, ZMQ_XPUB);
    zsocket_bind (backend, "tcp://*:5558");

    //  Subscribe to every single topic from publisher
    zsocket_set_subscribe (frontend, "");

    //  Store last instance of each topic in a cache
    zhash_t *cache = zhash_new ();
```

We route topic updates from frontend to backend, and we handle subscriptions by sending whatever we cached, if anything:

Example 68-1. Last Value Caching Proxy (lvcache.c) - main poll loop

```
        zmq_pollitem_t items [] = {
            { frontend, 0, ZMQ_POLLIN, 0 },
            { backend, 0, ZMQ_POLLIN, 0 }
        };
        if (zmq_poll (items, 2, 1000 * ZMQ_POLL_MSEC) == -1)
            break;              //  Interrupted

        //  Any new topic data we cache and then forward
        if (items [0].revents & ZMQ_POLLIN) {
            char *topic = zstr_recv (frontend);
            char *current = zstr_recv (frontend);
            if (!topic)
                break;
            char *previous = zhash_lookup (cache, topic);
```

```
                    if (previous) {
                        zhash_delete (cache, topic);
                        free (previous);
                    }
                    zhash_insert (cache, topic, current);
                    zstr_sendm (backend, topic);
                    zstr_send (backend, current);
                    free (topic);
                }
```

When we get a new subscription, we pull data from the cache:

Example 68-2. Last Value Caching Proxy (lvcache.c) - handle subscriptions

```
                zframe_t *frame = zframe_recv (backend);
                if (!frame)
                    break;
                //  Event is one byte 0=unsub or 1=sub, followed by topic
                byte *event = zframe_data (frame);
                if (event [0] == 1) {
                    char *topic = zmalloc (zframe_size (frame));
                    memcpy (topic, event + 1, zframe_size (frame) - 1);
                    printf ("Sending cached topic %s\n", topic);
                    char *previous = zhash_lookup (cache, topic);
                    if (previous) {
                        zstr_sendm (backend, topic);
                        zstr_send (backend, previous);
                    }
                    free (topic);
                }
                zframe_destroy (&frame);
            }
        }
        zctx_destroy (&context);
        zhash_destroy (&cache);
        return 0;
}
```

Now, run the proxy, and then the publisher:

```
./lvcache &
./pathopub tcp://localhost:5557
```

And now run as many instances of the subscriber as you want to try, each time connecting to the proxy on port 5558:

```
./pathosub tcp://localhost:5558
```

Each subscriber happily reports "Save Roger", and Gregor the Escaped Convict slinks back to his seat for dinner and a nice cup of hot milk, which is all he really wanted in the first place.

One note: by default, the XPUB socket does not report duplicate subscriptions, which is what you want when you're naively connecting an XPUB to an XSUB. Our example sneakily gets around this by using random topics so the chance of it not working is one in a million. In a real LVC proxy, you'll want to use the `ZMQ_XPUB_VERBOSE` option that we implement in Code Connected Volume 2 as an exercise.

Slow Subscriber Detection (Suicidal Snail Pattern)

A common problem you will hit when using the pub-sub pattern in real life is the slow subscriber. In an ideal world, we stream data at full speed from publishers to subscribers. In reality, subscriber applications are often written in interpreted languages, or just do a lot of work, or are just badly written, to the extent that they can't keep up with publishers.

How do we handle a slow subscriber? The ideal fix is to make the subscriber faster, but that might take work and time. Some of the classic strategies for handling a slow subscriber are:

- **Queue messages on the publisher**. This is what Gmail does when I don't read my email for a couple of hours. But in high-volume messaging, pushing queues upstream has the thrilling but unprofitable result of making publishers run out of memory and crash—especially if there are lots of subscribers and it's not possible to flush to disk for performance reasons.

- **Queue messages on the subscriber**. This is much better, and it's what ØMQ does by default if the network can keep up with things. If anyone's going to run out of memory and crash, it'll be the subscriber rather than the publisher, which is fair. This is perfect for "peaky" streams where a subscriber can't keep up for a while, but can catch up when the stream slows down. However, it's no answer to a subscriber that's simply too slow in general.

- **Stop queuing new messages after a while**. This is what Gmail does when my mailbox overflows its precious gigabytes of space. New messages just get rejected or dropped. This is a great strategy from the perspective of the publisher, and it's what ØMQ does when the publisher sets a HWM. However, it still doesn't help us fix the slow subscriber. Now we just get gaps in our message stream.

- **Punish slow subscribers with disconnect**. This is what Hotmail (remember that?) did when I didn't log in for two weeks, which is why I was on my fifteenth Hotmail account when it hit me that there was perhaps a better way. It's a nice brutal strategy that forces subscribers to sit up and pay attention and would be ideal, but ØMQ doesn't do this, and there's no way to layer it on top because subscribers are invisible to publisher applications.

None of these classic strategies fit, so we need to get creative. Rather than disconnect the publisher, let's convince the subscriber to kill itself. This is the Suicidal Snail pattern. When a subscriber detects that it's running too slowly (where "too slowly" is presumably a configured option that really means "so slowly that if you ever get here, shout really loudly because I need to know, so I can fix this!"), it croaks and dies.

How can a subscriber detect this? One way would be to sequence messages (number them in order) and use a HWM at the publisher. Now, if the subscriber detects a gap (i.e., the numbering isn't consecutive), it knows something is wrong. We then tune the HWM to the "croak and die if you hit this" level.

There are two problems with this solution. One, if we have many publishers, how do we sequence messages? The solution is to give each publisher a unique ID and add that to the sequencing. Second, if subscribers use ZMQ_SUBSCRIBE filters, they will get gaps by definition. Our precious sequencing will be for nothing.

Some use cases won't use filters, and sequencing will work for them. But a more general solution is that the publisher timestamps each message. When a subscriber gets a message, it checks the time, and if the difference is more than, say, one second, it does the "croak and die" thing, possibly firing off a squawk to some operator console first.

The Suicide Snail pattern works especially when subscribers have their own clients and service-level agreements and need to guarantee certain maximum latencies. Aborting a subscriber may not seem like a constructive way to guarantee a maximum latency, but it's the assertion model. Abort today, and the problem will be fixed. Allow late data to flow downstream, and the problem may cause wider damage and take longer to appear on the radar.

Here is a minimal example of a Suicidal Snail:

Example 69. Suicidal Snail (suisnail.c)

```
//  Suicidal Snail

#include "czmq.h"

//  This is our subscriber. It connects to the publisher and subscribes
//  to everything. It sleeps for a short time between messages to
//  simulate doing too much work. If a message is more than one second
//  late, it croaks.

#define MAX_ALLOWED_DELAY    1000    //  msecs

static void
subscriber (void *args, zctx_t *ctx, void *pipe)
{
    //  Subscribe to everything
    void *subscriber = zsocket_new (ctx, ZMQ_SUB);
    zsockopt_set_subscribe (subscriber, "");
    zsocket_connect (subscriber, "tcp://localhost:5556");

    //  Get and process messages
    while (true) {
        char *string = zstr_recv (subscriber);
        printf("%s\n", string);
```

```
            int64_t clock;
            int terms = sscanf (string, "%" PRId64, &clock);
            assert (terms == 1);
            free (string);

            //  Suicide snail logic
            if (zclock_time () - clock > MAX_ALLOWED_DELAY) {
                fprintf (stderr, "E: subscriber cannot keep up, aborting\n");
                break;
            }
            //  Work for 1 msec plus some random additional time
            zclock_sleep (1 + randof (2));
        }
        zstr_send (pipe, "gone and died");
    }
```

This is our publisher task. It publishes a time-stamped message to its PUB socket every millisecond:

Example 69-1. Suicidal Snail (suisnail.c) - publisher task

```
static void
publisher (void *args, zctx_t *ctx, void *pipe)
{
    //  Prepare publisher
    void *publisher = zsocket_new (ctx, ZMQ_PUB);
    zsocket_bind (publisher, "tcp://*:5556");

    while (true) {
        //  Send current clock (msecs) to subscribers
        char string [20];
        sprintf (string, "%" PRId64, zclock_time ());
        zstr_send (publisher, string);
        char *signal = zstr_recv_nowait (pipe);
        if (signal) {
            free (signal);
            break;
        }
        zclock_sleep (1);              //  1msec wait
    }
}
```

The main task simply starts a client and a server, and then waits for the client to signal that it has died:

Example 69-2. Suicidal Snail (suisnail.c) - main task

```
int main (void)
{
    zctx_t *ctx = zctx_new ();
    void *pubpipe = zthread_fork (ctx, publisher, NULL);
```

```
        void *subpipe = zthread_fork (ctx, subscriber, NULL);
        free (zstr_recv (subpipe));
        zstr_send (pubpipe, "break");
        zclock_sleep (100);
        zctx_destroy (&ctx);
        return 0;
}
```

Here are some things to note about the Suicidal Snail example:

- The message here consists simply of the current system clock as a number of milliseconds. In a realistic application, you'd have at least a message header with the timestamp and a message body with data.
- The example has subscriber and publisher in a single process as two threads. In reality, they would be separate processes. Using threads is just convenient for the demonstration.

High-Speed Subscribers (Black Box Pattern)

Now lets look at one way to make our subscribers faster. A common use case for pub-sub is distributing large data streams like market data coming from stock exchanges. A typical setup would have a publisher connected to a stock exchange, taking price quotes, and sending them out to a number of subscribers. If there are a handful of subscribers, we could use TCP. If we have a larger number of subscribers, we'd probably use reliable multicast, i.e., PGM.

Let's imagine our feed has an average of 100,000 100-byte messages a second. That's a typical rate, after filtering market data we don't need to send on to subscribers. Now we decide to record a day's data (maybe 250 GB in 8 hours), and then replay it to a simulation network, i.e., a small group of subscribers. While 100K messages a second is easy for a ØMQ application, we want to replay it *much faster*.

So we set up our architecture with a bunch of boxes—one for the publisher and one for each subscriber. These are well-specified boxes—eight cores, twelve for the publisher.

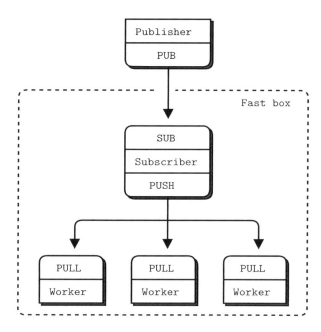

Figure 56. The Simple Black Box Pattern

And as we pump data into our subscribers, we notice two things:

1. When we do even the slightest amount of work with a message, it slows down our subscriber to the point where it can't catch up with the publisher again.
2. We're hitting a ceiling, at both publisher and subscriber, to around 6M messages a second, even after careful optimization and TCP tuning.

The first thing we have to do is break our subscriber into a multithreaded design so that we can do work with messages in one set of threads, while reading messages in another. Typically, we don't want to process every message the same way. Rather, the subscriber will filter some messages, perhaps by prefix key. When a message matches some criteria, the subscriber will call a worker to deal with it. In ØMQ terms, this means sending the message to a worker thread.

So the subscriber looks something like a queue device. We could use various sockets to connect the subscriber and workers. If we assume one-way traffic and workers that are all identical, we can use PUSH and PULL and delegate all the routing work to ØMQ (see figure 56). This is the simplest and fastest approach.

The subscriber talks to the publisher over TCP or PGM. The subscriber talks to its workers, which are all in the same process, over `inproc://`.

Now to break that ceiling. The subscriber thread hits 100% of CPU and because it is one thread, it cannot use more than one core. A single thread will always hit a ceiling, be it at 2M, 6M, or more messages per second. We want to split the work across multiple threads that can run in parallel.

The approach used by many high-performance products, which works here, is *sharding*. Using sharding, we split the work into parallel and independent streams, such as half of the topic keys in one stream, and half in another. We could use many streams, but performance won't scale unless we have free cores. So let's see how to shard into two streams (see figure 57).

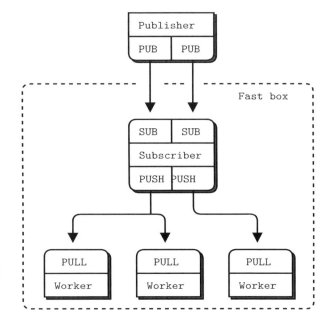

Figure 57. Mad Black Box Pattern

With two streams, working at full speed, we would configure ØMQ as follows:
- Two I/O threads, rather than one.
- Two network interfaces (NIC), one per subscriber.
- Each I/O thread bound to a specific NIC.

- Two subscriber threads, bound to specific cores.
- Two SUB sockets, one per subscriber thread.
- The remaining cores assigned to worker threads.
- Worker threads connected to both subscriber PUSH sockets.

Ideally, we want to match the number of fully-loaded threads in our architecture with the number of cores. When threads start to fight for cores and CPU cycles, the cost of adding more threads outweighs the benefits. There would be no benefit, for example, in creating more I/O threads.

Reliable Pub-Sub (Clone Pattern)

As a larger worked example, we'll take the problem of making a reliable pub-sub architecture. We'll develop this in stages. The goal is to allow a set of applications to share some common state. Here are our technical challenges:

- We have a large set of client applications, say thousands or tens of thousands.
- They will join and leave the network arbitrarily.
- These applications must share a single eventually-consistent *state*.
- Any application can update the state at any point in time.

Let's say that updates are reasonably low-volume. We don't have real time goals. The whole state can fit into memory. Some plausible use cases are:

- A configuration that is shared by a group of cloud servers.
- Some game state shared by a group of players.
- Exchange rate data that is updated in real time and available to applications.

Centralized Versus Decentralized

A first decision we have to make is whether we work with a central server or not. It makes a big difference in the resulting design. The trade-offs are these:

- Conceptually, a central server is simpler to understand because networks are not naturally symmetrical. With a central server, we avoid all questions of discovery, bind versus connect, and so on.
- Generally, a fully-distributed architecture is technically more challenging but ends up with simpler protocols. That is, each node must act as server and client in the right way, which is delicate. When done right, the results are simpler than using a central server. We saw this in the Freelance pattern in "Reliable Request-Reply Patterns".
- A central server will become a bottleneck in high-volume use cases. If handling scale in the order of millions of messages a second is required, we should aim for decentralization right away.

- Ironically, a centralized architecture will scale to more nodes more easily than a decentralized one. That is, it's easier to connect 10,000 nodes to one server than to each other.

So, for the Clone pattern we'll work with a *server* that publishes state updates and a set of *clients* that represent applications.

Representing State as Key-Value Pairs

We'll develop Clone in stages, solving one problem at a time. First, let's look at how to update a shared state across a set of clients. We need to decide how to represent our state, as well as the updates. The simplest plausible format is a key-value store, where one key-value pair represents an atomic unit of change in the shared state.

We have a simple pub-sub example in "Basics", the weather server and client. Let's change the server to send key-value pairs, and the client to store these in a hash table. This lets us send updates from one server to a set of clients using the classic pub-sub model (see figure 58).

An update is either a new key-value pair, a modified value for an existing key, or a deleted key. We can assume for now that the whole store fits in memory and that applications access it by key, such as by using a hash table or dictionary. For larger stores and some kind of persistence we'd probably store the state in a database, but that's not relevant here.

This is the server:

Example 70. Clone server, Model One (clonesrv1.c)

```
//  Clone server Model One

#include "kvsimple.c"

int main (void)
{
    //  Prepare our context and publisher socket
    zctx_t *ctx = zctx_new ();
    void *publisher = zsocket_new (ctx, ZMQ_PUB);
    zsocket_bind (publisher, "tcp://*:5556");
    zclock_sleep (200);

    zhash_t *kvmap = zhash_new ();
    int64_t sequence = 0;
    srandom ((unsigned) time (NULL));

    while (!zctx_interrupted) {
        //  Distribute as key-value message
        kvmsg_t *kvmsg = kvmsg_new (++sequence);
        kvmsg_fmt_key  (kvmsg, "%d", randof (10000));
        kvmsg_fmt_body (kvmsg, "%d", randof (1000000));
        kvmsg_send     (kvmsg, publisher);
        kvmsg_store    (&kvmsg, kvmap);
```

```
    }
    printf (" Interrupted\n%d messages out\n", (int) sequence);
    zhash_destroy (&kvmap);
    zctx_destroy (&ctx);
    return 0;
}
```

And here is the client:

Example 71. Clone client, Model One (clonecli1.c)

```
//  Clone client Model One

#include "kvsimple.c"

int main (void)
{
    //  Prepare our context and updates socket
    zctx_t *ctx = zctx_new ();
    void *updates = zsocket_new (ctx, ZMQ_SUB);
    zsockopt_set_subscribe (updates, "");
    zsocket_connect (updates, "tcp://localhost:5556");

    zhash_t *kvmap = zhash_new ();
    int64_t sequence = 0;

    while (true) {
        kvmsg_t *kvmsg = kvmsg_recv (updates);
        if (!kvmsg)
            break;          //  Interrupted
        kvmsg_store (&kvmsg, kvmap);
        sequence++;
    }
    printf (" Interrupted\n%d messages in\n", (int) sequence);
    zhash_destroy (&kvmap);
    zctx_destroy (&ctx);
    return 0;
}
```

Here are some things to note about this first model:

- All the hard work is done in a `kvmsg` class. This class works with key-value message objects, which are multipart ØMQ messages structured as three frames: a key (a ØMQ string), a sequence number (64-bit value, in network byte order), and a binary body (holds everything else).
- The server generates messages with a randomized 4-digit key, which lets us simulate a large but not enormous hash table (10K entries).
- We don't implement deletions in this version: all messages are inserts or updates.
- The server does a 200 millisecond pause after binding its socket. This is to prevent *slow joiner syndrome*, where the subscriber loses messages as it connects to the server's socket. We'll remove that in later versions of the Clone code.
- We'll use the terms *publisher* and *subscriber* in the code to refer to sockets. This will help later when we have multiple sockets doing different things.

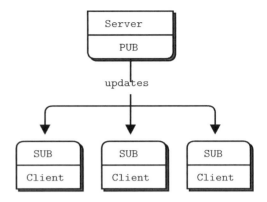

Figure 58. Publishing State Updates

Here is the `kvmsg` class, in the simplest form that works for now:

Example 72. Key-value message class (kvsimple.c)

```
//  kvsimple class - key-value message class for example applications

#include "kvsimple.h"
#include "zlist.h"

//  Keys are short strings
#define KVMSG_KEY_MAX   255

//  Message is formatted on wire as 4 frames:
//  frame 0: key (OMQ string)
//  frame 1: sequence (8 bytes, network order)
//  frame 2: body (blob)
#define FRAME_KEY       0
#define FRAME_SEQ       1
#define FRAME_BODY      2
#define KVMSG_FRAMES    3

//  The kvmsg class holds a single key-value message consisting of a
//  list of 0 or more frames:

struct _kvmsg {
```

```c
    // Presence indicators for each frame
    int present [KVMSG_FRAMES];
    // Corresponding OMQ message frames, if any
    zmq_msg_t frame [KVMSG_FRAMES];
    // Key, copied into safe C string
    char key [KVMSG_KEY_MAX + 1];
};
```

Here are the constructor and destructor for the class:

Example 72-1. Key-value message class (kvsimple.c) - constructor and destructor

```c
// Constructor, takes a sequence number for the new kvmsg instance:
kvmsg_t *
kvmsg_new (int64_t sequence)
{
    kvmsg_t
        *self;

    self = (kvmsg_t *) zmalloc (sizeof (kvmsg_t));
    kvmsg_set_sequence (self, sequence);
    return self;
}


// zhash_free_fn callback helper that does the low level destruction:
void
kvmsg_free (void *ptr)
{
    if (ptr) {
        kvmsg_t *self = (kvmsg_t *) ptr;
        // Destroy message frames if any
        int frame_nbr;
        for (frame_nbr = 0; frame_nbr < KVMSG_FRAMES; frame_nbr++)
            if (self->present [frame_nbr])
                zmq_msg_close (&self->frame [frame_nbr]);

        // Free object itself
        free (self);
    }
}

// Destructor
void
kvmsg_destroy (kvmsg_t **self_p)
{
    assert (self_p);
    if (*self_p) {
        kvmsg_free (*self_p);
        *self_p = NULL;
    }
}
```

This method reads a key-value message from socket, and returns a new `kvmsg` instance:

Example 72-2. Key-value message class (kvsimple.c) - recv method

```
kvmsg_t *
kvmsg_recv (void *socket)
{
    assert (socket);
    kvmsg_t *self = kvmsg_new (0);

    //  Read all frames off the wire, reject if bogus
    int frame_nbr;
    for (frame_nbr = 0; frame_nbr < KVMSG_FRAMES; frame_nbr++) {
        if (self->present [frame_nbr])
            zmq_msg_close (&self->frame [frame_nbr]);
        zmq_msg_init (&self->frame [frame_nbr]);
        self->present [frame_nbr] = 1;
        if (zmq_msg_recv (&self->frame [frame_nbr], socket, 0) == -1) {
            kvmsg_destroy (&self);
            break;
        }
        //  Verify multipart framing
        int rcvmore = (frame_nbr < KVMSG_FRAMES - 1)? 1: 0;
        if (zsockopt_rcvmore (socket) != rcvmore) {
            kvmsg_destroy (&self);
            break;
        }
    }
    return self;
}
```

This method sends a multiframe key-value message to a socket:

Example 72-3. Key-value message class (kvsimple.c) - send method

```
void
kvmsg_send (kvmsg_t *self, void *socket)
{
    assert (self);
    assert (socket);

    int frame_nbr;
    for (frame_nbr = 0; frame_nbr < KVMSG_FRAMES; frame_nbr++) {
        zmq_msg_t copy;
        zmq_msg_init (&copy);
        if (self->present [frame_nbr])
            zmq_msg_copy (&copy, &self->frame [frame_nbr]);
        zmq_msg_send (&copy, socket,
            (frame_nbr < KVMSG_FRAMES - 1)? ZMQ_SNDMORE: 0);
        zmq_msg_close (&copy);
```

    }
}

These methods let the caller get and set the message key, as a fixed string and as a printf formatted string:

Example 72-4. Key-value message class (kvsimple.c) - key methods

```
char *
kvmsg_key (kvmsg_t *self)
{
    assert (self);
    if (self->present [FRAME_KEY]) {
        if (!*self->key) {
            size_t size = zmq_msg_size (&self->frame [FRAME_KEY]);
            if (size > KVMSG_KEY_MAX)
                size = KVMSG_KEY_MAX;
            memcpy (self->key,
                zmq_msg_data (&self->frame [FRAME_KEY]), size);
            self->key [size] = 0;
        }
        return self->key;
    }
    else
        return NULL;
}

void
kvmsg_set_key (kvmsg_t *self, char *key)
{
    assert (self);
    zmq_msg_t *msg = &self->frame [FRAME_KEY];
    if (self->present [FRAME_KEY])
        zmq_msg_close (msg);
    zmq_msg_init_size (msg, strlen (key));
    memcpy (zmq_msg_data (msg), key, strlen (key));
    self->present [FRAME_KEY] = 1;
}

void
kvmsg_fmt_key (kvmsg_t *self, char *format, ...)
{
    char value [KVMSG_KEY_MAX + 1];
    va_list args;

    assert (self);
    va_start (args, format);
    vsnprintf (value, KVMSG_KEY_MAX, format, args);
    va_end (args);
    kvmsg_set_key (self, value);
}
```

These two methods let the caller get and set the message sequence number:

Example 72-5. Key-value message class (kvsimple.c) - sequence methods

```
int64_t
kvmsg_sequence (kvmsg_t *self)
{
    assert (self);
    if (self->present [FRAME_SEQ]) {
        assert (zmq_msg_size (&self->frame [FRAME_SEQ]) == 8);
        byte *source = zmq_msg_data (&self->frame [FRAME_SEQ]);
        int64_t sequence = ((int64_t) (source [0]) << 56)
                         + ((int64_t) (source [1]) << 48)
                         + ((int64_t) (source [2]) << 40)
                         + ((int64_t) (source [3]) << 32)
                         + ((int64_t) (source [4]) << 24)
                         + ((int64_t) (source [5]) << 16)
                         + ((int64_t) (source [6]) << 8)
                         +  (int64_t) (source [7]);
        return sequence;
    }
    else
        return 0;
}

void
kvmsg_set_sequence (kvmsg_t *self, int64_t sequence)
{
    assert (self);
    zmq_msg_t *msg = &self->frame [FRAME_SEQ];
    if (self->present [FRAME_SEQ])
        zmq_msg_close (msg);
    zmq_msg_init_size (msg, 8);

    byte *source = zmq_msg_data (msg);
    source [0] = (byte) ((sequence >> 56) & 255);
    source [1] = (byte) ((sequence >> 48) & 255);
    source [2] = (byte) ((sequence >> 40) & 255);
    source [3] = (byte) ((sequence >> 32) & 255);
    source [4] = (byte) ((sequence >> 24) & 255);
    source [5] = (byte) ((sequence >> 16) & 255);
    source [6] = (byte) ((sequence >> 8)  & 255);
    source [7] = (byte) ((sequence)       & 255);

    self->present [FRAME_SEQ] = 1;
}
```

These methods let the caller get and set the message body as a fixed string and as a printf formatted string:

Example 72-6. Key-value message class (kvsimple.c) - message body methods

```
byte *
kvmsg_body (kvmsg_t *self)
{
    assert (self);
    if (self->present [FRAME_BODY])
        return (byte *) zmq_msg_data (&self->frame [FRAME_BODY]);
    else
        return NULL;
}

void
kvmsg_set_body (kvmsg_t *self, byte *body, size_t size)
{
    assert (self);
    zmq_msg_t *msg = &self->frame [FRAME_BODY];
    if (self->present [FRAME_BODY])
        zmq_msg_close (msg);
    self->present [FRAME_BODY] = 1;
    zmq_msg_init_size (msg, size);
    memcpy (zmq_msg_data (msg), body, size);
}

void
kvmsg_fmt_body (kvmsg_t *self, char *format, ...)
{
    char value [255 + 1];
    va_list args;

    assert (self);
    va_start (args, format);
    vsnprintf (value, 255, format, args);
    va_end (args);
    kvmsg_set_body (self, (byte *) value, strlen (value));
}
```

This method returns the body size of the most recently read message, if any exists:

Example 72-7. Key-value message class (kvsimple.c) - size method

```
size_t
kvmsg_size (kvmsg_t *self)
{
    assert (self);
    if (self->present [FRAME_BODY])
        return zmq_msg_size (&self->frame [FRAME_BODY]);
    else
```

```
        return 0;
}
```

This method stores the key-value message into a hash map, unless the key and value are both null. It nullifies the kvmsg reference so that the object is owned by the hash map, not the caller:

Example 72-8. Key-value message class (kvsimple.c) - store method

```
void
kvmsg_store (kvmsg_t **self_p, zhash_t *hash)
{
    assert (self_p);
    if (*self_p) {
        kvmsg_t *self = *self_p;
        assert (self);
        if (self->present [FRAME_KEY]
        &&  self->present [FRAME_BODY]) {
            zhash_update (hash, kvmsg_key (self), self);
            zhash_freefn (hash, kvmsg_key (self), kvmsg_free);
        }
        *self_p = NULL;
    }
}
```

This method prints the key-value message to stderr for debugging and tracing:

Example 72-9. Key-value message class (kvsimple.c) - dump method

```
void
kvmsg_dump (kvmsg_t *self)
{
    if (self) {
        if (!self) {
            fprintf (stderr, "NULL");
            return;
        }
        size_t size = kvmsg_size (self);
        byte  *body = kvmsg_body (self);
        fprintf (stderr, "[seq:%" PRId64 "]", kvmsg_sequence (self));
        fprintf (stderr, "[key:%s]", kvmsg_key (self));
        fprintf (stderr, "[size:%zd] ", size);
        int char_nbr;
        for (char_nbr = 0; char_nbr < size; char_nbr++)
            fprintf (stderr, "%02X", body [char_nbr]);
        fprintf (stderr, "\n");
    }
    else
        fprintf (stderr, "NULL message\n");
}
```

It's good practice to have a self-test method that tests the class; this also shows how it's used in applications:

Example 72-10. Key-value message class (kvsimple.c) - test method

```c
int
kvmsg_test (int verbose)
{
    kvmsg_t
        *kvmsg;

    printf (" * kvmsg: ");

    //  Prepare our context and sockets
    zctx_t *ctx = zctx_new ();
    void *output = zsocket_new (ctx, ZMQ_DEALER);
    int rc = zmq_bind (output, "ipc://kvmsg_selftest.ipc");
    assert (rc == 0);
    void *input = zsocket_new (ctx, ZMQ_DEALER);
    rc = zmq_connect (input, "ipc://kvmsg_selftest.ipc");
    assert (rc == 0);

    zhash_t *kvmap = zhash_new ();

    //  Test send and receive of simple message
    kvmsg = kvmsg_new (1);
    kvmsg_set_key  (kvmsg, "key");
    kvmsg_set_body (kvmsg, (byte *) "body", 4);
    if (verbose)
        kvmsg_dump (kvmsg);
    kvmsg_send (kvmsg, output);
    kvmsg_store (&kvmsg, kvmap);

    kvmsg = kvmsg_recv (input);
    if (verbose)
        kvmsg_dump (kvmsg);
    assert (streq (kvmsg_key (kvmsg), "key"));
    kvmsg_store (&kvmsg, kvmap);

    //  Shutdown and destroy all objects
    zhash_destroy (&kvmap);
    zctx_destroy (&ctx);

    printf ("OK\n");
    return 0;
}
```

Later, we'll make a more sophisticated kvmsg class that will work in in real applications.

Both the server and client maintain hash tables, but this first model only works properly if we start all clients before the server and the clients never crash. That's very artificial.

Getting an Out-of-Band Snapshot

So now we have our second problem: how to deal with late-joining clients or clients that crash and then restart.

In order to allow a late (or recovering) client to catch up with a server, it has to get a snapshot of the server's state. Just as we've reduced "message" to mean "a sequenced key-value pair", we can reduce "state" to mean "a hash table". To get the server state, a client opens a DEALER socket and asks for it explicitly (see figure 59).

To make this work, we have to solve a problem of timing. Getting a state snapshot will take a certain time, possibly fairly long if the snapshot is large. We need to correctly apply updates to the snapshot. But the server won't know when to start sending us updates. One way would be to start subscribing, get a first update, and then ask for "state for update N". This would require the server storing one snapshot for each update, which isn't practical.

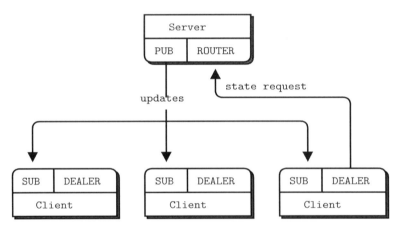

Figure 59. State Replication

So we will do the synchronization in the client, as follows:

- The client first subscribes to updates and then makes a state request. This guarantees that the state is going to be newer than the oldest update it has.
- The client waits for the server to reply with state, and meanwhile queues all updates. It does this simply by not reading them: ØMQ keeps them queued on the socket queue.
- When the client receives its state update, it begins once again to read updates. However, it discards any updates that are older than the state update. So if the state update includes updates up to 200, the client will discard updates up to 201.
- The client then applies updates to its own state snapshot.

It's a simple model that exploits ØMQ's own internal queues. Here's the server:

Example 73. Clone server, Model Two (clonesrv2.c)

```c
//  Clone server - Model Two

//  Lets us build this source without creating a library
#include "kvsimple.c"

static int s_send_single (const char *key, void *data, void *args);
static void state_manager (void *args, zctx_t *ctx, void *pipe);

int main (void)
{
    //  Prepare our context and sockets
    zctx_t *ctx = zctx_new ();
    void *publisher = zsocket_new (ctx, ZMQ_PUB);
    zsocket_bind (publisher, "tcp://*:5557");

    int64_t sequence = 0;
    srandom ((unsigned) time (NULL));

    //  Start state manager and wait for synchronization signal
    void *updates = zthread_fork (ctx, state_manager, NULL);
    free (zstr_recv (updates));

    while (!zctx_interrupted) {
        //  Distribute as key-value message
        kvmsg_t *kvmsg = kvmsg_new (++sequence);
        kvmsg_fmt_key  (kvmsg, "%d", randof (10000));
        kvmsg_fmt_body (kvmsg, "%d", randof (1000000));
        kvmsg_send     (kvmsg, publisher);
        kvmsg_send     (kvmsg, updates);
        kvmsg_destroy (&kvmsg);
    }
    printf (" Interrupted\n%d messages out\n", (int) sequence);
    zctx_destroy (&ctx);
    return 0;
}

//  Routing information for a key-value snapshot
typedef struct {
    void *socket;           //  ROUTER socket to send to
    zframe_t *identity;     //  Identity of peer who requested state
} kvroute_t;

//  Send one state snapshot key-value pair to a socket
//  Hash item data is our kvmsg object, ready to send
static int
s_send_single (const char *key, void *data, void *args)
{
```

```
    kvroute_t *kvroute = (kvroute_t *) args;
    //  Send identity of recipient first
    zframe_send (&kvroute->identity,
        kvroute->socket, ZFRAME_MORE + ZFRAME_REUSE);
    kvmsg_t *kvmsg = (kvmsg_t *) data;
    kvmsg_send (kvmsg, kvroute->socket);
    return 0;
}
```

The state manager task maintains the state and handles requests from clients for snapshots:

Example 73-1. Clone server, Model Two (clonesrv2.c) - state manager

```
static void
state_manager (void *args, zctx_t *ctx, void *pipe)
{
    zhash_t *kvmap = zhash_new ();

    zstr_send (pipe, "READY");
    void *snapshot = zsocket_new (ctx, ZMQ_ROUTER);
    zsocket_bind (snapshot, "tcp://*:5556");

    zmq_pollitem_t items [] = {
        { pipe, 0, ZMQ_POLLIN, 0 },
        { snapshot, 0, ZMQ_POLLIN, 0 }
    };
    int64_t sequence = 0;       //  Current snapshot version number
    while (!zctx_interrupted) {
        int rc = zmq_poll (items, 2, -1);
        if (rc == -1 && errno == ETERM)
            break;              //  Context has been shut down

        //  Apply state update from main thread
        if (items [0].revents & ZMQ_POLLIN) {
            kvmsg_t *kvmsg = kvmsg_recv (pipe);
            if (!kvmsg)
                break;          //  Interrupted
            sequence = kvmsg_sequence (kvmsg);
            kvmsg_store (&kvmsg, kvmap);
        }
        //  Execute state snapshot request
        if (items [1].revents & ZMQ_POLLIN) {
            zframe_t *identity = zframe_recv (snapshot);
            if (!identity)
                break;          //  Interrupted

            //  Request is in second frame of message
            char *request = zstr_recv (snapshot);
            if (streq (request, "ICANHAZ?"))
                free (request);
```

```
                else {
                    printf ("E: bad request, aborting\n");
                    break;
                }
                //  Send state snapshot to client
                kvroute_t routing = { snapshot, identity };

                //  For each entry in kvmap, send kvmsg to client
                zhash_foreach (kvmap, s_send_single, &routing);

                //  Now send END message with sequence number
                printf ("Sending state shapshot=%d\n", (int) sequence);
                zframe_send (&identity, snapshot, ZFRAME_MORE);
                kvmsg_t *kvmsg = kvmsg_new (sequence);
                kvmsg_set_key  (kvmsg, "KTHXBAI");
                kvmsg_set_body (kvmsg, (byte *) "", 0);
                kvmsg_send     (kvmsg, snapshot);
                kvmsg_destroy (&kvmsg);
            }
        }
        zhash_destroy (&kvmap);
    }
```

And here is the client:

Example 74. Clone client, Model Two (clonecli2.c)

```
//  Clone client - Model Two

//  Lets us build this source without creating a library
#include "kvsimple.c"

int main (void)
{
    //  Prepare our context and subscriber
    zctx_t *ctx = zctx_new ();
    void *snapshot = zsocket_new (ctx, ZMQ_DEALER);
    zsocket_connect (snapshot, "tcp://localhost:5556");
    void *subscriber = zsocket_new (ctx, ZMQ_SUB);
    zsockopt_set_subscribe (subscriber, "");
    zsocket_connect (subscriber, "tcp://localhost:5557");

    zhash_t *kvmap = zhash_new ();

    //  Get state snapshot
    int64_t sequence = 0;
    zstr_send (snapshot, "ICANHAZ?");
    while (true) {
        kvmsg_t *kvmsg = kvmsg_recv (snapshot);
        if (!kvmsg)
            break;          //  Interrupted
```

```c
            if (streq (kvmsg_key (kvmsg), "KTHXBAI")) {
                sequence = kvmsg_sequence (kvmsg);
                printf ("Received snapshot=%d\n", (int) sequence);
                kvmsg_destroy (&kvmsg);
                break;          // Done
            }
            kvmsg_store (&kvmsg, kvmap);
        }
        // Now apply pending updates, discard out-of-sequence messages
        while (!zctx_interrupted) {
            kvmsg_t *kvmsg = kvmsg_recv (subscriber);
            if (!kvmsg)
                break;          // Interrupted
            if (kvmsg_sequence (kvmsg) > sequence) {
                sequence = kvmsg_sequence (kvmsg);
                kvmsg_store (&kvmsg, kvmap);
            }
            else
                kvmsg_destroy (&kvmsg);
        }
        zhash_destroy (&kvmap);
        zctx_destroy (&ctx);
        return 0;
    }
```

Here are some things to note about these two programs:

- The server uses two tasks. One thread produces the updates (randomly) and sends these to the main PUB socket, while the other thread handles state requests on the ROUTER socket. The two communicate across PAIR sockets over an `inproc://` connection.

- The client is really simple. In C, it consists of about fifty lines of code. A lot of the heavy lifting is done in the kvmsg class. Even so, the basic Clone pattern is easier to implement than it seemed at first.

- We don't use anything fancy for serializing the state. The hash table holds a set of kvmsg objects, and the server sends these, as a batch of messages, to the client requesting state. If multiple clients request state at once, each will get a different snapshot.

- We assume that the client has exactly one server to talk to. The server must be running; we do not try to solve the question of what happens if the server crashes.

Right now, these two programs don't do anything real, but they correctly synchronize state. It's a neat example of how to mix different patterns: PAIR-PAIR, PUB-SUB, and ROUTER-DEALER.

Republishing Updates from Clients

In our second model, changes to the key-value store came from the server itself. This is a centralized model that is useful, for example if we have a central configuration file we want to distribute, with local caching on each node. A more interesting model takes updates from clients, not the server. The server thus becomes a stateless broker. This gives us some benefits:

- We're less worried about the reliability of the server. If it crashes, we can start a new instance and feed it new values.
- We can use the key-value store to share knowledge between active peers.

To send updates from clients back to the server, we could use a variety of socket patterns. The simplest plausible solution is a PUSH-PULL combination (see figure 60).

Why don't we allow clients to publish updates directly to each other? While this would reduce latency, it would remove the guarantee of consistency. You can't get consistent shared state if you allow the order of updates to change depending on who receives them. Say we have two clients, changing different keys. This will work fine. But if the two clients try to change the same key at roughly the same time, they'll end up with different notions of its value.

There are a few strategies for obtaining consistency when changes happen in multiple places at once. We'll use the approach of centralizing all change. No matter the precise timing of the changes that clients make, they are all pushed through the server, which enforces a single sequence according to the order in which it gets updates.

By mediating all changes, the server can also add a unique sequence number to all updates. With unique sequencing, clients can detect the nastier failures, including network congestion and queue overflow. If a client discovers that its incoming message stream has a hole, it can take action. It seems sensible that the client contact the server and ask for the missing messages, but in practice that isn't useful. If there are holes, they're caused by network stress, and adding more stress to the network will make things worse. All the client can do is warn its users that it is "unable to continue", stop, and not restart until someone has manually checked the cause of the problem.

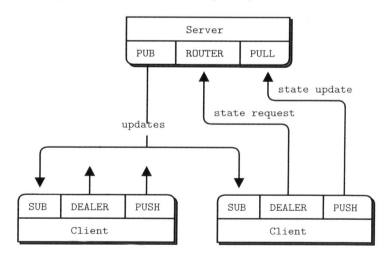

Figure 60. Republishing Updates

We'll now generate state updates in the client. Here's the server:

Example 75. Clone server, Model Three (clonesrv3.c)

```
//  Clone server - Model Three

//  Lets us build this source without creating a library
#include "kvsimple.c"

//  Routing information for a key-value snapshot
typedef struct {
    void *socket;           //  ROUTER socket to send to
    zframe_t *identity;     //  Identity of peer who requested state
} kvroute_t;

//  Send one state snapshot key-value pair to a socket
//  Hash item data is our kvmsg object, ready to send
static int
s_send_single (const char *key, void *data, void *args)
{
    kvroute_t *kvroute = (kvroute_t *) args;
    //  Send identity of recipient first
    zframe_send (&kvroute->identity,
        kvroute->socket, ZFRAME_MORE + ZFRAME_REUSE);
    kvmsg_t *kvmsg = (kvmsg_t *) data;
    kvmsg_send (kvmsg, kvroute->socket);
    return 0;
}

int main (void)
{
    //  Prepare our context and sockets
    zctx_t *ctx = zctx_new ();
    void *snapshot = zsocket_new (ctx, ZMQ_ROUTER);
    zsocket_bind (snapshot, "tcp://*:5556");
    void *publisher = zsocket_new (ctx, ZMQ_PUB);
    zsocket_bind (publisher, "tcp://*:5557");
    void *collector = zsocket_new (ctx, ZMQ_PULL);
    zsocket_bind (collector, "tcp://*:5558");
```

The body of the main task collects updates from clients and publishes them back out to clients:

Example 75-1. Clone server, Model Three (clonesrv3.c) - body of main task

```
    int64_t sequence = 0;
    zhash_t *kvmap = zhash_new ();

    zmq_pollitem_t items [] = {
        { collector, 0, ZMQ_POLLIN, 0 },
        { snapshot, 0, ZMQ_POLLIN, 0 }
```

```
    };
    while (!zctx_interrupted) {
        int rc = zmq_poll (items, 2, 1000 * ZMQ_POLL_MSEC);

        //  Apply state update sent from client
        if (items [0].revents & ZMQ_POLLIN) {
            kvmsg_t *kvmsg = kvmsg_recv (collector);
            if (!kvmsg)
                break;          //  Interrupted
            kvmsg_set_sequence (kvmsg, ++sequence);
            kvmsg_send (kvmsg, publisher);
            kvmsg_store (&kvmsg, kvmap);
            printf ("I: publishing update %5d\n", (int) sequence);
        }
        //  Execute state snapshot request
        if (items [1].revents & ZMQ_POLLIN) {
            zframe_t *identity = zframe_recv (snapshot);
            if (!identity)
                break;          //  Interrupted

            //  Request is in second frame of message
            char *request = zstr_recv (snapshot);
            if (streq (request, "ICANHAZ?"))
                free (request);
            else {
                printf ("E: bad request, aborting\n");
                break;
            }
            //  Send state snapshot to client
            kvroute_t routing = { snapshot, identity };

            //  For each entry in kvmap, send kvmsg to client
            zhash_foreach (kvmap, s_send_single, &routing);

            //  Now send END message with sequence number
            printf ("I: sending shapshot=%d\n", (int) sequence);
            zframe_send (&identity, snapshot, ZFRAME_MORE);
            kvmsg_t *kvmsg = kvmsg_new (sequence);
            kvmsg_set_key  (kvmsg, "KTHXBAI");
            kvmsg_set_body (kvmsg, (byte *) "", 0);
            kvmsg_send     (kvmsg, snapshot);
            kvmsg_destroy (&kvmsg);
        }
    }
    printf (" Interrupted\n%d messages handled\n", (int) sequence);
    zhash_destroy (&kvmap);
    zctx_destroy (&ctx);

    return 0;
}
```

And here is the client:

Example 76. Clone client, Model Three (clonecli3.c)

```
//  Clone client - Model Three

//  Lets us build this source without creating a library
#include "kvsimple.c"

int main (void)
{
    //  Prepare our context and subscriber
    zctx_t *ctx = zctx_new ();
    void *snapshot = zsocket_new (ctx, ZMQ_DEALER);
    zsocket_connect (snapshot, "tcp://localhost:5556");
    void *subscriber = zsocket_new (ctx, ZMQ_SUB);
    zsockopt_set_subscribe (subscriber, "");
    zsocket_connect (subscriber, "tcp://localhost:5557");
    void *publisher = zsocket_new (ctx, ZMQ_PUSH);
    zsocket_connect (publisher, "tcp://localhost:5558");

    zhash_t *kvmap = zhash_new ();
    srandom ((unsigned) time (NULL));
```

We first request a state snapshot:

Example 76-1. Clone client, Model Three (clonecli3.c) - getting a state snapshot

```
    zstr_send (snapshot, "ICANHAZ?");
    while (true) {
        kvmsg_t *kvmsg = kvmsg_recv (snapshot);
        if (!kvmsg)
            break;          //  Interrupted
        if (streq (kvmsg_key (kvmsg), "KTHXBAI")) {
            sequence = kvmsg_sequence (kvmsg);
            printf ("I: received snapshot=%d\n", (int) sequence);
            kvmsg_destroy (&kvmsg);
            break;          //  Done
        }
        kvmsg_store (&kvmsg, kvmap);
    }
```

Now we wait for updates from the server and every so often, we send a random key-value update to the server:

Example 76-2. Clone client, Model Three (clonecli3.c) - processing state updates

```
    int64_t alarm = zclock_time () + 1000;
    while (!zctx_interrupted) {
        zmq_pollitem_t items [] = { { subscriber, 0, ZMQ_POLLIN, 0 } };
        int tickless = (int) ((alarm - zclock_time ()));
        if (tickless < 0)
```

```
                    tickless = 0;
            int rc = zmq_poll (items, 1, tickless * ZMQ_POLL_MSEC);
            if (rc == -1)
                break;              //  Context has been shut down

            if (items [0].revents & ZMQ_POLLIN) {
                kvmsg_t *kvmsg = kvmsg_recv (subscriber);
                if (!kvmsg)
                    break;          //  Interrupted

                //  Discard out-of-sequence kvmsgs, incl. heartbeats
                if (kvmsg_sequence (kvmsg) > sequence) {
                    sequence = kvmsg_sequence (kvmsg);
                    kvmsg_store (&kvmsg, kvmap);
                    printf ("I: received update=%d\n", (int) sequence);
                }
                else
                    kvmsg_destroy (&kvmsg);
            }
            //  If we timed out, generate a random kvmsg
            if (zclock_time () >= alarm) {
                kvmsg_t *kvmsg = kvmsg_new (0);
                kvmsg_fmt_key  (kvmsg, "%d", randof (10000));
                kvmsg_fmt_body (kvmsg, "%d", randof (1000000));
                kvmsg_send     (kvmsg, publisher);
                kvmsg_destroy (&kvmsg);
                alarm = zclock_time () + 1000;
            }
        }
        printf (" Interrupted\n%d messages in\n", (int) sequence);
        zhash_destroy (&kvmap);
        zctx_destroy (&ctx);
        return 0;
    }
```

Here are some things to note about this third design:

- The server has collapsed to a single task. It manages a PULL socket for incoming updates, a ROUTER socket for state requests, and a PUB socket for outgoing updates.

- The client uses a simple tickless timer to send a random update to the server once a second. In a real implementation, we would drive updates from application code.

Working with Subtrees

As we grow the number of clients, the size of our shared store will also grow. It stops being reasonable to send everything to every client. This is the classic story with pub-sub: when you have a very small number of clients, you can send every message to all clients. As you grow the architecture, this becomes inefficient. Clients specialize in different areas.

So even when working with a shared store, some clients will want to work only with a part of that store, which we call a *subtree*. The client has to request the subtree when it makes a state request, and it must specify the same subtree when it subscribes to updates.

There are a couple of common syntaxes for trees. One is the *path hierarchy*, and another is the *topic tree*. These look like this:

- Path hierarchy: /some/list/of/paths
- Topic tree: some.list.of.topics

We'll use the path hierarchy, and extend our client and server so that a client can work with a single subtree. Once you see how to work with a single subtree you'll be able to extend this yourself to handle multiple subtrees, if your use case demands it.

Here's the server implementing subtrees, a small variation on Model Three:

Example 77. Clone server, Model Four (clonesrv4.c)

```
//  Clone server - Model Four

//  Lets us build this source without creating a library
#include "kvsimple.c"

//  Routing information for a key-value snapshot
typedef struct {
    void *socket;           //  ROUTER socket to send to
    zframe_t *identity;     //  Identity of peer who requested state
    char *subtree;          //  Client subtree specification
} kvroute_t;

//  Send one state snapshot key-value pair to a socket
//  Hash item data is our kvmsg object, ready to send
static int
s_send_single (const char *key, void *data, void *args)
{
    kvroute_t *kvroute = (kvroute_t *) args;
    kvmsg_t *kvmsg = (kvmsg_t *) data;
    if (strlen (kvroute->subtree) <= strlen (kvmsg_key (kvmsg))
    &&  memcmp (kvroute->subtree,
                kvmsg_key (kvmsg), strlen (kvroute->subtree)) == 0) {
        //  Send identity of recipient first
        zframe_send (&kvroute->identity,
            kvroute->socket, ZFRAME_MORE + ZFRAME_REUSE);
        kvmsg_send (kvmsg, kvroute->socket);
    }
    return 0;
}
```

```
// The main task is identical to clonesrv3 except for where it
// handles subtrees.
...
            // Request is in second frame of message
            char *request = zstr_recv (snapshot);
            char *subtree = NULL;
            if (streq (request, "ICANHAZ?")) {
                free (request);
                subtree = zstr_recv (snapshot);
            }
...
            // Send state snapshot to client
            kvroute_t routing = { snapshot, identity, subtree };
...
            // Now send END message with sequence number
            printf ("I: sending shapshot=%d\n", (int) sequence);
            zframe_send (&identity, snapshot, ZFRAME_MORE);
            kvmsg_t *kvmsg = kvmsg_new (sequence);
            kvmsg_set_key  (kvmsg, "KTHXBAI");
            kvmsg_set_body (kvmsg, (byte *) subtree, 0);
            kvmsg_send     (kvmsg, snapshot);
            kvmsg_destroy (&kvmsg);
            free (subtree);
        }
    }
...
```

And here is the corresponding client:

Example 78. Clone client, Model Four (clonecli4.c)

```
//  Clone client - Model Four

//  Lets us build this source without creating a library
#include "kvsimple.c"

//  This client is identical to clonecli3 except for where we
//  handles subtrees.
#define SUBTREE "/client/"
...
    zsocket_connect (subscriber, "tcp://localhost:5557");
    zsockopt_set_subscribe (subscriber, SUBTREE);
...
    //  We first request a state snapshot:
    int64_t sequence = 0;
    zstr_sendm (snapshot, "ICANHAZ?");
    zstr_send  (snapshot, SUBTREE);
...
        //  If we timed out, generate a random kvmsg
        if (zclock_time () >= alarm) {
            kvmsg_t *kvmsg = kvmsg_new (0);
```

```
                kvmsg_fmt_key  (kvmsg, "%s%d", SUBTREE, randof (10000));
                kvmsg_fmt_body (kvmsg, "%d", randof (1000000));
                kvmsg_send     (kvmsg, publisher);
                kvmsg_destroy (&kvmsg);
                alarm = zclock_time () + 1000;
        }
...
```

Ephemeral Values

An ephemeral value is one that expires automatically unless regularly refreshed. If you think of Clone being used for a registration service, then ephemeral values would let you do dynamic values. A node joins the network, publishes its address, and refreshes this regularly. If the node dies, its address eventually gets removed.

The usual abstraction for ephemeral values is to attach them to a *session*, and delete them when the session ends. In Clone, sessions would be defined by clients, and would end if the client died. A simpler alternative is to attach a *time to live* (TTL) to ephemeral values, which the server uses to expire values that haven't been refreshed in time.

A good design principle that I use whenever possible is to *not invent concepts that are not absolutely essential*. If we have very large numbers of ephemeral values, sessions will offer better performance. If we use a handful of ephemeral values, it's fine to set a TTL on each one. If we use masses of ephemeral values, it's more efficient to attach them to sessions and expire them in bulk. This isn't a problem we face at this stage, and may never face, so sessions go out the window.

Now we will implement ephemeral values. First, we need a way to encode the TTL in the key-value message. We could add a frame. The problem with using ØMQ frames for properties is that each time we want to add a new property, we have to change the message structure. It breaks compatibility. So let's add a properties frame to the message, and write the code to let us get and put property values.

Next, we need a way to say, "delete this value". Up until now, servers and clients have always blindly inserted or updated new values into their hash table. We'll say that if the value is empty, that means "delete this key".

Here's a more complete version of the kvmsg class, which implements the properties frame (and adds a UUID frame, which we'll need later on). It also handles empty values by deleting the key from the hash, if necessary:

Example 79. Key-value message class: full (kvmsg.c)

```
//  kvmsg class - key-value message class for example applications

#include "kvmsg.h"
#include <uuid/uuid.h>
#include "zlist.h"

//  Keys are short strings
```

```
#define KVMSG_KEY_MAX    255

//  Message is formatted on wire as 4 frames:
//  frame 0: key (OMQ string)
//  frame 1: sequence (8 bytes, network order)
//  frame 2: uuid (blob, 16 bytes)
//  frame 3: properties (OMQ string)
//  frame 4: body (blob)
#define FRAME_KEY       0
#define FRAME_SEQ       1
#define FRAME_UUID      2
#define FRAME_PROPS     3
#define FRAME_BODY      4
#define KVMSG_FRAMES    5

//  Structure of our class
struct _kvmsg {
    //  Presence indicators for each frame
    int present [KVMSG_FRAMES];
    //  Corresponding OMQ message frames, if any
    zmq_msg_t frame [KVMSG_FRAMES];
    //  Key, copied into safe C string
    char key [KVMSG_KEY_MAX + 1];
    //  List of properties, as name=value strings
    zlist_t *props;
    size_t props_size;
};
```

These two helpers serialize a list of properties to and from a message frame:

Example 79-1. Key-value message class: full (kvmsg.c) - property encoding

```
static void
s_encode_props (kvmsg_t *self)
{
    zmq_msg_t *msg = &self->frame [FRAME_PROPS];
    if (self->present [FRAME_PROPS])
        zmq_msg_close (msg);

    zmq_msg_init_size (msg, self->props_size);
    char *prop = zlist_first (self->props);
    char *dest = (char *) zmq_msg_data (msg);
    while (prop) {
        strcpy (dest, prop);
        dest += strlen (prop);
        *dest++ = '\n';
        prop = zlist_next (self->props);
    }
    self->present [FRAME_PROPS] = 1;
}
```

```c
static void
s_decode_props (kvmsg_t *self)
{
    zmq_msg_t *msg = &self->frame [FRAME_PROPS];
    self->props_size = 0;
    while (zlist_size (self->props))
        free (zlist_pop (self->props));

    size_t remainder = zmq_msg_size (msg);
    char *prop = (char *) zmq_msg_data (msg);
    char *eoln = memchr (prop, '\n', remainder);
    while (eoln) {
        *eoln = 0;
        zlist_append (self->props, strdup (prop));
        self->props_size += strlen (prop) + 1;
        remainder -= strlen (prop) + 1;
        prop = eoln + 1;
        eoln = memchr (prop, '\n', remainder);
    }
}
```

Here are the constructor and destructor for the class:

Example 79-2. Key-value message class: full (kvmsg.c) - constructor and destructor

```c
//  Constructor, takes a sequence number for the new kvmsg instance:
kvmsg_t *
kvmsg_new (int64_t sequence)
{
    kvmsg_t
        *self;

    self = (kvmsg_t *) zmalloc (sizeof (kvmsg_t));
    self->props = zlist_new ();
    kvmsg_set_sequence (self, sequence);
    return self;
}

//  zhash_free_fn callback helper that does the low level destruction:
void
kvmsg_free (void *ptr)
{
    if (ptr) {
        kvmsg_t *self = (kvmsg_t *) ptr;
        //  Destroy message frames if any
        int frame_nbr;
        for (frame_nbr = 0; frame_nbr < KVMSG_FRAMES; frame_nbr++)
            if (self->present [frame_nbr])
                zmq_msg_close (&self->frame [frame_nbr]);
```

```
            //  Destroy property list
            while (zlist_size (self->props))
                free (zlist_pop (self->props));
            zlist_destroy (&self->props);

            //  Free object itself
            free (self);
        }
    }

    //  Destructor
    void
    kvmsg_destroy (kvmsg_t **self_p)
    {
        assert (self_p);
        if (*self_p) {
            kvmsg_free (*self_p);
            *self_p = NULL;
        }
    }
```

This method reads a key-value message from the socket and returns a new kvmsg instance:

Example 79-3. Key-value message class: full (kvmsg.c) - recv method

```
    kvmsg_t *
    kvmsg_recv (void *socket)
    {
        //  This method is almost unchanged from kvsimple
        ...
        if (self)
            s_decode_props (self);
        return self;
    }

    //  Send key-value message to socket; any empty frames are sent as such.
    void
    kvmsg_send (kvmsg_t *self, void *socket)
    {
        assert (self);
        assert (socket);

        s_encode_props (self);
        //  The rest of the method is unchanged from kvsimple
        ...
```

This method duplicates a kvmsg instance, returns the new instance:

Example 79-4. Key-value message class: full (kvmsg.c) - dup method

```
kvmsg_t *
kvmsg_dup (kvmsg_t *self)
{
    kvmsg_t *kvmsg = kvmsg_new (0);
    int frame_nbr;
    for (frame_nbr = 0; frame_nbr < KVMSG_FRAMES; frame_nbr++) {
        if (self->present [frame_nbr]) {
            zmq_msg_t *src = &self->frame [frame_nbr];
            zmq_msg_t *dst = &kvmsg->frame [frame_nbr];
            zmq_msg_init_size (dst, zmq_msg_size (src));
            memcpy (zmq_msg_data (dst),
                    zmq_msg_data (src), zmq_msg_size (src));
            kvmsg->present [frame_nbr] = 1;
        }
    }
    kvmsg->props_size = zlist_size (self->props);
    char *prop = (char *) zlist_first (self->props);
    while (prop) {
        zlist_append (kvmsg->props, strdup (prop));
        prop = (char *) zlist_next (self->props);
    }
    return kvmsg;
}

// The key, sequence, body, and size methods are the same as in kvsimple.
...
```

These methods get and set the UUID for the key-value message:

Example 79-5. Key-value message class: full (kvmsg.c) - UUID methods

```
byte *
kvmsg_uuid (kvmsg_t *self)
{
    assert (self);
    if (self->present [FRAME_UUID]
    &&  zmq_msg_size (&self->frame [FRAME_UUID]) == sizeof (uuid_t))
        return (byte *) zmq_msg_data (&self->frame [FRAME_UUID]);
    else
        return NULL;
}

// Sets the UUID to a randomly generated value
void
kvmsg_set_uuid (kvmsg_t *self)
{
    assert (self);
```

```
        zmq_msg_t *msg = &self->frame [FRAME_UUID];
        uuid_t uuid;
        uuid_generate (uuid);
        if (self->present [FRAME_UUID])
            zmq_msg_close (msg);
        zmq_msg_init_size (msg, sizeof (uuid));
        memcpy (zmq_msg_data (msg), uuid, sizeof (uuid));
        self->present [FRAME_UUID] = 1;
}
```

These methods get and set a specified message property:

Example 79-6. Key-value message class: full (kvmsg.c) - property methods

```
//  Get message property, return "" if no such property is defined.
char *
kvmsg_get_prop (kvmsg_t *self, char *name)
{
    assert (strchr (name, '=') == NULL);
    char *prop = zlist_first (self->props);
    size_t namelen = strlen (name);
    while (prop) {
        if (strlen (prop) > namelen
        &&  memcmp (prop, name, namelen) == 0
        &&  prop [namelen] == '=')
            return prop + namelen + 1;
        prop = zlist_next (self->props);
    }
    return "";
}


//  Set message property. Property name cannot contain '='. Max length of
//  value is 255 chars.
void
kvmsg_set_prop (kvmsg_t *self, char *name, char *format, ...)
{
    assert (strchr (name, '=') == NULL);

    char value [255 + 1];
    va_list args;
    assert (self);
    va_start (args, format);
    vsnprintf (value, 255, format, args);
    va_end (args);

    //  Allocate name=value string
    char *prop = malloc (strlen (name) + strlen (value) + 2);

    //  Remove existing property if any
    sprintf (prop, "%s=", name);
    char *existing = zlist_first (self->props);
```

```
        while (existing) {
            if (memcmp (prop, existing, strlen (prop)) == 0) {
                self->props_size -= strlen (existing) + 1;
                zlist_remove (self->props, existing);
                free (existing);
                break;
            }
            existing = zlist_next (self->props);
        }
        //  Add new name=value property string
        strcat (prop, value);
        zlist_append (self->props, prop);
        self->props_size += strlen (prop) + 1;
    }
}
```

This method stores the key-value message into a hash map, unless the key and value are both null. It nullifies the `kvmsg` reference so that the object is owned by the hash map, not the caller:

Example 79-7. Key-value message class: full (kvmsg.c) - store method

```
void
kvmsg_store (kvmsg_t **self_p, zhash_t *hash)
{
    assert (self_p);
    if (*self_p) {
        kvmsg_t *self = *self_p;
        assert (self);
        if (kvmsg_size (self)) {
            if (self->present [FRAME_KEY]
            &&  self->present [FRAME_BODY]) {
                zhash_update (hash, kvmsg_key (self), self);
                zhash_freefn (hash, kvmsg_key (self), kvmsg_free);
            }
        }
        else
            zhash_delete (hash, kvmsg_key (self));

        *self_p = NULL;
    }
}
```

This method extends the `kvsimple` implementation with support for message properties:

Example 79-8. Key-value message class: full (kvmsg.c) - dump method

```
void
kvmsg_dump (kvmsg_t *self)
{
    ...
```

```
            fprintf (stderr, "[size:%zd] ", size);
            if (zlist_size (self->props)) {
                fprintf (stderr, "[");
                char *prop = zlist_first (self->props);
                while (prop) {
                    fprintf (stderr, "%s;", prop);
                    prop = zlist_next (self->props);
                }
                fprintf (stderr, "]");
            }
...
```

This method is the same as in kvsimple with added support for the uuid and property features of kvmsg:

Example 79-9. Key-value message class: full (kvmsg.c) - test method

```
int
kvmsg_test (int verbose)
{
...
    //  Test send and receive of simple message
    kvmsg = kvmsg_new (1);
    kvmsg_set_key  (kvmsg, "key");
    kvmsg_set_uuid (kvmsg);
    kvmsg_set_body (kvmsg, (byte *) "body", 4);
    if (verbose)
        kvmsg_dump (kvmsg);
    kvmsg_send (kvmsg, output);
    kvmsg_store (&kvmsg, kvmap);

    kvmsg = kvmsg_recv (input);
    if (verbose)
        kvmsg_dump (kvmsg);
    assert (streq (kvmsg_key (kvmsg), "key"));
    kvmsg_store (&kvmsg, kvmap);

    //  Test send and receive of message with properties
    kvmsg = kvmsg_new (2);
    kvmsg_set_prop (kvmsg, "prop1", "value1");
    kvmsg_set_prop (kvmsg, "prop2", "value1");
    kvmsg_set_prop (kvmsg, "prop2", "value2");
    kvmsg_set_key  (kvmsg, "key");
    kvmsg_set_uuid (kvmsg);
    kvmsg_set_body (kvmsg, (byte *) "body", 4);
    assert (streq (kvmsg_get_prop (kvmsg, "prop2"), "value2"));
    if (verbose)
        kvmsg_dump (kvmsg);
    kvmsg_send (kvmsg, output);
    kvmsg_destroy (&kvmsg);
```

```
        kvmsg = kvmsg_recv (input);
        if (verbose)
            kvmsg_dump (kvmsg);
        assert (streq (kvmsg_key (kvmsg), "key"));
        assert (streq (kvmsg_get_prop (kvmsg, "prop2"), "value2"));
        kvmsg_destroy (&kvmsg);
    ...
```

The Model Five client is almost identical to Model Four. It uses the full kvmsg class now, and sets a randomized ttl property (measured in seconds) on each message:

```
    kvmsg_set_prop (kvmsg, "ttl", "%d", randof (30));
```

Using a Reactor

Until now, we have used a poll loop in the server. In this next model of the server, we switch to using a reactor. In C, we use CZMQ's zloop class. Using a reactor makes the code more verbose, but easier to understand and build out because each piece of the server is handled by a separate reactor handler.

We use a single thread and pass a server object around to the reactor handlers. We could have organized the server as multiple threads, each handling one socket or timer, but that works better when threads don't have to share data. In this case all work is centered around the server's hashmap, so one thread is simpler.

There are three reactor handlers:

- One to handle snapshot requests coming on the ROUTER socket;
- One to handle incoming updates from clients, coming on the PULL socket;
- One to expire ephemeral values that have passed their TTL.

Example 80. Clone server, Model Five (clonesrv5.c)

```
//  Clone server - Model Five

//  Lets us build this source without creating a library
#include "kvmsg.c"

//  zloop reactor handlers
static int s_snapshots  (zloop_t *loop, zmq_pollitem_t *poller, void *args);
static int s_collector  (zloop_t *loop, zmq_pollitem_t *poller, void *args);
static int s_flush_ttl  (zloop_t *loop, zmq_pollitem_t *poller, void *args);

//  Our server is defined by these properties
typedef struct {
    zctx_t *ctx;                //  Context wrapper
    zhash_t *kvmap;             //  Key-value store
    zloop_t *loop;              //  zloop reactor
    int port;                   //  Main port we're working on
    int64_t sequence;           //  How many updates we're at
    void *snapshot;             //  Handle snapshot requests
```

```
        void *publisher;           //  Publish updates to clients
        void *collector;           //  Collect updates from clients
    } clonesrv_t;

    int main (void)
    {
        clonesrv_t *self = (clonesrv_t *) zmalloc (sizeof (clonesrv_t));
        self->port = 5556;
        self->ctx = zctx_new ();
        self->kvmap = zhash_new ();
        self->loop = zloop_new ();
        zloop_set_verbose (self->loop, FALSE);

        //  Set up our clone server sockets
        self->snapshot  = zsocket_new (self->ctx, ZMQ_ROUTER);
        zsocket_bind (self->snapshot, "tcp://*:%d", self->port);
        self->publisher = zsocket_new (self->ctx, ZMQ_PUB);
        zsocket_bind (self->publisher, "tcp://*:%d", self->port + 1);
        self->collector = zsocket_new (self->ctx, ZMQ_PULL);
        zsocket_bind (self->collector, "tcp://*:%d", self->port + 2);

        //  Register our handlers with reactor
        zmq_pollitem_t poller = { 0, 0, ZMQ_POLLIN };
        poller.socket = self->snapshot;
        zloop_poller (self->loop, &poller, s_snapshots, self);
        poller.socket = self->collector;
        zloop_poller (self->loop, &poller, s_collector, self);
        zloop_timer (self->loop, 1000, 0, s_flush_ttl, self);

        //  Run reactor until process interrupted
        zloop_start (self->loop);

        zloop_destroy (&self->loop);
        zhash_destroy (&self->kvmap);
        zctx_destroy (&self->ctx);
        free (self);
        return 0;
    }
```

We handle ICANHAZ? requests by sending snapshot data to the client that requested it:

Example 80-1. Clone server, Model Five (clonesrv5.c) - send snapshots

```
    //  Routing information for a key-value snapshot
    typedef struct {
        void *socket;           //  ROUTER socket to send to
        zframe_t *identity;     //  Identity of peer who requested state
        char *subtree;          //  Client subtree specification
    } kvroute_t;
```

```
// We call this function for each key-value pair in our hash table
static int
s_send_single (const char *key, void *data, void *args)
{
    kvroute_t *kvroute = (kvroute_t *) args;
    kvmsg_t *kvmsg = (kvmsg_t *) data;
    if (strlen (kvroute->subtree) <= strlen (kvmsg_key (kvmsg))
    &&  memcmp (kvroute->subtree,
                kvmsg_key (kvmsg), strlen (kvroute->subtree)) == 0) {
        zframe_send (&kvroute->identity,    // Choose recipient
            kvroute->socket, ZFRAME_MORE + ZFRAME_REUSE);
        kvmsg_send (kvmsg, kvroute->socket);
    }
    return 0;
}
```

This is the reactor handler for the snapshot socket; it accepts just the ICANHAZ? request and replies with a state snapshot ending with a KTHXBAI message:

Example 80-2. Clone server, Model Five (clonesrv5.c) - snapshot handler

```
static int
s_snapshots (zloop_t *loop, zmq_pollitem_t *poller, void *args)
{
    clonesrv_t *self = (clonesrv_t *) args;

    zframe_t *identity = zframe_recv (poller->socket);
    if (identity) {
        // Request is in second frame of message
        char *request = zstr_recv (poller->socket);
        char *subtree = NULL;
        if (streq (request, "ICANHAZ?")) {
            free (request);
            subtree = zstr_recv (poller->socket);
        }
        else
            printf ("E: bad request, aborting\n");

        if (subtree) {
            // Send state socket to client
            kvroute_t routing = { poller->socket, identity, subtree };
            zhash_foreach (self->kvmap, s_send_single, &routing);

            // Now send END message with sequence number
            zclock_log ("I: sending shapshot=%d", (int) self->sequence);
            zframe_send (&identity, poller->socket, ZFRAME_MORE);
            kvmsg_t *kvmsg = kvmsg_new (self->sequence);
            kvmsg_set_key  (kvmsg, "KTHXBAI");
            kvmsg_set_body (kvmsg, (byte *) subtree, 0);
            kvmsg_send     (kvmsg, poller->socket);
            kvmsg_destroy (&kvmsg);
```

Code Connected Volume 1 - Chapter 5. Advanced Pub-Sub Patterns   283

```
            free (subtree);
        }
        zframe_destroy (&identity);
    }
    return 0;
}
```

We store each update with a new sequence number, and if necessary, a time-to-live. We publish updates immediately on our publisher socket:

Example 80-3. Clone server, Model Five (clonesrv5.c) - collect updates

```
static int
s_collector (zloop_t *loop, zmq_pollitem_t *poller, void *args)
{
    clonesrv_t *self = (clonesrv_t *) args;

    kvmsg_t *kvmsg = kvmsg_recv (poller->socket);
    if (kvmsg) {
        kvmsg_set_sequence (kvmsg, ++self->sequence);
        kvmsg_send (kvmsg, self->publisher);
        int ttl = atoi (kvmsg_get_prop (kvmsg, "ttl"));
        if (ttl)
            kvmsg_set_prop (kvmsg, "ttl",
                "%" PRId64, zclock_time () + ttl * 1000);
        kvmsg_store (&kvmsg, self->kvmap);
        zclock_log ("I: publishing update=%d", (int) self->sequence);
    }
    return 0;
}
```

At regular intervals, we flush ephemeral values that have expired. This could be slow on very large data sets:

Example 80-4. Clone server, Model Five (clonesrv5.c) - flush ephemeral values

```
//  If key-value pair has expired, delete it and publish the
//  fact to listening clients.
static int
s_flush_single (const char *key, void *data, void *args)
{
    clonesrv_t *self = (clonesrv_t *) args;

    kvmsg_t *kvmsg = (kvmsg_t *) data;
    int64_t ttl;
    sscanf (kvmsg_get_prop (kvmsg, "ttl"), "%" PRId64, &ttl);
    if (ttl && zclock_time () >= ttl) {
        kvmsg_set_sequence (kvmsg, ++self->sequence);
        kvmsg_set_body (kvmsg, (byte *) "", 0);
        kvmsg_send (kvmsg, self->publisher);
        kvmsg_store (&kvmsg, self->kvmap);
```

```
            zclock_log ("I: publishing delete=%d", (int) self->sequence);
        }
        return 0;
    }

    static int
    s_flush_ttl (zloop_t *loop, zmq_pollitem_t *poller, void *args)
    {
        clonesrv_t *self = (clonesrv_t *) args;
        if (self->kvmap)
            zhash_foreach (self->kvmap, s_flush_single, args);
        return 0;
    }
```

Adding the Binary Star Pattern for Reliability

The Clone models we've explored up to now have been relatively simple. Now we're going to get into unpleasantly complex territory, which has me getting up for another espresso. You should appreciate that making "reliable" messaging is complex enough that you always need to ask, "Do we actually need this?" before jumping into it. If you can get away with unreliable or with "good enough" reliability, you can make a huge win in terms of cost and complexity. Sure, you may lose some data now and then. It is often a good trade-off. Having said, that, and... sips... because the espresso is really good, let's jump in.

As you play with the last model, you'll stop and restart the server. It might look like it recovers, but of course it's applying updates to an empty state instead of the proper current state. Any new client joining the network will only get the latest updates instead of the full historical record.

What we want is a way for the server to recover from being killed, or crashing. We also need to provide backup in case the server is out of commission for any length of time. When someone asks for "reliability", ask them to list the failures they want to handle. In our case, these are:

- The server process crashes and is automatically or manually restarted. The process loses its state and has to get it back from somewhere.
- The server machine dies and is offline for a significant time. Clients have to switch to an alternate server somewhere.
- The server process or machine gets disconnected from the network, e.g., a switch dies or a datacenter gets knocked out. It may come back at some point, but in the meantime clients need an alternate server.

Our first step is to add a second server. We can use the Binary Star pattern from "Reliable Request-Reply Patterns" to organize these into primary and backup. Binary Star is a reactor, so it's useful that we already refactored the last server model into a reactor style.

We need to ensure that updates are not lost if the primary server crashes. The simplest technique is to send them to both servers. The backup server can then act as a client, and keep its state synchronized by receiving updates as all clients do. It'll also get new updates from clients. It can't yet store these in its hash table, but it can hold onto them for a while.

So, Model Six introduces the following changes over Model Five:
- We use a pub-sub flow instead of a push-pull flow for client updates sent to the servers. This takes care of fanning out the updates to both servers. Otherwise we'd have to use two DEALER sockets.
- We add heartbeats to server updates (to clients), so that a client can detect when the primary server has died. It can then switch over to the backup server.
- We connect the two servers using the Binary Star bstar reactor class. Binary Star relies on the clients to vote by making an explicit request to the server they consider active. We'll use snapshot requests as the voting mechanism.
- We make all update messages uniquely identifiable by adding a UUID field. The client generates this, and the server propagates it back on republished updates.
- The passive server keeps a "pending list" of updates that it has received from clients, but not yet from the active server; or updates it's received from the active server, but not yet from the clients. The list is ordered from oldest to newest, so that it is easy to remove updates off the head.

It's useful to design the client logic as a finite state machine. The client cycles through three states:
- The client opens and connects its sockets, and then requests a snapshot from the first server. To avoid request storms, it will ask any given server only twice. One request might get lost, which would be bad luck. Two getting lost would be carelessness.
- The client waits for a reply (snapshot data) from the current server, and if it gets it, it stores it. If there is no reply within some timeout, it fails over to the next server.

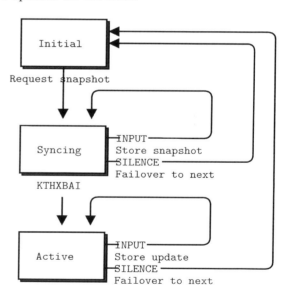

Figure 61. Clone Client Finite State Machine

- When the client has gotten its snapshot, it waits for and processes updates. Again, if it doesn't hear anything from the server within some timeout, it fails over to the next server.

The client loops forever. It's quite likely during startup or failover that some clients may be trying to talk to the primary server while others are trying to talk to the backup server. The Binary Star state machine handles this (see figure 61), hopefully accurately. It's hard to prove software correct; instead we hammer it until we can't prove it wrong.

Failover happens as follows:

- The client detects that primary server is no longer sending heartbeats, and concludes that it has died. The client connects to the backup server and requests a new state snapshot.
- The backup server starts to receive snapshot requests from clients, and detects that primary server has gone, so it takes over as primary.
- The backup server applies its pending list to its own hash table, and then starts to process state snapshot requests.

When the primary server comes back online, it will:

- Start up as passive server, and connect to the backup server as a Clone client.
- Start to receive updates from clients, via its SUB socket.

We make a few assumptions:

- At least one server will keep running. If both servers crash, we lose all server state and there's no way to recover it.
- Multiple clients do not update the same hash keys at the same time. Client updates will arrive at the two servers in a different order. Therefore, the backup server may apply updates from its pending list in a different order than the primary server would or did. Updates from one client will always arrive in the same order on both servers, so that is safe.

Thus the architecture for our high-availability server pair using the Binary Star pattern has two servers and a set of clients that talk to both servers (see figure 62).

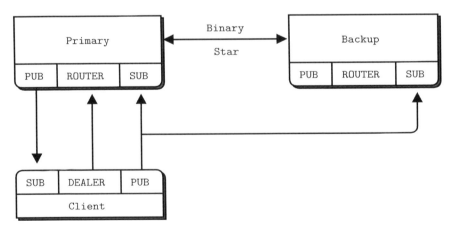

Figure 62. High-availability Clone Server Pair

Here is the sixth and last model of the Clone server:

Example 81. Clone server, Model Six (clonesrv6.c)

```
//  Clone server Model Six

//  Lets us build this source without creating a library
#include "bstar.c"
#include "kvmsg.c"
```

We define a set of reactor handlers and our server object structure:

Example 81-1. Clone server, Model Six (clonesrv6.c) - definitions

```
//  Bstar reactor handlers
static int
    s_snapshots    (zloop_t *loop, zmq_pollitem_t *poller, void *args);
static int
    s_collector    (zloop_t *loop, zmq_pollitem_t *poller, void *args);
static int
    s_flush_ttl    (zloop_t *loop, zmq_pollitem_t *poller, void *args);
static int
    s_send_hugz    (zloop_t *loop, zmq_pollitem_t *poller, void *args);
static int
    s_new_active   (zloop_t *loop, zmq_pollitem_t *poller, void *args);
static int
    s_new_passive  (zloop_t *loop, zmq_pollitem_t *poller, void *args);
static int
    s_subscriber   (zloop_t *loop, zmq_pollitem_t *poller, void *args);

//  Our server is defined by these properties
typedef struct {
    zctx_t *ctx;                //  Context wrapper
    zhash_t *kvmap;             //  Key-value store
    bstar_t *bstar;             //  Bstar reactor core
    int64_t sequence;           //  How many updates we're at
    int port;                   //  Main port we're working on
    int peer;                   //  Main port of our peer
    void *publisher;            //  Publish updates and hugz
    void *collector;            //  Collect updates from clients
    void *subscriber;           //  Get updates from peer
    zlist_t *pending;           //  Pending updates from clients
    Bool primary;               //  TRUE if we're primary
    Bool active;                //  TRUE if we're active
    Bool passive;                //  TRUE if we're passive
} clonesrv_t;
```

The main task parses the command line to decide whether to start as a primary or backup server. We're using the Binary Star pattern for reliability. This interconnects the two servers so they can agree on which one is primary and which one is backup. To allow the two servers to run on the same box, we use different ports for primary and backup. Ports 5003/5004 are used to interconnect the servers. Ports 5556/5566 are used to receive voting events (snapshot requests in the clone pattern). Ports 5557/5567 are used by the publisher, and ports 5558/5568 are used by the collector:

Example 81-2. Clone server, Model Six (clonesrv6.c) - main task setup

```
int main (int argc, char *argv [])
{
    clonesrv_t *self = (clonesrv_t *) zmalloc (sizeof (clonesrv_t));
    if (argc == 2 && streq (argv [1], "-p")) {
        zclock_log ("I: primary active, waiting for backup (passive)");
        self->bstar = bstar_new (BSTAR_PRIMARY, "tcp://*:5003",
                                 "tcp://localhost:5004");
        bstar_voter (self->bstar, "tcp://*:5556",
                     ZMQ_ROUTER, s_snapshots, self);
        self->port = 5556;
        self->peer = 5566;
        self->primary = TRUE;
    }
    else
    if (argc == 2 && streq (argv [1], "-b")) {
        zclock_log ("I: backup passive, waiting for primary (active)");
        self->bstar = bstar_new (BSTAR_BACKUP, "tcp://*:5004",
                                 "tcp://localhost:5003");
        bstar_voter (self->bstar, "tcp://*:5566",
                     ZMQ_ROUTER, s_snapshots, self);
        self->port = 5566;
        self->peer = 5556;
        self->primary = FALSE;
    }
    else {
        printf ("Usage: clonesrv4 { -p | -b }\n");
        free (self);
        exit (0);
    }
    // Primary server will become first active
    if (self->primary)
        self->kvmap = zhash_new ();

    self->ctx = zctx_new ();
    self->pending = zlist_new ();
    bstar_set_verbose (self->bstar, TRUE);

    // Set up our clone server sockets
    self->publisher = zsocket_new (self->ctx, ZMQ_PUB);
    self->collector = zsocket_new (self->ctx, ZMQ_SUB);
```

```
    zsockopt_set_subscribe (self->collector, "");
    zsocket_bind (self->publisher, "tcp://*:%d", self->port + 1);
    zsocket_bind (self->collector, "tcp://*:%d", self->port + 2);

    //  Set up our own clone client interface to peer
    self->subscriber = zsocket_new (self->ctx, ZMQ_SUB);
    zsockopt_set_subscribe (self->subscriber, "");
    zsocket_connect (self->subscriber,
                     "tcp://localhost:%d", self->peer + 1);
```

After we've setup our sockets, we register our binary star event handlers, and then start the bstar reactor. This finishes when the user presses Ctrl-C or when the process receives a SIGINT interrupt:

Example 81-3. Clone server, Model Six (clonesrv6.c) - main task body

```
    //  Register state change handlers
    bstar_new_active (self->bstar, s_new_active, self);
    bstar_new_passive (self->bstar, s_new_passive, self);

    //  Register our other handlers with the bstar reactor
    zmq_pollitem_t poller = { self->collector, 0, ZMQ_POLLIN };
    zloop_poller (bstar_zloop (self->bstar), &poller, s_collector, self);
    zloop_timer  (bstar_zloop (self->bstar), 1000, 0, s_flush_ttl, self);
    zloop_timer  (bstar_zloop (self->bstar), 1000, 0, s_send_hugz, self);

    //  Start the bstar reactor
    bstar_start (self->bstar);

    //  Interrupted, so shut down
    while (zlist_size (self->pending)) {
        kvmsg_t *kvmsg = (kvmsg_t *) zlist_pop (self->pending);
        kvmsg_destroy (&kvmsg);
    }
    zlist_destroy (&self->pending);
    bstar_destroy (&self->bstar);
    zhash_destroy (&self->kvmap);
    zctx_destroy (&self->ctx);
    free (self);

    return 0;
}

//  We handle ICANHAZ? requests exactly as in the clonesrv5 example.
...
```

The collector is more complex than in the clonesrv5 example because the way it processes updates depends on whether we're active or passive. The active applies them immediately to its kvmap, whereas the passive queues them as pending:

Example 81-4. Clone server, Model Six (clonesrv6.c) - collect updates

```
//  If message was already on pending list, remove it and return TRUE,
//  else return FALSE.
static int
s_was_pending (clonesrv_t *self, kvmsg_t *kvmsg)
{
    kvmsg_t *held = (kvmsg_t *) zlist_first (self->pending);
    while (held) {
        if (memcmp (kvmsg_uuid (kvmsg),
                    kvmsg_uuid (held), sizeof (uuid_t)) == 0) {
            zlist_remove (self->pending, held);
            return TRUE;
        }
        held = (kvmsg_t *) zlist_next (self->pending);
    }
    return FALSE;
}

static int
s_collector (zloop_t *loop, zmq_pollitem_t *poller, void *args)
{
    clonesrv_t *self = (clonesrv_t *) args;

    kvmsg_t *kvmsg = kvmsg_recv (poller->socket);
    if (kvmsg) {
        if (self->active) {
            kvmsg_set_sequence (kvmsg, ++self->sequence);
            kvmsg_send (kvmsg, self->publisher);
            int ttl = atoi (kvmsg_get_prop (kvmsg, "ttl"));
            if (ttl)
                kvmsg_set_prop (kvmsg, "ttl",
                    "%" PRId64, zclock_time () + ttl * 1000);
            kvmsg_store (&kvmsg, self->kvmap);
            zclock_log ("I: publishing update=%d", (int) self->sequence);
        }
        else {
            //  If we already got message from active, drop it, else
            //  hold on pending list
            if (s_was_pending (self, kvmsg))
                kvmsg_destroy (&kvmsg);
            else
                zlist_append (self->pending, kvmsg);
        }
    }
    return 0;
}
```

```
// We purge ephemeral values using exactly the same code as in
// the previous clonesrv5 example.
...
```

We send a HUGZ message once a second to all subscribers so that they can detect if our server dies. They'll then switch over to the backup server, which will become active:

Example 81-5. Clone server, Model Six (clonesrv6.c) - heartbeating

```
static int
s_send_hugz (zloop_t *loop, zmq_pollitem_t *poller, void *args)
{
    clonesrv_t *self = (clonesrv_t *) args;

    kvmsg_t *kvmsg = kvmsg_new (self->sequence);
    kvmsg_set_key  (kvmsg, "HUGZ");
    kvmsg_set_body (kvmsg, (byte *) "", 0);
    kvmsg_send     (kvmsg, self->publisher);
    kvmsg_destroy (&kvmsg);

    return 0;
}
```

When we switch from passive to active, we apply our pending list so that our kvmap is up-to-date. When we switch to passive, we wipe our kvmap and grab a new snapshot from the active server:

Example 81-6. Clone server, Model Six (clonesrv6.c) - handling state changes

```
static int
s_new_active (zloop_t *loop, zmq_pollitem_t *unused, void *args)
{
    clonesrv_t *self = (clonesrv_t *) args;

    self->active = TRUE;
    self->passive = FALSE;

    //  Stop subscribing to updates
    zmq_pollitem_t poller = { self->subscriber, 0, ZMQ_POLLIN };
    zloop_poller_end (bstar_zloop (self->bstar), &poller);

    //  Apply pending list to own hash table
    while (zlist_size (self->pending)) {
        kvmsg_t *kvmsg = (kvmsg_t *) zlist_pop (self->pending);
        kvmsg_set_sequence (kvmsg, ++self->sequence);
        kvmsg_send (kvmsg, self->publisher);
        kvmsg_store (&kvmsg, self->kvmap);
        zclock_log ("I: publishing pending=%d", (int) self->sequence);
    }
    return 0;
```

```
}

static int
s_new_passive (zloop_t *loop, zmq_pollitem_t *unused, void *args)
{
    clonesrv_t *self = (clonesrv_t *) args;

    zhash_destroy (&self->kvmap);
    self->active = FALSE;
    self->passive = TRUE;

    //  Start subscribing to updates
    zmq_pollitem_t poller = { self->subscriber, 0, ZMQ_POLLIN };
    zloop_poller (bstar_zloop (self->bstar), &poller, s_subscriber, self);

    return 0;
}
```

When we get an update, we create a new kvmap if necessary, and then add our update to our kvmap. We're always passive in this case:

Example 81-7. Clone server, Model Six (clonesrv6.c) - subscriber handler

```
static int
s_subscriber (zloop_t *loop, zmq_pollitem_t *poller, void *args)
{
    clonesrv_t *self = (clonesrv_t *) args;
    //  Get state snapshot if necessary
    if (self->kvmap == NULL) {
        self->kvmap = zhash_new ();
        void *snapshot = zsocket_new (self->ctx, ZMQ_DEALER);
        zsocket_connect (snapshot, "tcp://localhost:%d", self->peer);
        zclock_log ("I: asking for snapshot from: tcp://localhost:%d",
                    self->peer);
        zstr_sendm (snapshot, "ICANHAZ?");
        zstr_send (snapshot, ""); // blank subtree to get all
        while (true) {
            kvmsg_t *kvmsg = kvmsg_recv (snapshot);
            if (!kvmsg)
                break;          //  Interrupted
            if (streq (kvmsg_key (kvmsg), "KTHXBAI")) {
                self->sequence = kvmsg_sequence (kvmsg);
                kvmsg_destroy (&kvmsg);
                break;          //  Done
            }
            kvmsg_store (&kvmsg, self->kvmap);
        }
        zclock_log ("I: received snapshot=%d", (int) self->sequence);
        zsocket_destroy (self->ctx, snapshot);
    }
    //  Find and remove update off pending list
```

```
        kvmsg_t *kvmsg = kvmsg_recv (poller->socket);
        if (!kvmsg)
            return 0;

        if (strneq (kvmsg_key (kvmsg), "HUGZ")) {
            if (!s_was_pending (self, kvmsg)) {
                //  If active update came before client update, flip it
                //  around, store active update (with sequence) on pending
                //  list and use to clear client update when it comes later
                zlist_append (self->pending, kvmsg_dup (kvmsg));
            }
            //  If update is more recent than our kvmap, apply it
            if (kvmsg_sequence (kvmsg) > self->sequence) {
                self->sequence = kvmsg_sequence (kvmsg);
                kvmsg_store (&kvmsg, self->kvmap);
                zclock_log ("I: received update=%d", (int) self->sequence);
            }
            else
                kvmsg_destroy (&kvmsg);
        }
        else
            kvmsg_destroy (&kvmsg);

        return 0;
    }
```

This model is only a few hundred lines of code, but it took quite a while to get working. To be accurate, building Model Six took about a full week of "Sweet god, this is just too complex for an example" hacking. We've assembled pretty much everything and the kitchen sink into this small application. We have failover, ephemeral values, subtrees, and so on. What surprised me was that the upfront design was pretty accurate. Still the details of writing and debugging so many socket flows is quite challenging.

The reactor-based design removes a lot of the grunt work from the code, and what remains is simpler and easier to understand. We reuse the bstar reactor from "Reliable Request-Reply Patterns". The whole server runs as one thread, so there's no inter-thread weirdness going on—just a structure pointer (self) passed around to all handlers, which can do their thing happily. One nice side effect of using reactors is that the code, being less tightly integrated into a poll loop, is much easier to reuse. Large chunks of Model Six are taken from Model Five.

I built it piece by piece, and got each piece working *properly* before going onto the next one. Because there are four or five main socket flows, that meant quite a lot of debugging and testing. I debugged just by dumping messages to the console. Don't use classic debuggers to step through ØMQ applications; you need to see the message flows to make any sense of what is going on.

For testing, I always try to use Valgrind, which catches memory leaks and invalid memory accesses. In C, this is a major concern, as you can't delegate to a garbage collector. Using proper and consistent abstractions like kvmsg and CZMQ helps enormously.

The Clustered Hashmap Protocol

While the server is pretty much a mashup of the previous model plus the Binary Star pattern, the client is quite a lot more complex. But before we get to that, let's look at the final protocol. I've written this up as a specification on the ZeroMQ RFC website as the Clustered Hashmap Protocol[22].

Roughly, there are two ways to design a complex protocol such as this one. One way is to separate each flow into its own set of sockets. This is the approach we used here. The advantage is that each flow is simple and clean. The disadvantage is that managing multiple socket flows at once can be quite complex. Using a reactor makes it simpler, but still, it makes a lot of moving pieces that have to fit together correctly.

The second way to make such a protocol is to use a single socket pair for everything. In this case, I'd have used ROUTER for the server and DEALER for the clients, and then done everything over that connection. It makes for a more complex protocol but at least the complexity is all in one place. In Code Connected Volume 2 we'll look at an example of a protocol done over a ROUTER-DEALER combination.

Let's look at CHP in more detail now. Note that "SHOULD", "MUST" and "MAY" are key words we use in protocol specifications to indicate requirement levels.

Goals

CHP is meant to provide a basis for reliable pub-sub across a cluster of clients connected over a ØMQ network. It defines a "hashmap" abstraction consisting of key-value pairs. Any client can modify any key-value pair at any time, and changes are propagated to all clients. A client can join the network at any time.

Architecture

CHP connects a set of client applications and a set of servers. Clients connect to the server. Clients do not see each other. Clients can come and go arbitrarily.

Ports and Connections

The server MUST open three ports as follows:

- A SNAPSHOT port (ØMQ ROUTER socket) at port number P.
- A PUBLISHER port (ØMQ PUB socket) at port number P + 1.
- A COLLECTOR port (ØMQ SUB socket) at port number P + 2.

The client SHOULD open at least two connections:

- A SNAPSHOT connection (ØMQ DEALER socket) to port number P.
- A SUBSCRIBER connection (ØMQ SUB socket) to port number P + 1.

The client MAY open a third connection, if it wants to update the hashmap:

- A PUBLISHER connection (ØMQ PUB socket) to port number P + 2.

---

22 http://rfc.zeromq.org/spec:12

This extra frame is not shown in the commands explained below.

State Synchronization

The client MUST start by sending a ICANHAZ command to its snapshot connection. This command consists of two frames as follows:

```
ICANHAZ command
-----------------------------------
Frame 0: "ICANHAZ?"
Frame 1: subtree specification
```

Both frames are ØMQ strings. The subtree specification MAY be empty. If not empty, it consists of a slash followed by one or more path segments, ending in a slash.

The server MUST respond to a ICANHAZ command by sending zero or more KVSYNC commands to its snapshot port, followed with a KTHXBAI command. The server MUST prefix each command with the identity of the client, as provided by ØMQ with the ICANHAZ command. The KVSYNC command specifies a single key-value pair as follows:

```
KVSYNC command
-----------------------------------
Frame 0: key, as OMQ string
Frame 1: sequence number, 8 bytes in network order
Frame 2: <empty>
Frame 3: <empty>
Frame 4: value, as blob
```

The sequence number has no significance and may be zero.

The KTHXBAI command takes this form:

```
KTHXBAI command
-----------------------------------
Frame 0: "KTHXBAI"
Frame 1: sequence number, 8 bytes in network order
Frame 2: <empty>
Frame 3: <empty>
Frame 4: subtree specification
```

The sequence number MUST be the highest sequence number of the KVSYNC commands previously sent.

When the client has received a KTHXBAI command, it SHOULD start to receive messages from its subscriber connection and apply them.

Server-to-Client Updates

When the server has an update for its hashmap it MUST broadcast this on its publisher socket as a KVPUB command. The KVPUB command has this form:

```
KVPUB command
------------------------------------
Frame 0: key, as OMQ string
Frame 1: sequence number, 8 bytes in network order
Frame 2: UUID, 16 bytes
Frame 3: properties, as OMQ string
Frame 4: value, as blob
```

The sequence number MUST be strictly incremental. The client MUST discard any KVPUB commands whose sequence numbers are not strictly greater than the last KTHXBAI or KVPUB command received.

The UUID is optional and frame 2 MAY be empty (size zero). The properties field is formatted as zero or more instances of "name=value" followed by a newline character. If the key-value pair has no properties, the properties field is empty.

If the value is empty, the client SHOULD delete its key-value entry with the specified key.

In the absence of other updates the server SHOULD send a HUGZ command at regular intervals, e.g., once per second. The HUGZ command has this format:

```
HUGZ command
------------------------------------
Frame 0: "HUGZ"
Frame 1: 00000000
Frame 2: <empty>
Frame 3: <empty>
Frame 4: <empty>
```

The client MAY treat the absence of HUGZ as an indicator that the server has crashed (see Reliability below).

Client-to-Server Updates

When the client has an update for its hashmap, it MAY send this to the server via its publisher connection as a KVSET command. The KVSET command has this form:

```
KVSET command
------------------------------------
Frame 0: key, as OMQ string
Frame 1: sequence number, 8 bytes in network order
Frame 2: UUID, 16 bytes
Frame 3: properties, as OMQ string
Frame 4: value, as blob
```

The sequence number has no significance and may be zero. The UUID SHOULD be a universally unique identifier, if a reliable server architecture is used.

If the value is empty, the server MUST delete its key-value entry with the specified key.

The server SHOULD accept the following properties:

- `ttl`: specifies a time-to-live in seconds. If the KVSET command has a `ttl` property, the server SHOULD delete the key-value pair and broadcast a KVPUB with an empty value in order to delete this from all clients when the TTL has expired.

Reliability

CHP may be used in a dual-server configuration where a backup server takes over if the primary server fails. CHP does not specify the mechanisms used for this failover but the Binary Star pattern may be helpful.

To assist server reliability, the client MAY:

- Set a UUID in every KVSET command.
- Detect the lack of HUGZ over a time period and use this as an indicator that the current server has failed.
- Connect to a backup server and re-request a state synchronization.

Scalability and Performance

CHP is designed to be scalable to large numbers (thousands) of clients, limited only by system resources on the broker. Because all updates pass through a single server, the overall throughput will be limited to some millions of updates per second at peak, and probably less.

Security

CHP does not implement any authentication, access control, or encryption mechanisms and should not be used in any deployment where these are required.

Building a Multithreaded Stack and API

The client stack we've used so far isn't smart enough to handle this protocol properly. As soon as we start doing heartbeats, we need a client stack that can run in a background thread. In the Freelance pattern at the end of "Reliable Request-Reply Patterns" we used a multithreaded API but didn't explain it in detail. It turns out that multithreaded APIs are quite useful when you start to make more complex ØMQ protocols like CHP.

If you make a nontrivial protocol and you expect applications to implement it properly, most developers will get it wrong most of the time. You're going to be left with a lot of unhappy people complaining that your protocol is too complex, too fragile, and too hard to use. Whereas if you give them a simple API to call, you have some chance of them buying in.

Our multithreaded API consists of a frontend object and a background agent, connected by two PAIR sockets (see figure 63). Connecting two PAIR sockets like this is so useful that your high-level binding should probably do what CZMQ does, which is package a "create new thread with a pipe that I can use to send messages to it" method.

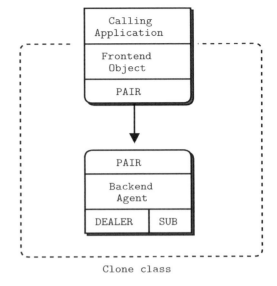

Figure 63. Multithreaded API

The multithreaded APIs that we see in this book all take the same form:

- The constructor for the object (clone_new) creates a context and starts a background thread connected with a pipe. It holds onto one end of the pipe so it can send commands to the background thread.
- The background thread starts an *agent* that is essentially a zmq_poll loop reading from the pipe socket and any other sockets (here, the DEALER and SUB sockets).
- The main application thread and the background thread now communicate only via ØMQ messages. By convention, the frontend sends string commands so that each method on the class turns into a message sent to the backend agent, like this:

```
void
clone_connect (clone_t *self, char *address, char *service)
{
    assert (self);
    zmsg_t *msg = zmsg_new ();
    zmsg_addstr (msg, "CONNECT");
    zmsg_addstr (msg, address);
    zmsg_addstr (msg, service);
    zmsg_send (&msg, self->pipe);
}
```

- If the method needs a return code, it can wait for a reply message from the agent.
- If the agent needs to send asynchronous events back to the frontend, we add a recv method to the class, which waits for messages on the frontend pipe.

- We may want to expose the frontend pipe socket handle to allow the class to be integrated into further poll loops. Otherwise any `recv` method would block the application.

The clone class has the same structure as the `flcliapi` class from "Reliable Request-Reply Patterns" and adds the logic from the last model of the Clone client. Without ØMQ, this kind of multithreaded API design would be weeks of really hard work. With ØMQ, it was a day or two of work.

The actual API methods for the clone class are quite simple:

```
//  Create a new clone class instance
clone_t *
    clone_new (void);

//  Destroy a clone class instance
void
    clone_destroy (clone_t **self_p);

//  Define the subtree, if any, for this clone class
void
    clone_subtree (clone_t *self, char *subtree);

//  Connect the clone class to one server
void
    clone_connect (clone_t *self, char *address, char *service);

//  Set a value in the shared hashmap
void
    clone_set (clone_t *self, char *key, char *value, int ttl);

//  Get a value from the shared hashmap
char *
    clone_get (clone_t *self, char *key);
```

So here is Model Six of the clone client, which has now become just a thin shell using the clone class:

Example 82. Clone client, Model Six (clonecli6.c)

```
//  Clone client Model Six

//  Lets us build this source without creating a library
#include "clone.c"
#define SUBTREE "/client/"

int main (void)
{
    //  Create distributed hash instance
    clone_t *clone = clone_new ();

    //  Specify configuration
```

```
        clone_subtree (clone, SUBTREE);
        clone_connect (clone, "tcp://localhost", "5556");
        clone_connect (clone, "tcp://localhost", "5566");

        //  Set random tuples into the distributed hash
        while (!zctx_interrupted) {
            //  Set random value, check it was stored
            char key [255];
            char value [10];
            sprintf (key, "%s%d", SUBTREE, randof (10000));
            sprintf (value, "%d", randof (1000000));
            clone_set (clone, key, value, randof (30));
            sleep (1);
        }
        clone_destroy (&clone);
        return 0;
    }
```

Note the connect method, which specifies one server endpoint. Under the hood, we're in fact talking to three ports. However, as the CHP protocol says, the three ports are on consecutive port numbers:

- The server state router (ROUTER) is at port P.
- The server updates publisher (PUB) is at port P + 1.
- The server updates subscriber (SUB) is at port P + 2.

So we can fold the three connections into one logical operation (which we implement as three separate ØMQ connect calls).

Let's end with the source code for the clone stack. This is a complex piece of code, but easier to understand when you break it into the frontend object class and the backend agent. The frontend sends string commands ("SUBTREE", "CONNECT", "SET", "GET") to the agent, which handles these commands as well as talking to the server(s). Here is the agent's logic:

1. Start up by getting a snapshot from the first server
2. When we get a snapshot switch to reading from the subscriber socket.
3. If we don't get a snapshot then fail over to the second server.
4. Poll on the pipe and the subscriber socket.
5. If we got input on the pipe, handle the control message from the frontend object.
6. If we got input on the subscriber, store or apply the update.
7. If we didn't get anything from the server within a certain time, fail over.
8. Repeat until the process is interrupted by Ctrl-C.

And here is the actual clone class implementation:

Example 83. Clone class (clone.c)

```
// clone class - Clone client API stack (multithreaded)

#include "clone.h"
// If no server replies within this time, abandon request
#define GLOBAL_TIMEOUT  4000    //  msecs


// =====================================================================
// Synchronous part, works in our application thread

// Structure of our class

struct _clone_t {
    zctx_t *ctx;                // Our context wrapper
    void *pipe;                 // Pipe through to clone agent
};


// This is the thread that handles our real clone class
static void clone_agent (void *args, zctx_t *ctx, void *pipe);
```

Here are the constructor and destructor for the clone class. Note that we create a context specifically for the pipe that connects our frontend to the backend agent:

Example 83-1. Clone class (clone.c) - constructor and destructor

```
clone_t *
clone_new (void)
{
    clone_t
        *self;

    self = (clone_t *) zmalloc (sizeof (clone_t));
    self->ctx = zctx_new ();
    self->pipe = zthread_fork (self->ctx, clone_agent, NULL);
    return self;
}

void
clone_destroy (clone_t **self_p)
{
    assert (self_p);
    if (*self_p) {
        clone_t *self = *self_p;
        zctx_destroy (&self->ctx);
        free (self);
        *self_p = NULL;
    }
}
```

Specify subtree for snapshot and updates, which we must do before connecting to a server as the subtree specification is sent as the first command to the server. Sends a [SUBTREE][subtree] command to the agent:

Example 83-2. Clone class (clone.c) - subtree method

```
void clone_subtree (clone_t *self, char *subtree)
{
    assert (self);
    zmsg_t *msg = zmsg_new ();
    zmsg_addstr (msg, "SUBTREE");
    zmsg_addstr (msg, subtree);
    zmsg_send (&msg, self->pipe);
}
```

Connect to a new server endpoint. We can connect to at most two servers. Sends [CONNECT][endpoint][service] to the agent:

Example 83-3. Clone class (clone.c) - connect method

```
void
clone_connect (clone_t *self, char *address, char *service)
{
    assert (self);
    zmsg_t *msg = zmsg_new ();
    zmsg_addstr (msg, "CONNECT");
    zmsg_addstr (msg, address);
    zmsg_addstr (msg, service);
    zmsg_send (&msg, self->pipe);
}
```

Set a new value in the shared hashmap. Sends a [SET][key][value][ttl] command through to the agent which does the actual work:

Example 83-4. Clone class (clone.c) - set method

```
void
clone_set (clone_t *self, char *key, char *value, int ttl)
{
    char ttlstr [10];
    sprintf (ttlstr, "%d", ttl);

    assert (self);
    zmsg_t *msg = zmsg_new ();
    zmsg_addstr (msg, "SET");
    zmsg_addstr (msg, key);
    zmsg_addstr (msg, value);
    zmsg_addstr (msg, ttlstr);
    zmsg_send (&msg, self->pipe);
}
```

Look up value in distributed hash table. Sends [GET][key] to the agent and waits for a value response. If there is no value available, will eventually return NULL:

Example 83-5. Clone class (clone.c) - get method

```
char *
clone_get (clone_t *self, char *key)
{
    assert (self);
    assert (key);
    zmsg_t *msg = zmsg_new ();
    zmsg_addstr (msg, "GET");
    zmsg_addstr (msg, key);
    zmsg_send (&msg, self->pipe);

    zmsg_t *reply = zmsg_recv (self->pipe);
    if (reply) {
        char *value = zmsg_popstr (reply);
        zmsg_destroy (&reply);
        return value;
    }
    return NULL;
}
```

The backend agent manages a set of servers, which we implement using our simple class model:

Example 83-6. Clone class (clone.c) - working with servers

```
typedef struct {
    char *address;              //  Server address
    int port;                   //  Server port
    void *snapshot;             //  Snapshot socket
    void *subscriber;           //  Incoming updates
    uint64_t expiry;            //  When server expires
    uint requests;              //  How many snapshot requests made?
} server_t;

static server_t *
server_new (zctx_t *ctx, char *address, int port, char *subtree)
{
    server_t *self = (server_t *) zmalloc (sizeof (server_t));

    zclock_log ("I: adding server %s:%d...", address, port);
    self->address = strdup (address);
    self->port = port;

    self->snapshot = zsocket_new (ctx, ZMQ_DEALER);
    zsocket_connect (self->snapshot, "%s:%d", address, port);
    self->subscriber = zsocket_new (ctx, ZMQ_SUB);
    zsocket_connect (self->subscriber, "%s:%d", address, port + 1);
```

```
        zsockopt_set_subscribe (self->subscriber, subtree);
        return self;
}

static void
server_destroy (server_t **self_p)
{
    assert (self_p);
    if (*self_p) {
        server_t *self = *self_p;
        free (self->address);
        free (self);
        *self_p = NULL;
    }
}
```

Here is the implementation of the backend agent itself:

Example 83-7. Clone class (clone.c) - backend agent class

```
//  Number of servers to which we will talk to
#define SERVER_MAX     2

//  Server considered dead if silent for this long
#define SERVER_TTL     5000    //  msecs

//  States we can be in
#define STATE_INITIAL     0    //  Before asking server for state
#define STATE_SYNCING     1    //  Getting state from server
#define STATE_ACTIVE      2    //  Getting new updates from server

typedef struct {
    zctx_t *ctx;                //  Context wrapper
    void *pipe;                 //  Pipe back to application
    zhash_t *kvmap;             //  Actual key/value table
    char *subtree;              //  Subtree specification, if any
    server_t *server [SERVER_MAX];
    uint nbr_servers;           //  0 to SERVER_MAX
    uint state;                 //  Current state
    uint cur_server;            //  If active, server 0 or 1
    int64_t sequence;           //  Last kvmsg processed
    void *publisher;            //  Outgoing updates
} agent_t;

static agent_t *
agent_new (zctx_t *ctx, void *pipe)
{
    agent_t *self = (agent_t *) zmalloc (sizeof (agent_t));
    self->ctx = ctx;
    self->pipe = pipe;
    self->kvmap = zhash_new ();
```

```
        self->subtree = strdup ("");
        self->state = STATE_INITIAL;
        self->publisher = zsocket_new (self->ctx, ZMQ_PUB);
        return self;
    }

    static void
    agent_destroy (agent_t **self_p)
    {
        assert (self_p);
        if (*self_p) {
            agent_t *self = *self_p;
            int server_nbr;
            for (server_nbr = 0; server_nbr < self->nbr_servers; server_nbr++)
                server_destroy (&self->server [server_nbr]);
            zhash_destroy (&self->kvmap);
            free (self->subtree);
            free (self);
            *self_p = NULL;
        }
    }
```

Here we handle the different control messages from the frontend; SUBTREE, CONNECT, SET, and GET:

Example 83-8. Clone class (clone.c) - handling a control message

```
    static int
    agent_control_message (agent_t *self)
    {
        zmsg_t *msg = zmsg_recv (self->pipe);
        char *command = zmsg_popstr (msg);
        if (command == NULL)
            return -1;      // Interrupted

        if (streq (command, "SUBTREE")) {
            free (self->subtree);
            self->subtree = zmsg_popstr (msg);
        }
        else
        if (streq (command, "CONNECT")) {
            char *address = zmsg_popstr (msg);
            char *service = zmsg_popstr (msg);
            if (self->nbr_servers < SERVER_MAX) {
                self->server [self->nbr_servers++] = server_new (
                    self->ctx, address, atoi (service), self->subtree);
                //  We broadcast updates to all known servers
                zsocket_connect (self->publisher, "%s:%d",
                    address, atoi (service) + 2);
            }
            else
```

```
            zclock_log ("E: too many servers (max. %d)", SERVER_MAX);
        free (address);
        free (service);
    }
    else
```

When we set a property, we push the new key-value pair onto all our connected servers:

Example 83-9. Clone class (clone.c) - set and get commands

```
        char *key = zmsg_popstr (msg);
        char *value = zmsg_popstr (msg);
        char *ttl = zmsg_popstr (msg);
        zhash_update (self->kvmap, key, (byte *) value);
        zhash_freefn (self->kvmap, key, free);

        //  Send key-value pair on to server
        kvmsg_t *kvmsg = kvmsg_new (0);
        kvmsg_set_key  (kvmsg, key);
        kvmsg_set_uuid (kvmsg);
        kvmsg_fmt_body (kvmsg, "%s", value);
        kvmsg_set_prop (kvmsg, "ttl", ttl);
        kvmsg_send     (kvmsg, self->publisher);
        kvmsg_destroy (&kvmsg);
        free (ttl);
        free (key);             //  Value is owned by hash table
    }
    else
    if (streq (command, "GET")) {
        char *key = zmsg_popstr (msg);
        char *value = zhash_lookup (self->kvmap, key);
        if (value)
            zstr_send (self->pipe, value);
        else
            zstr_send (self->pipe, "");
        free (key);
        free (value);
    }
    free (command);
    zmsg_destroy (&msg);
    return 0;
}
```

The asynchronous agent manages a server pool and handles the request-reply dialog when the application asks for it:

Example 83-10. Clone class (clone.c) - backend agent

```
static void
clone_agent (void *args, zctx_t *ctx, void *pipe)
```

```
{
    agent_t *self = agent_new (ctx, pipe);

    while (true) {
        zmq_pollitem_t poll_set [] = {
            { pipe, 0, ZMQ_POLLIN, 0 },
            { 0,    0, ZMQ_POLLIN, 0 }
        };
        int poll_timer = -1;
        int poll_size = 2;
        server_t *server = self->server [self->cur_server];
        switch (self->state) {
            case STATE_INITIAL:
                //  In this state we ask the server for a snapshot,
                //  if we have a server to talk to...
                if (self->nbr_servers > 0) {
                    zclock_log ("I: waiting for server at %s:%d...",
                        server->address, server->port);
                    if (server->requests < 2) {
                        zstr_sendm (server->snapshot, "ICANHAZ?");
                        zstr_send  (server->snapshot, self->subtree);
                        server->requests++;
                    }
                    server->expiry = zclock_time () + SERVER_TTL;
                    self->state = STATE_SYNCING;
                    poll_set [1].socket = server->snapshot;
                }
                else
                    poll_size = 1;
                break;

            case STATE_SYNCING:
                //  In this state we read from snapshot and we expect
                //  the server to respond, else we fail over.
                poll_set [1].socket = server->snapshot;
                break;

            case STATE_ACTIVE:
                //  In this state we read from subscriber and we expect
                //  the server to give hugz, else we fail over.
                poll_set [1].socket = server->subscriber;
                break;
        }
        if (server) {
            poll_timer = (server->expiry - zclock_time ())
                       * ZMQ_POLL_MSEC;
            if (poll_timer < 0)
                poll_timer = 0;
        }
```

We're ready to process incoming messages; if nothing at all comes from our server within the timeout, that means the server is dead:

Example 83-11. Clone class (clone.c) - client poll loop

```
        int rc = zmq_poll (poll_set, poll_size, poll_timer);
        if (rc == -1)
            break;              // Context has been shut down

        if (poll_set [0].revents & ZMQ_POLLIN) {
            if (agent_control_message (self))
                break;          // Interrupted
        }
        else
        if (poll_set [1].revents & ZMQ_POLLIN) {
            kvmsg_t *kvmsg = kvmsg_recv (poll_set [1].socket);
            if (!kvmsg)
                break;          // Interrupted

            //  Anything from server resets its expiry time
            server->expiry = zclock_time () + SERVER_TTL;
            if (self->state == STATE_SYNCING) {
                //  Store in snapshot until we're finished
                server->requests = 0;
                if (streq (kvmsg_key (kvmsg), "KTHXBAI")) {
                    self->sequence = kvmsg_sequence (kvmsg);
                    self->state = STATE_ACTIVE;
                    zclock_log ("I: received from %s:%d snapshot=%d",
                        server->address, server->port,
                        (int) self->sequence);
                    kvmsg_destroy (&kvmsg);
                }
                else
                    kvmsg_store (&kvmsg, self->kvmap);
            }
            else
            if (self->state == STATE_ACTIVE) {
                //  Discard out-of-sequence updates, incl. hugz
                if (kvmsg_sequence (kvmsg) > self->sequence) {
                    self->sequence = kvmsg_sequence (kvmsg);
                    kvmsg_store (&kvmsg, self->kvmap);
                    zclock_log ("I: received from %s:%d update=%d",
                        server->address, server->port,
                        (int) self->sequence);
                }
                else
                    kvmsg_destroy (&kvmsg);
            }
        }
        else {
            //  Server has died, failover to next
```

```
                zclock_log ("I: server at %s:%d didn't give hugz",
                    server->address, server->port);
                self->cur_server = (self->cur_server + 1) % self->nbr_servers;
                self->state = STATE_INITIAL;
            }
        }
        agent_destroy (&self);
    }
```

Postface

Tales from Out There

I asked some of the contributors to this book to tell us what they were doing with ØMQ. Here are their stories.

Rob Gagnon's Story

"We use ØMQ to assist in aggregating thousands of events occurring every minute across our global network of telecommunications servers so that we can accurately report and monitor for situations that require our attention. ØMQ made the development of the system not only easier, but faster to develop, and more robust and fault-tolerant than we had originally planned in our original design.

"We're able to easily add and remove clients from the network without the loss of any message. If we need to enhance the server portion of our system, we can stop and restart it as well, without having to worry about stopping all of the clients first. The built-in buffering of ØMQ makes this all possible."

Tom van Leeuwen's Story

"I was looking for creating some kind of service bus connecting all kinds of services together. There were already some products that implemented a broker, but they did not have the functionality I wanted/needed. By accident I stumbled upon ØMQ which is awesome. It's very lightweight, lean, simple and easy to follow since the zguide is very complete and reads very well. I've actually implemented the Titanic pattern and the Majordomo broker with some additions (client/worker authentication and workers sending a catalog explaining what they provide and how they should be addressed).

"The beautiful thing about ØMQ is the fact that it is a library and not an application. You can mold it however you like and it simply puts boring things like queuing, reconnecting, tcp sockets and such to the background, making sure you can concentrate on what is important for you. I've implemented all kinds of workers/clients and the broker in Ruby, because that is the main language we use for development, but also some php clients to connect to the bus from existing php webapps. We use this service bus for cloud services connecting all kinds of platform devices to a service bus exposing functionality for automation.

"ØMQ is very easy to understand and if you spend a day in the zguide, you'll have good knowledge of how it works. I'm a network engineer, not a software developer, but managed to create a very nice solution for our automation needs! ØMQ: Thank you very much!"

Michael Jakl's Story

"We use ØMQ for distributing millions of documents per day in our distributed processing pipeline. We started out with big message queuing brokers that had their own respective issues and problems. In the quest of simplifying our architecture, we chose ØMQ to do the wiring. So far it had a huge impact in how our architecture scales and how easy it is to change/move the components. The plethora of language bindings lets us choose the right tool for the job without sacrificing interoperability in our system. We don't use a lot of sockets (less than 10 in our whole application), but that's all we needed to split a huge monolithic application into small independent parts.

"All in all, ØMQ lets me keep my sanity and helps my customers to stay within budget."

Vadim Shalts's Story

"I am team leader in the company ActForex, which develops software for financial markets. Due to the nature of our domain, we need to process large volumes of prices quickly. In addition, it's extremely critical to minimize latency in processing orders and prices. Achieve a high throughput is not enough. Everything must be handled in a soft real time with a predictable ultra low latency per price. The system consists of multiple components which exchanging messages. Each price can take a lot of processing stages, each of which increases total latency. As a consequence, low and predictable latency of messaging between components becomes a key factor of our architecture.

"We investigated different solutions to find suitable for our needs. We tried different message brokers (RabbitMQ, ActiveMQ Apollo, Kafka), but failed to reach a low and predictable latency with any of them. In the end, we have chosen ZeroMQ used in conjunction with ZooKeeper for service discovery. Complex coordination with ZeroMQ requires a relatively large effort and a good understanding, as a result of the natural complexity of multi-threading. We found that external agent like ZooKeeper is better choice for service discovery and coordination while ZeroMQ can be used primary for simple messaging. ZeroMQ perfectly fit into our architecture. It allowed us to achieve the desired latency using minimal efforts. It saved us from a bottleneck in the processing of messages and made processing time very stable and predictable.

"I can decidedly recommend ZeroMQ for solutions where low latency is important."

How This Book Happened

When I set out to write a ZeroMQ book, we were still debating the pros and cons of forks and pull requests in the ØMQ community. Today, for what it's worth, this argument seems settled: the "liberal" policy which we adopted for libzmq in early 2012 broke our dependency on a single prime author, and opened the floor to dozens of new contributors. More profoundly, it allowed us to move to a gently organic evolutionary model, very different from the older forced-march model.

The reason I was confident this would work was that our work on this book had, for a year or more, shown the way. True, the text is my own work, which is perhaps as it should be. Writing is not programming. When we write, we tell a story and one doesn't want different voices telling one tale, it feels strange.

For me the real long-term value of the book is the repository of examples: about 65,000 lines of code in 24 different languages. It's partly about making ØMQ accessible to more people. People already refer to the Python and PHP example repositories—two of the most complete—when they want to tell others how to learn ØMQ. But it's also about learning programming languages.

Here's a loop of code in Tcl:

```
while {1} {
    # Process all parts of the message
    zmq message message
    frontend recv_msg message
    set more [frontend getsockopt RCVMORE]
    backend send_msg message [expr {$more?"SNDMORE":""}]
    message close
    if {!$more} {
        break ; # Last message part
    }
}
```

And here's the same loop in Lua:

```
while true do
    --  Process all parts of the message
    local msg = frontend:recv()
    if (frontend:getopt(zmq.RCVMORE) == 1) then
        backend:send(msg, zmq.SNDMORE)
    else
        backend:send(msg, 0)
        break;      -- Last message part
    end
end
```

And this particular example (rrbroker) is in C#, C++, CL, Clojure, Erlang, F#, Go, Haskell, Haxe, Java, Lua, Node.js, Perl, PHP, Python, Ruby, Scala, Tcl, and of course C. This code base, all provided as open source under the MIT/X11 license, may form the basis for other books, or projects.

But what this collection of translations says most profoundly is this: the language you choose is a detail, even a distraction. The power of ØMQ lies in the patterns it gives you and lets you build, and these transcend the comings and goings of languages. My goal as a software and social architect is to build structures that can last generations. There seems no point in aiming for mere decades.

Removing Friction

I'll explain the technical tool chain we used in terms of the friction we removed. In this book we're telling a story and the goal is to reach as many people as possible, as cheaply and smoothly as we can.

The core idea was to host the text and examples on GitHub and make it easy for anyone to contribute. It turned out to be more complex than that, however.

Let's start with the division of labor. I'm a good writer and can produce endless amounts of decent text quickly. But what was impossible for me was to provide the examples in other languages. Since the core ØMQ API is in C, it seemed logical to write the original examples in C. Also, C is a neutral choice; it's perhaps the only language that doesn't create strong emotions.

How to encourage people to make translations of the examples? We tried a few approaches and finally what worked best was to offer a "choose your language" link on every single example, in the text, which took people either to the translation, or to a page explaining how they could contribute. The way it usually works is that as people learn ØMQ in their preferred language, they contribute a handful of translations, or fixes to the existing ones.

At the same time I noticed a few people quite determinedly translating *every single* example. This was mainly binding authors who realized that the examples were a great way to encourage people to use their bindings. For their efforts, I extended the scripts to produce language-specific versions of the book. Instead of including the C code, we'd include the Python, or PHP code. Lua and Haxe also got their dedicated Guides.

Once we have an idea of who works on what, we know how to structure the work itself. It's clear that to write and test an example, what you want to work on is *source code*. So we import this source code when we build the book, and that's how we make language-specific versions.

I like to write in a plain text format. It's fast and works well with source control systems like git. Since the main platform for our websites is Wikidot, I write using Wikidot's very readable markup format.

At least in the first chapters, it was important to draw pictures to explain the flow of messages between peers. Making diagrams by hand is a lot of work, and when we want to get final output in different formats, image conversion becomes a chore. I started with Ditaa, which turns text diagrams into PNGs, then later switched to asciitosvg, which produces SVG files, which are rather better. Having the graphics in the markup text, also as text, makes it remarkably easy to work.

By now you'll realize that the toolchain we use is highly customized, though it uses a lot of external tools. All are available on Ubuntu, which is a mercy, and the whole custom toolchain is in the zguide repository in the bin subdirectory.

Let's walk through the editing and publishing process. Here is how we produce the online version:

```
bin/buildguide
```

Which works as follows:

- The original text sits in a series of text files (one per chapter).
- The examples sit in the examples subdirectory, classified per language.
- We take the text, and process this using a custom Perl script, mkwikidot, into a set of Wikidot-ready files.
- We do this for each of the languages that get their own Guide version.
- We extract the graphics and calls asciitosvg and rasterize on each one to produce image files, which it stores in the images subdirectory.
- We extract inline listings (which are not translated) and stores these in the listings subdirectory.
- We use pygmentize on each example and listing to create a marked-up page in Wikidot format.
- We upload all changed files to the online wiki using the Wikidot API.

Doing this from scratch takes a while. So we store the SHA1 signatures of every image, listing, example, and text file, and only process and upload changes, and that makes it easy to publish a new version of the text when people make new contributions.

To produce the PDF and Epub formats we do this:

```
bin/buildpdfs
```

Which works as follows:

- We use the custom mkdocbook Perl program on the input files to produce a DocBook output.
- We push the DocBook format through docbook2ps and ps2pdf to create clean PDFs, in each language.
- We push the DocBook format though db2epub to create Epub books, and in each language.
- We upload the PDFs to the public wiki using the Wikidot API.

It's important, when you create a community project, to lower the "change latency", i.e., the time it takes for people to see their work live. Or at least, to see that you've accepted their pull request. If that is more than a day or two, you've often lost your contributor's interest.

Licensing

I want people to reuse this text in their own work: in presentations, articles, and even other books. However, the deal is that if they remix my work, others can remix theirs.

I'd like credit, and have no argument against others making money from their remixes. Thus, the text is licensed under cc-by-sa.

For the examples, we started with GPL, but it rapidly became clear this wasn't workable. The point of examples is to give people reusable code fragments so they will use ØMQ more widely, and if these are GPL that won't happen. We switched to MIT/X11, even for the larger and more complex examples that conceivably would work as LGPL.

However when we started turning the examples into stand-alone projects (as with Majordomo), we used the LGPL. Again, remixability trumps dissemination. Licenses are tools, use them with intent, not ideology.

Code Connected Volume 2

That's the end of Volume 1. If you've worked your way through the examples and understood how they work, thank you for your patience and hard work. You can now rank yourself as a professional-grade ØMQ developer.

In the next volume, "Code Connected Volume 2", we'll take it to the next level. Writing code is one thing. Making successful products is something else. In the next book you'll learn how to do large-scale software architecture. I'll introduce a set of techniques of software development, and demonstrate them with worked examples, starting with ØMQ itself and ending with a general-purpose framework for distributed applications (Zyre). These techniques are independent of license, though open source amplifies them.

Made in the USA
Lexington, KY
18 May 2013